THE DEMOCRAT

Voters cannot answer simple survey questions about politics. Legislators cannot recall the details of legislation. Jurors cannot comprehend legal arguments. Observations such as these are plentiful, and several generations of pundits and scholars have used these observations to claim that voters, legislators, and jurors are incompetent. Are these claims correct? Do voters, jurors, and legislators who lack political information make bad decisions?

In *The Democratic Dilemma,* Professors Arthur Lupia and Mathew McCubbins explain how citizens make decisions about complex issues. Combining insights from economics, political science, and the cognitive sciences, they develop theories and experiments about learning and choice. They use these tools to identify the requirements for reasoned choice – the choice that a citizen would make if he or she possessed a certain (perhaps greater) level of knowledge. The results clarify debates about voter, juror, and legislator competence and also reveal how the design of political institutions affects citizens' abilities to govern themselves effectively.

POLITICAL ECONOMY OF INSTITUTIONS AND DECISIONS

Editors
James E. Alt, *Harvard University*
Douglass C. North, *Washington University of St. Louis*

THE
DEMOCRATIC
DILEMMA

CAN CITIZENS LEARN WHAT
THEY NEED TO KNOW?

ARTHUR LUPIA

University of California, San Diego

MATHEW D. McCUBBINS

University of California, San Diego

CAMBRIDGE
UNIVERSITY PRESS

PUBLISHED BY THE PRESS SYNDICATE OF THE UNIVERSITY OF CAMBRIDGE
The Pitt Building, Trumpington Street, Cambridge CB2 1RP, United Kingdom

CAMBRIDGE UNIVERSITY PRESS
The Edinburgh Building, Cambridge CB2 2RU, United Kingdom
40 West 20th Street, New York, NY 10011-4211, USA
10 Stamford Road, Oakleigh, Melbourne 3166, Australia

First published 1998

Typeset in Sabon

Library of Congress Cataloging-in-Publication Data
Lupia, Arthur (date)
The democratic dilemma : can citizens learn what they need
to know? / Arthur Lupia, Mathew D. McCubbins.
p.   cm. – (Political economy of institutions and decisions)
Includes bibliographical references and indexes.
ISBN 0-521-58448-5. – ISBN 0-521-58593-7 (pbk.)
1. Political socialization.   2. Civics.   I. McCubbins, Mathew D.
(Mathew Daniel) (date).   II. Title.   III. Series.
JA76.L86   1998
306.2 – dc21   97-18130
CIP

A catalog record for this book is available from
the British Library.

ISBN 0 521 58448 5 hardback
ISBN 0 521 58593 7 paperback

Transferred to digital printing 2003

in loving memory of
Mae Slack and H. W. McCubbins

Contents

Contents

Tables and Figures

FIGURES

Series Editors' Preface

The Cambridge series on the Political Economy of Institutions and Decisions is built around attempts to answer two central questions: How do institutions evolve in response to individual incentives, strategies, and choices, and how do institutions affect the performance of political and economic systems? The scope of the series is comparative and historical rather than international or specifically American, and the focus is positive rather than normative.

This innovative, highly ambitious book develops and tests theories about how people can resolve a dilemma of modern democracy: that complexity seems to impose intolerable information burdens on people seeking to make informed choices. Of course, people use all sorts of shortcuts to inform themselves, and indeed they can often reason without being immersed in detail. But when or under what circumstances does limited-information reasoning work out well for the chooser? When can voters reach enlightened decisions on complex questions? Thinking about bureaucracy and organizational behavior, when does delegation work? Lupia and McCubbins provide a unified answer to these and many other similar questions. They do so by developing a general model of communication and persuasion that gives the necessary and sufficient conditions under which agents' actions are informative, or under which shortcuts cannot hurt, analyzing in detail the roles of common interests, verification, and penalties for lying.

But they do much more than construct a formal model. They also test the insights the model provides using data collected experimentally, in a manner consistent with the premises and findings of cognitive psychology. The book thus provides a pathbreaking analysis of information and persuasion in contemporary politics and lays a foundation for exciting future interdisciplinary empirical work.

Acknowledgments

The Democratic Dilemma draws from the lessons of a wide array of scholarship to provide a cohesive and positive statement about the political consequences of limited information. Skilled practitioners in many different disciplines have challenged us to give the strongest possible argument while expressing ourselves to a wide academic audience. As a result, we supplement our formal arguments, mathematical models, laboratory experiments, and national surveys with metaphors, analogies, and anecdotes that specialists and nonspecialists alike can understand.

We owe many debts of gratitude. We acknowledge the support of the National Science Foundation and its Political Science Program, through grant SBR-9422831. Dr. Lupia acknowledges a UCSD COR grant for partial support of the research reported here, and for a grant, administered by Paul Sniderman, for the 1994 Multi-Investigator Survey, from the National Science Foundation, number SBR-9309946. Early drafts of this book were written while Dr. McCubbins was a Fellow at the Center for Advanced Study in the Behavioral Sciences. Dr. McCubbins is grateful for the financial support for this fellowship, provided by the National Science Foundation, grant SBR-9022192.

We presented portions of this book at many conferences and seminars and received comments and advice for which we are grateful. Two seminars, lasting several days each, were especially useful to us in revising this book. The first was at the Department of Government, Harvard University, in May 1995; the second was at the Hoover Institution of Stanford University in January 1996. We thank Jim Alt, Barry Weingast, and Doug North for these opportunities.

We received comments on this manuscript from nearly one hundred people. We thank all of them and will repay our debt in kind. Of these, several scholars showed tremendous determination and ingenuity of argument in their efforts to steer the course of this project. To these individuals we owe a special debt: Jim Alt, Randall Calvert, Gary Cox, Vince Crawford, Daniel Diermeier, John Ferejohn, Elisabeth Gerber, Gary Jacobson,

Acknowledgments

James Kuklinski, Douglass North, Samuel Popkin, Kenneth Shepsle, Joel Sobel, Paul Sniderman, Tracy Strong, Mark Turner, Peter Tyack, Barry Weingast, and Oliver Williamson.

We also owe a great debt to a number of hard-working research assistants: Scott Basinger, Morganne Beck, Greg Bovitz, Andrea Campbell, Carola Clift, Michael Ensley, Jennifer Nicoll, Julie Pope, and Robert Schwartz. Perhaps more than that of any other individual, we are grateful for the hard work and keen insight of James Druckman.

Finally, we owe a debt of gratitude to our children, Francesca, Colin, and Kenny. They were often our first experimental subjects and were the source of many of our examples.

1

Knowledge and the Foundation
of Democracy

> Knowledge will forever govern ignorance: And a people who mean to be their own Governors, must arm themselves with the power which knowledge gives. A popular Government, without popular information, or the means of acquiring it, is but a Prologue to a Farce or a Tragedy; or, perhaps both.
>
>   – James Madison[1]

The founders of the American republic, and many of their contemporaries around the world, believed that democracy requires citizens to make reasoned choices. Reasoned choice, in turn, requires that people know the consequences of their actions.

Can voters, legislators, and jurors make reasoned choices? Many observers conclude that they cannot. The evidence for this conclusion is substantial – study after study documents the breadth and depth of citizen ignorance. Making matters worse is the fact that many people acquire what little information they have from thirty-minute news summaries, thirty-second political advertisements, or eight-second sound bites. From this evidence, it seems very likely that "Men of factious tempers, of local prejudices, or of sinister designs, may, by intrigue, by corruption, or by any other means, first obtain the suffrages, and then betray the interests, of the people" (Madison, *Federalist* 10).

It is widely believed that there is a mismatch between the requirements of democracy and most people's ability to meet these requirements. If this mismatch is too prevalent, then effective self-governance is impossible. The *democratic dilemma* is that the people who are called upon to make reasoned choices may not be capable of doing so.

In this book, we concede that people lack political information. We also concede that this ignorance can allow people "of sinister designs"

[1] From Hunt (1910: 103). Madison expressed similar beliefs in *Federalist* 57 and in a speech before the Virginia Ratifying Convention, where he argued that it is necessary that the people possess the "virtue and intelligence to select men of virtue and wisdom" (Riemer 1986: 40).

to deceive and betray the underinformed. We do not concede, however, that democracy *must* succumb to these threats. Rather, we conclude that:

- Reasoned choice does not require full information; rather, it requires the ability to predict the consequences of actions. We define this ability as knowledge.[2]
- People *choose* to disregard most of the information they could acquire and base virtually all of their decisions on remarkably little information.
- People often *substitute* the advice of others for the information they lack. This substitution can give people the capacity for reasoned choice.
- Relying on the advice of others involves tradeoffs. Although it decreases the costs of acquiring knowledge, it also introduces the possibility of deception.
- A person who wants to gain knowledge from the advice of others must choose to follow some advice while ignoring other advice. People make these choices in systematic and predictable ways.
- Political institutions can help people choose which advice to follow and which advice to ignore. Institutions do this when they *clarify* the incentives of advice givers.
- Understanding how people learn not only helps us better identify when presumed democratic dilemmas are real but also shows us how we might begin to resolve these dilemmas.

In the remainder of this chapter we foreshadow our argument and provide a road map of the rest of the book.

---

[2]There exists a centuries-old debate about what democracy *should* do. This debate has involved many great minds, is wide ranging, and is totally unresolved. We do not believe ourselves capable of resolving this debate. However, we strongly believe that we can make the debate more constructive. We can do so by clarifying the relationship between what information people have and what types of decisions they can make. Our book is firmly about determining the capabilities of people who lack political information. It is designed to resolve debates about how much information voters, jurors, and legislators need in order to perform certain tasks. So, although our book may help to clarify debates about what democracy should do, it will not resolve these debates.

We mention this because our relationship to the debate about what democracy should do motivates our definition of reasoned choice. Our definition of reasoned choice allows the reader to define an amount of knowledge that is required for reasoned choice. Some readers may argue that a reasoned choice requires knowledge of very technical matters, whereas others may argue that a reasoned choice requires less knowledge. Note that the difference between these viewpoints reduces to different views on what democracy should do. Therefore, our definition of reasoned choice is purposefully precise with respect to the relationship between information, knowledge, and choice and is purposefully vague with respect to most normative debates about what democracies *should* do.

Knowledge and Democracy

DEMOCRACY, DELEGATION, AND REASONED CHOICE

Democracy is a method of government based upon the choices of the people. In all modern democracies, the people elect or appoint others to represent them. Legislative assemblies, executives, commissions, judges, and juries are empowered by the people to make collective decisions on their behalf. These delegations form the foundation of democracy.

But there are dangers. As Dahl (1967: 21) warns, the principal danger is that uninformed decision makers, by failing to delegate well, will transform democracy into a *tyranny of experts*: "there are decisions that require me to *delegate* authority to others . . . but if I delegate, may I not, in practice, end up with a kind of aristocracy of experts, or even false experts?"

Must democracy become a tyranny of experts? Many observers answer yes, because those who delegate seem uninformed when compared with those to whom they delegate.

The principal democratic delegation, that of the people electing their governors, seems most susceptible to tyranny. Cicero's observation that "in the common people there is no wisdom, no penetration, no power of judgment" is an apt summary of modern voting studies (see Berelson 1952, Campbell et al. 1960, Converse 1964, Kinder and Sears 1985, Lane and Sears 1964, Luskin 1987, McClosky 1964, Neuman 1986, Schattschneider 1960, Schumpeter 1942, Zaller 1992, Zaller and Feldman 1992; for a survey, see Delli Carpini and Keeter 1996). Many scholars argue that voters, because of their obstinance or their inability to educate themselves, become the unwitting puppets of campaign and media puppet-masters (Bennett 1992, Sabato 1991). Iyengar (1987: 816) summarizes the literature on voting and elections: "the low level of political knowledge and the absence of ideological reasoning has lent credence to the charges that popular control of government is illusory." These studies suggest that voters who lack information cannot use elections to control their governors.

Other observers make similar arguments about elected representatives. Weber, for example, argues that legislators cannot control bureaucrats:

Under normal conditions, the power position of a fully developed bureaucracy is always overtowering. The "political master" finds himself in the position of the "dilettante" who stands opposite the "expert," facing the trained official who stands within the management of administration. This holds whether the "master" whom the bureaucracy serves is a "people," equipped with the weapons of "legislative initiative," the "referendum," and the right to remove officials, or a parliament, elected on a more aristocratic or more "democratic" basis and equipped with the right to vote a lack of confidence, or with the actual authority to vote it. (Weber quoted in Gerth and Mills 1946: 232)

3

Niskanen (1971) continues that public officials' inability to contend with the complexities of modern legislation places them at the mercy of self-serving special interests and bureaucrats. Lowi (1979: xii) concludes, "actual policy-making will not come from voter preferences or congressional enactments but from a process of tripartite bargaining between the specialized administrators, relevant members of Congress, and the representatives of self-selected organized interests."

Jurors also seem to lack the information they need. Posner (1995: 52), for example, argues, "As American law and society become ever more complex, the jury's cognitive limitations will become ever more palpable and socially costly." Other observers characterize the legal system, not as a forum where citizens make reasoned choices, but as a stage for emotional appeals where style and deception overwhelm knowledge. As Abramson (1994: 3) laments,

The gap between the complexity of modern litigation and the qualifications of jurors has widened to frightening proportions. The average jury rarely understands the expert testimony in an anti-trust suit, a medical malpractice case, or an insanity defense. Nor do most jurors know the law or comprehend the judge's crash course of instructions on it. Trial by jury has thus become trial by ignorance.

Although the critiques of democracy's delegations are myriad and diverse, all have a common conclusion – *reasoned choice does not govern delegation.* As Schumpeter (1942: 262) argues, "the typical citizen drops down to a lower level of mental performance as soon as he enters the political field. He argues and analyzes in a way which he would readily recognize as infantile within the sphere of his real interests. He becomes a primitive again. His thinking is associative and affective. . . . [T]his may prove fatal to the nation."

If voters, legislators, and jurors lack the capability to delegate effectively, then democracy may be "but a prologue to a farce or a tragedy." Like the scholars just quoted, we find this possibility alarming. Unlike these scholars, however, we argue that the capabilities of the people and the requirements of democracy are not as mismatched as many critics would have us believe. In what follows, we will identify the conditions under which this mismatch does and does not exist.

A PREVIEW OF OUR THEORY

We argue that *limited information need not prevent people from making reasoned choices.* Of course, we are not the first analysts to make this type of argument. In the 1950s, for example, Berelson, Lazarfeld, and McPhee (1954) and Downs (1957) argued that voters rely on opinion leaders and political parties to overcome their information shortfalls.

4

More recently, a generation of scholars led by Fiorina (1981), Kuklinski, Metlay, and May (1982), Calvert (1985), Grofman and Norrander (1990), the contributors to Ferejohn and Kuklinski (1990), Popkin (1991), Sniderman, Brody, and Tetlock (1991), and the contributors to Lodge and McGraw (1995) has further countered the view that the "democratic citizen is expected to be well informed about political affairs" (Berelson, Lazarsfeld, and McPhee 1954: 308). Collectively, these scholars have demonstrated that voters can use a wide range of simple cues as substitutes for complex information. We concur with the basic insight of each of these studies – people can use substitutes for encyclopedic information.

However, we want to do more than argue that limited information need not prevent people from making reasoned choices. We want to argue that *there are specific conditions under which people who have limited information can make reasoned choices.* Therefore, in addition to showing that people *can* use cues, we want to answer questions about *when and how* people use cues, *when* cues are effective substitutes for detailed information, and *when* cues are detrimental. To understand who is (and who is not) capable of reasoned choice, we must be able to answer questions such as:

- When do people use simple cues?
- When do people ignore simple cues and seek more detailed information instead?
- When are simple cues sufficient for reasoned choice?
- When can people who offer simple cues manipulate or deceive those who use them?
- What factors determine why a person relies on some simple cues while ignoring many others?
- How do political institutions affect the use and effectiveness of simple cues?

To answer these questions, we construct theories of attention, persuasion, and delegation. Like all theories, ours build upon the ideas of others. Our theories' lineage is most directly traced to economic games of incomplete information (e.g., Harsanyi 1967, 1968a, 1968b), signaling models (e.g., McKelvey and Ordeshook 1986, Spence 1973; see also Banks 1991), and strategic communication models (Crawford and Sobel 1982; see also Calvert 1986, Farrell and Gibbons 1989). However, our theory also contains premises that are common to theories of communication and learning in cognitive science (e.g., Churchland and Sejnowski 1992, Simon 1955) and theories of persuasion in social psychology (e.g., Eagly and Chaiken 1993, McGuire 1969, Petty and Cacioppo 1986). As a result, our theory has the rare advantage of being relevant to the usually separate debates on

5

learning, communication, and choice held in cognitive science, economics, political science, and psychology. Next, we describe our theory and preview the answers it gives to the questions listed previously.

Knowledge and Information

We begin in Chapter 2 by developing a theory of attention. The purpose of our theory is to explain how humans cope with complexity and scarcity. As Simon (1979: 3) argues, "human thinking powers are very modest when compared with the complexities of the environments in which human beings live." Making matters worse is the fact that many of the resources people need to survive are scarce.

Ironically, for many political issues, information is not scarce; rather it is the cognitive resources that a person can use to process information that are scarce. For example, political information appears in the newspapers, in the mail, on community bulletin boards, and on television and radio and is relayed to us in person by friends and family. People often lack the time and energy needed to make sense of all this information. As a consequence, people often have only incomplete information. Fortunately, reasoned choice does not require complete information. Instead, it requires *knowledge: the ability to predict the consequences of actions.*[3]

Implicit in many critiques of democracy is the claim that people who lack *information* are incapable of reasoned choice. By contrast, we argue that people who lack information solve enormously complex problems every day. They do so by making effective use of the information available to them, sorting that which is useful from that which is not.

Information is useful only if it helps people avoid costly mistakes. By contrast, if more information does not lead people to change their decisions, then it provides no instrumental benefit and they should ignore it. Indeed, ignoring useless information is necessary for humans and other species to survive and prosper (Churchland and Sejnowski 1992).

Those who find such statements surprising should consider the almost boundless range of actions, both mundane and grand, for which people ignore available information. For example, people take medication without knowing all of the conditions under which it might be harmful. They also buy houses based on limited information about the neighborhoods around them and with little or no information about the neighbors. People

[3]For example, knowing which of two products is "better" than the other is often sufficient for us to make the same choice we would have made had we been completely informed about each product.

6

make choices in this way not because the information is unavailable but because the costs of paying attention to it exceed the value of its use.[4]

Although reasoned choice does not require complete information, it does require the ability to predict the consequences of actions. In many cases, simple pieces of information can provide the knowledge people need. For example, to navigate a busy intersection successfully, you must *know* where all of the other cars are going to be sure that you can avoid crashing into them. Advocates of complete information might argue that successful automotive navigation requires as much information as you can gather about the intentions of other drivers and the speed, acceleration, direction, and mass of their cars. At many intersections, however, there is a simple substitute for *all* of this information – a traffic signal. At these intersections, traffic signals are substitutes for more complex information and reduce the amount of information required to make a reasoned choice. At intersections without working traffic signals or other simple cues, reasoned choices require more information. Using similar logic, it follows that limited information precludes reasoned choice only if people are stuck at complex political intersections and lack access to effective political traffic signals.

Persuasion, Enlightenment, and Deception

People who want to make reasoned choices need knowledge. There are two ways to acquire knowledge. The first way is to draw from personal experience. People who exercise this option use their own observations of the past to derive predictions about the future consequences of their actions. The second way is to learn from others. People who exercise this option substitute other people's observations of the past for the personal experience they lack.

In many political settings, only the second option is available. This is true because politics is often abstract and its consequences are remote. In these settings, personal experience does not provide sufficient knowledge for reasoned choice. For many political decisions, reasoned choice requires learning from others.

There are many explanations of how people learn from others. Indeed, a generation of scholars, starting with Knight, Simon, Berelson et al.

---

[4]Furthermore, beyond being useless, some types of information cause people to make the wrong (i.e., welfare-reducing) choices when they would have otherwise made the right (i.e., welfare-increasing) ones with less information. For example, a person who votes for Jones instead of Smith because a newspaper endorses Jones may regret having attended to this additional information when Jones later opposes a policy that both she and Smith support.

and Downs, suggest numerous heuristics – simple means for generating information substitutes.[5] Examples include opinion leaders (Berelson, Lazarsfeld, and McPhee 1954), party identification (Downs 1957), biased information providers (Calvert 1985), campaign events (Popkin 1991), campaign information (Lodge, Steenbergen, and Brau 1995), history (Downs 1957, Fiorina 1981, Key 1966), polls (McKelvey and Ordeshook 1986), costly action (Lupia 1992), "fire alarms" (McCubbins and Schwartz 1984), people who have similar interests (Krehbiel 1991; Sniderman, Brody, and Tetlock 1991), demographics (Popkin et al. 1976), competition (Milgrom and Roberts 1986), interest group endorsements (Lupia 1994), and the media (Iyengar and Kinder 1987; Page, Shapiro, and Dempsey 1987).

Individually, each of these explanations of how we learn from others is valuable and enlightening. Each reveals a source of the judgmental shortcuts that people undoubtedly use. However, as Sniderman, Brody, and Tetlock (1991: 70) argue, "The most serious risk is that . . . every correlation between independent and dependent variables [is] taken as evidence of a new judgmental shortcut." We agree. We need a theory that explains when or how people choose among the shortcuts listed in the preceding paragraph. To understand how people learn from others, we must be able to explain *how people choose whom to believe*.

In Chapter 3, we explain *how* people learn from others. This explanation answers questions such as "Who can learn from whom?" In Chapter 4, we explain *what* people learn from others. This explanation answers such questions as "When is learning from others a sufficient substitute for personal experience as the basis of reasoned choice?" and "When does relying on the testimony of others prevent reasoned choice?"

In Chapters 3 and 4, we show that learning from others is no trivial matter. To see why, notice that any attempt to learn from others leads to one of three possible outcomes.

- The first outcome is *enlightenment*. When someone furnishes us with knowledge, we become enlightened. Enlightenment, then, is the process of becoming enlightened. If we initially lack knowledge sufficient for reasoned choice and can obtain such knowledge only from others, then we can make reasoned decisions only if others enlighten us.
- The second outcome is *deception*. Deception is the process by which the testimony we hear reduces our ability to predict accurately the consequences of our actions. For example, we are deceived when someone lies to us *and* we believe that individual.
- The third outcome is that we *learn nothing*. When we learn nothing, our beliefs go unchanged and we gain no knowledge.

[5]Also, see Key (1966) and Tversky and Kahneman (1974).

Both enlightenment and deception, in turn, require *persuasion: a successful attempt to change the beliefs of another.* The key to understanding whether people become enlightened or deceived by the testimony of others is to understand the conditions under which they can persuade one another.

Most scholars of communication and politics, dating back to Aristotle, focus on a speaker's *internal character* (e.g., honesty, ideology, or reputation) as a necessary condition for persuasion. If a speaker lacks the right character, then these scholars conclude that the speaker will not be persuasive. In Chapter 3, we present a different set of necessary and sufficient conditions for persuasion. We argue that persuasion need not be contingent upon personal character; rather, *persuasion requires that a listener perceive a speaker to be both knowledgeable and trustworthy.* Although a perception of trust can arise from a positive evaluation of a speaker's character, we show that *external forces can substitute for character* and can thus generate persuasion in contexts where it would not otherwise occur.

An example of an external force that generates trust and persuasion is a listener's observation of a speaker's costly effort. From this observation, the listener can learn about the intensity of a speaker's preferences. This particular condition is also very much like the adage that actions speak louder than words. When speaker costs have this effect, they can provide a basis for trust by providing listeners with a window to speaker incentives.

To see how costly effort affects persuasion, consider the following situation. First, suppose that a listener knows a speaker to have one of three possible motivations – he is a conservative with intense preferences, a conservative with non-intense preferences, or a liberal with non-intense preferences. Second, suppose that the listener does not know which of the three motivations the speaker actually has. Third, suppose that the listener can make a reasoned choice only if he or she knows whether the speaker is liberal or conservative. Fourth, suppose that if the listener observes that the speaker paid a quarter of his or her income to affect a policy outcome, then the listener can conclude that the speaker has intense preferences. If all four suppositions are true, then the speaker's costly effort persuades the listener. As a result, the listener can make a reasoned choice because she can infer that the speaker is a conservative.

Another example of a trust-inducing external force is a penalty for lying. Penalties for lying, whether explicit, such as fines for perjury, or implicit, such as the loss of a valued reputation, can also generate trust by revealing a speaker's incentives. That is, although a listener may believe that a speaker has an interest in deception, the presence of a penalty for lying may lead the listener to believe that certain types of lies are prohibitively costly, rendering certain types of statements very likely to be true.

Our conditions for persuasion show when forces such as costly effort and penalties for lying are, and are not, effective substitutes for a speaker's character.[6] These conditions reveal that you do not necessarily learn more from people who are like you, nor do you learn more from people you like. This is why most people turn to financial advisors, instead of their mothers, when dealing with mutual funds, and back to Mom when seeking advice about child rearing.

Unlike most well-known theories of persuasion and strategic communication, our conditions for persuasion also clarify how and when people suffer as a result of substituting simple cues for complex information. For example, our theory allows us to identify conditions under which a speaker can deceive a listener (i.e., conditions under which a speaker lies *and* a listener believes the lie). These conditions are important because many critics of democracy claim that uninformed citizens are ripe for manipulation at the hands of slick political salesmen.

We will show that deception requires a number of factors that are not trivially satisfied. More important, in Chapters 4 and 10, we will use the conditions for deception that we identify as the basis for showing how certain political institutions can be redesigned to reduce the dangers of deception.

More generally, our conditions for persuasion show why some statements are persuasive and others are not. The obvious reason for these differences is that statements vary in content. The less obvious reason is that the context under which a speaker makes a statement also affects persuasion considerably. Two people making precisely the same statement may not be equally persuasive if only one is subject to penalties for lying.

Our conditions for persuasion further imply that not everyone can persuade. People listen to some speakers and not others. They read some books and not others. They buy some products even though the manufacturers spend very little money on advertising while refusing to buy others supported by celebrity endorsements. Similarly, people respond to the advice of some experts or interest groups and not that of others. Our conditions for persuasion explain how people make these choices.

Our results also reveal the bounds on the effectiveness of the heuristics mentioned earlier. Consider, for example, the use of ideology as a heuristic. When there is a high correlation between a speaker's ideology and that speaker's knowledge and trustworthiness, then people are likely to find ideological cues useful. By contrast, when there is no clear correlation,

---

[6]A third external force that can induce a listener to trust a speaker arises when the speaker's statements are subject to some chance of being externally verified.

ideology is useless. Similar arguments can be made about other heuristics, such as party, reputation, and likability. In sum, *concepts such as reputation, party, or ideology are useful heuristics only if they convey information about knowledge and trust. The converse of this statement is not true* – knowledge and trust are the fundamental factors that make cues persuasive; the other factors are not.

In Chapter 4, we shift our focus from identifying the conditions for persuasion to identifying how the design of political institutions can affect the incidence of enlightenment and deception. The key to enlightenment is that a listener has accurate beliefs about the speaker's knowledge and incentives. The key to deception is that the listener has inaccurate beliefs about these factors.[7] When nature, cultural norms, or the structure of political institutions provides listeners with a window to a speaker's interests, knowledge, and incentives, then the context is ripe for enlightenment. Otherwise people who attempt to learn from others are likely to be deceived. We conclude Chapter 4 by arguing that reasoned choice is impossible only when there is limited information and the conditions for enlightenment do not exist and cannot be created. Together, Chapters 3 and 4 clarify the relationship between limited information and reasoned choice.

Successful Delegation and the Institutions of Knowledge

In Chapter 5 we use the lessons of Chapters 2, 3, and 4 to clarify the political consequences of limited information. We begin with the observation that modern democracy requires delegation. We then show that delegation has three possible consequences – it can succeed, it can fail, or it can have no effect. We deem delegation to have succeeded when an agent (the person or persons to whom authority is delegated) enhances the welfare of a principal (the person or persons who did the delegating). We deem delegation to have failed when an agent reduces a principal's welfare. Delegation has no effect when an agent's actions do not affect a principal's welfare.

Two reasons are commonly cited for the failure of delegation: principals and agents have *conflicting interests* over the outcome of delegation, and agents have *expertise* regarding the consequences of the delegation that principals do not (for a survey, see Kiewiet and McCubbins 1991, Miller 1992). When delegation occurs under these conditions, agents are

[7]If you know a false statement is coming, then it is optimal to ignore what the speaker is saying. Therefore, you can be deceived only if you mistake a false statement for a true one.

11

free to take any action that suits them, irrespective of the consequences for the principal, and the principal cannot cause them to do otherwise.

We find that delegation succeeds if two conditions are satisfied: the knowledge condition and the incentive condition. The knowledge condition is satisfied in one of two ways. First, it is satisfied when the principal's personal experience allows her to distinguish beneficial from detrimental agent actions. Second, it is satisfied when the principal can obtain this knowledge from others. Therefore, the knowledge condition does not require the principal to know everything the agent knows; it requires only that the principal know enough to distinguish welfare-enhancing from welfare-decreasing agent actions.

The incentive condition is satisfied when the agent and the principal have at least some goals in common. In many cases, satisfaction of the knowledge condition is sufficient for satisfaction of the incentive condition: A principal who becomes enlightened with respect to the consequences of delegation either can motivate the agent to take actions that enhance her welfare or can reject the agent's actions that do not enhance her welfare.

We find that the outcome of delegation is not determined by whether or not the principal can match the agent's technical expertise. Instead, it is determined by the principal's ability to use the testimony of others effectively. If the principal has this ability, then delegation can succeed despite the information she lacks. If the principal lacks information about the agent and lacks the ability to learn from others, then delegation is doomed.

Moreover, we argue that, if democratic principals can create the context in which knowledgeable and persuasive speakers can inform them of the consequences of their agent's actions, then they can facilitate successful delegation. We argue that institutions, such as administrative procedure, rules of evidence, and statutory law, provide the context in which principals can learn about their agent's actions. Institutions can, if properly structured, offer principals a way to better judge their agent's actions. When institutions are poorly designed, or the incentives they induce are opaque, then the political consequence of limited information is likely to be failed delegation. By contrast, when these institutions properly and clearly structure incentives, then they facilitate enlightenment, reasoned choice, and successful delegation even in complex circumstances.

Conclusion

The mismatch between what delegation demands and citizens' capabilities constitutes the democratic dilemma. If people are not capable of reasoned political choices, then effective self-governance is an illusion. After observing that voters, legislators, and jurors are ignorant of many of the details of the decisions they face, many scholars and political commentators conclude that the illusion is real and argue for some type of reform. If their conclusion is correct, then effective self-governance may indeed require political reform. If their conclusion is incorrect, their reforms may restrain the truly competent and do more harm than good.

Other scholars have argued that people are quite capable of making complex decisions with very little information. They point to instances in which people use heuristics and conclude that such heuristics are sufficient for reasoned choice. If these conclusions are correct, then successful delegation does not require reform and the critics mentioned previously are akin to democracy's Chicken Littles. If, however, these latter conclusions are incorrect, then the optimistic scholars are akin to democracy's Pollyannas, advocating the perpetuation of ineffective and harmful systems of governance.

Both sides of this debate recognize that people are often ignorant about the details of the choices they make. They also both recognize the existence of information shortcuts, cues, and heuristics. What is missing from this debate is an understanding of when ignorance of details prevents reasoned choice, how people choose among potential heuristics, and when these heuristics provide effective substitutes for the detailed information people lack. Only when we have these understandings will we be able to make constructive use of the common observation that people lack information. At that point, we can separate the Chicken Littles from the Pollyannas and build effective solutions to the democratic dilemma.

PLAN OF THE BOOK

This book has three parts. In Part I, containing Chapters 2 through 5, we develop the theories just described.

In Part II, which contains Chapters 6 through 9, we test the crucial hypotheses about learning, persuasion, reasoned choice, and delegation that we produce in Part I. In Chapter 6, we define a set of standards for empirical research that motivates the experiments we conduct. In Chapters 7 and 8, we describe a series of laboratory experiments. In Chapter 7, we use laboratory experiments to evaluate the predictive strength of our conditions for persuasion, enlightenment, and deception. In Chapter 8, we use laboratory experiments to evaluate our theoretical predictions about delegation. In Chapter 9, we describe a survey experiment about persuasion.

In Part III, which contains Chapter 10 and a brief afterword, we describe our theories' and experiments' implications for the effect and design of political institutions. In Chapter 10, we examine democratic institutions from the United States and elsewhere and show how they do or do not provide the context for successful delegation. At the end of Chapter 10 and in our Afterword, we discuss how to reform institutions in order to stack the deck in favor of reasoned choice and successful delegation.

PART I

Theory

2

How People Learn

The acquisition of information must be analyzed, since it is itself the result of decisions.

– Arrow (1974: 48)

Most citizens have scant information about politics. Indeed, after attending to their families, jobs, hobbies, social commitments, and various other demands, most people have little time left to inform themselves about the events on Capitol Hill, in the state capitol, or in city hall.

The claim that citizens lack political information has a long and respected history.[1] Four decades of survey research show that citizens cannot recall basic political facts (e.g., Delli Carpini and Keeter 1991), do not have a consistent understanding of ideological abstractions (e.g., Converse 1964), and fail to recall or recognize the names of their elected representatives (e.g., Jacobson 1992, Neuman 1986).[2]

Pundits and scholars use survey data to conclude that *citizens who lack information are incapable of reasoned choice.*[3] Lane and Sears (1964: 116), for example, argue that "Most people have very modest conceptual equipment for the political thinking they do; most are insufficiently informed to rely very much on their own resources for their political decisions."

Other observers make similar arguments about legislators. In a single legislative session, lawmakers consider hundreds, if not thousands, of

[1]Political commentators (e.g., Greider 1992, Herbert 1995, Lippmann 1922) and social scientists (e.g., Campbell et al. 1960, Parsons 1967, Schumpeter 1942, Smith 1989) alike have lamented the ignorance of the citizenry. For a different perspective, however, see Nie, Verba, and Petrocik (1976).

[2]Smith (1989: 159) attests to the volume of such studies in the following passage: "In the early years of survey research, there were a fair number of information questions. Indeed, one of the most important early findings of survey researchers was how little the public knew about politics. . . . The public's lack of information was so well established that scholars lost interest in studying the subject."

[3]See, for example, Campbell et al. (1960), Greider (1992), Herbert (1995), Lippmann (1922), Parsons (1967), Schumpeter (1942), Smith (1989).

17

policy proposals. Because legislators have limited time and energy, they cannot be well informed about most of these proposals. As Krehbiel (1991: 65) explains, "The premise that legislators often do not know the precise consequence of the policies they enact is evident not only in newspapers but also in the empirical research on Congress." Many scholars conclude that legislators' limited information allows expert bureaucrats to dominate the policymaking process (Freeman 1955, Lowi 1979, Ripley 1983, Smith 1988, Weber 1946, Wilson 1885).[4]

We say that a choice is reasoned if it is based upon an accurate prediction about a choice's consequence, and we reject the conclusion that people who lack information are incapable of reasoned choice. We reject this conclusion because it is based on an erroneous, though prevalent, assumption. The assumption is that people can make reliable predictions about the consequences of their actions *only if* they know a detailed set of facts about these actions. If this assumption is true, then it must also be true that reasoned choices can be made only by *ambulatory encyclopedias* – people who can store and quickly retrieve a detailed set of facts about every decision they make. If, however, the assumption is false, then even individuals who cannot answer simple survey questions or explain the details of proposed legislation may nevertheless be capable of reasoned choice.

In this chapter, we present a theory of how people collect and use information. We use the theory to show that some widely held assumptions and conclusions about the behavioral consequences of limited information are false. Our theory builds on well-established premises from the cognitive and social sciences. In particular, recent cognitive science research leads us to replace the erroneous assumption stated previously with two new assumptions.

The first new assumption is that *learning is active and goal oriented*. This is one of the most basic lessons of cognitive science. Though we seem to learn many things without even trying, the simple fact is that humans usually choose when and what to learn. This finding is consistent over time and across individuals.[5]

The second new assumption incorporates the process by which people use limited information to draw complex inferences. Cognitive scientists

[4]This view is not limited to the U.S. Congress. Some scholars of parliamentary democracy use similar logic to conclude that party leaders, bureaucrats, or ministers implement policy with little regard for the interests of backbenchers (i.e., "rank and file" Members of Parliament) or their constituents (Johnson 1975, Meny 1990, Mezey 1979, Savoie 1990).
[5]See Holland et al. (1986), Kandel, Schwartz, and Jessel (1995), and Newell (1990) for reviews of this literature and elaborations of the argument that learning is goal oriented.

call this process *connectionism*.[6] Connectionism is the way that people systematically *connect* current observations of their physical world to physical or emotional feedback from experience. Connectionist models show how people systematically attribute meaning to new or relevant objects by connecting them with objects, events, or people that they have encountered before.

For instance, you may have a theory that dark clouds produce rain. So, when you see a dark cloud, a connection leads you to infer that rain is coming. If your goal is to stay dry, then your observation leads you to seek cover. Taking this action does not require that you watch a weather report or that you obtain a degree in meteorology; instead, it merely requires that you connect an observation (you see dark clouds) to a previous observation or theory (clouds produce rain). If you are goal oriented (you desire to stay dry), then you use the connection (rain is coming) to act accordingly (seek cover).

As Churchland (1995: 15) explains, connectionist activity underlies "all of the distinctive cognitive properties displayed in living creatures, such as:

- the capacity for recognizing features or patterns through a veil of noise and distortion, or given only partial information;
- the capacity for seeing complex analogies;
- the capacity for recalling relevant information, instantly, as it bears on novel circumstances;
- the capacity for focusing attention on different features of one's sensory input . . ."

Without a process like connectionism, reasoned choice requires encyclopedic information. With such a process, reasoned choice requires less information.

Our theory of information acquisition and processing allows us to reject the conclusion that limited information prevents reasoned choice. We show that under a surprisingly broad set of conditions, people can use limited amounts of information to solve complex problems. For example, suppose that a particular set of facts is sufficient for a reasoned choice (e.g., suppose that knowing Bill Clinton's position on one hundred political issues is sufficient for a reasoned choice). A person who does not know these facts and cannot access any other facts or connections that

---

[6]Some readers may recognize a similarity between the cognitive scientists' connectionism and social psychology's schema. Undoubtedly, the causal mechanisms underlying each are quite similar. Unlike schema, whose existence and general properties are often badly defined, cognitive scientists have conducted extensive research on the conditions under which new connections will and will not be made. Churchland and Sejnowski (1992), Clark (1993), Jackendoff (1994), and McCauley (1996) provide recent reviews and critiques of this research.

allow him or her to make the same choice cannot make a reasoned choice. If, however, there exists another, perhaps simpler, set of facts or connections that is sufficient for the person to make the same choice (e.g., Bill Clinton is endorsed by the National Education Association), then knowing the initial set of facts is not a prerequisite for reasoned choice.

This cognitive perspective also generates a more sensible way to interpret data on citizens' limited information. Many social scientists argue that people who cannot give detailed reasons for what they have done do not really understand what they have done. However, that people cannot explain or have forgotten *why* they do what they do is a general fact of life. As Churchland (1995: 22) further notes:

Humans are famously bad at describing their sensations – of tastes, of aromas, of feelings – but we are famously good at discriminating, enjoying, and suffering them. . . . And yet, while we all participate in the richness of sensory life, we struggle to communicate to others all but its coarsest features. Our capacity for verbal description comes nowhere near our capacity for sensory discrimination.

Therefore, we should expect even people who make reasoned political decisions to be unable to answer detailed questions about their choices (see Fiorina 1981; Lodge 1995; Lodge, Steenbergen, and Brau 1995 for related arguments). It follows that a person's inability to answer detailed survey questions correctly may reveal nothing about the quality of his or her decisions (i.e., it may reveal nothing about whether these decisions are the same ones that person would have made had he or she been an ambulatory encyclopedia). We use similar logic to argue the following points.

1. Learning is *active:* People choose when and what to learn.
2. Knowledge is the ability to predict accurately the consequences of choices, and information is the data from which knowledge may be derived. Therefore, knowledge requires information, but large amounts of information do not ensure knowledge.
3. Information is valuable *only* when it improves the accuracy of predictions about the consequences of choices.[7]
4. Reasoned choice requires only that people make accurate predictions about the consequences of their choices.

The remainder of the chapter continues as follows: First, we describe our theory of information acquisition and choice. Our theory has two parts. The first part is a model of attention. This model explains how

[7]Here is where we separate ourselves from "rational ignorance" models (e.g., Downs 1957). "Rational ignorance" models argue that the costs of acquiring information often outweigh the positive benefits of acquiring it. Although we agree, we also argue that, aside from the costs of obtaining and processing information, the benefit of obtaining information may be zero or negative.

people decide when to gather information and what information to gather. The second part is a theory of how people use the information they have. We then conclude that people who possess only a few simple facts about politics can make a wide range of reasoned choices.

The world is complex. We adapt to complexity by learning. Many people believe that human learning processes are automatic and passive. They believe that we learn much like the apocryphal Newton under the apple tree, minding our own business while knowledge simply falls on our heads. This belief is prevalent because we seem to accomplish much in life with very little forethought.

The strongest evidence that learning is automatic and passive is that many activities that we now take for granted seem to have come about "naturally." To cite a few examples: We walk from our parking spaces to our offices without thinking about either the directions or the mechanisms of self-ambulation, we drive home from work while thinking about many other things, we buy a brand of toothpaste without contemplating either all other brands or our brand's chemical structure, and we tie our shoelaces without reflection. That we do not *seem* to think about these activities leads many of us to feel that we just naturally learn how to do things – that learning is more or less automatic.

At one time, however, all of these tasks were new and difficult for us. When we move to a new city, we must be careful to read street signs, follow maps, and identify landmarks that help us avoid time-consuming mistakes. Similarly, there was a time when our parents had to help us tie our shoelaces. Then something changed. Through a series of experiment-like trials, sometimes few and sometimes many, we made a new connection between the particular and the general. Certain tasks went from being a mystery to becoming "automatic."[8]

[8]A variant of these beliefs is that many things we do are a matter of instinct, not learning. This is a misconception. Instincts are automatic physical reactions such as an eye blink or a knee jerk. In contrast, learning is knowledge gained through experience (which can be incidental or active) or practice (which is active and not incidental). Indeed, some seemingly "instinctual" behaviors are learned through experience and practice. Consider an example from the study of vision. The first time that people try on a new pair of prescription glasses, they have trouble seeing. Several hours or days later they have no such trouble. What changed to allow clearer vision? What did not change was the physical structure of the eye or the eyeglasses. What changed was the product of active learning – through trial and error, people *learn* how to use the new glasses for the purpose of focusing. What seems automatic is at least partially learned.

That we do things such as drive to the office automatically does not imply that at one time we did not think carefully about it. Indeed, most of us can remember trying alternate routes to work. This is but one indication that learning is not automatic. Another is the number of VCRs in the homes of well-educated people that blink "12:00" and have never been programmed.

We argue that human learning is not automatic. To see this, consider three simple facts. First, learning requires effort. Second, effort is a scarce resource for everyone. Third, and a consequence of the first two facts, *people choose* what and when to learn. Thus, *learning is active.*

How we actively direct our scarce cognitive resources determines what we can learn. *Attention* is a prerequisite for learning anything. However, attention is scarce. In general, when we pay attention to one stimulus, we do so at the expense of paying attention to other stimuli. For instance, at noisy gatherings we often *choose* to pay attention to one conversation at the expense of attending to another (Jackendoff 1980). When visiting Disneyland, we listen for our children's screams (of delight or otherwise) but not the screams of others. If we want to exit a room, we attend to the location of a door instead of attending to the color of an end table. Survival requires that we make good use of our limited attention.

The Purpose of Paying Attention

Relative to our ability to comprehend it, our environment is very complex. This is one reason that it actually takes concentration to read this book. As you read it, you are choosing to ignore other things that are within your ken, such as the voices of people in the next room or the shuffle of feet outside your door. As much as you might like to pay attention to many factors at once, you cannot. You must develop a means for choosing among stimuli.

To understand the means people use for choosing among stimuli, we must identify the purpose of attention. To do this, we introduce two premises. The first premise is that *scarcity* is a ubiquitous feature of the human condition. As a result, people nearly always have *choices* to make. The second premise is that the ability to experience pain and pleasure is another ubiquitous feature of the human condition.

Many variations in pain and pleasure come from interactions with the environment. Some interactions, such as eating an apple, yield pleasure; others, such as stepping on a tack, cause pain.[9] If pain and pleasure

---

[9]In general, people *do not know the precise causes of the pain and pleasure that they feel.* However, this does not prevent them from feeling either. Unlike their causes, pain and pleasure do not have to be conceptualized or explained – they are basic elements of the human condition.

22

correlate with environmental factors, and if people desire to avoid pain and experience pleasure, then they have an incentive to learn about their environment and to base their choices on what they learn. Therefore, the purpose of directing scarce attention is to avoid the risk of future pain and increase the opportunity for future pleasure. In essence, we assume that people are goal oriented (i.e., *rational*) and that the purpose of paying attention is to make reasoned choices.[10]

Rationality. Our definition of rationality departs from the definitions commonly employed by economists and political scientists. Many of these definitions confound rationality and omniscience, assuming that rational actors must be limitless calculators. By contrast, our definition is consistent with that of *Webster's New Collegiate Dictionary. Webster's* defines *rational* as "a: having reason or understanding b: relating to, based on, or agreeable to reason . . ." and defines *reason* as "the proper exercise of the mind."

We define rationality to mean all human behavior that is directed toward the pursuit of pleasure and the avoidance of pain. At times, this behavior is reflexive, such as the act of pulling one's hand away from a flame.[11] At other times, this pursuit is quite complicated, such as when we select candidates or political parties to support.

Complex problems and limited cognitive capacities do not imply that people cannot be rational.[12] Rather, these facts imply just the opposite.

---

[10]Our definition implies that rationality and concern for others are not mutually exclusive. People who do things out of concern for others act self-interestedly. This must be true because people *choose* whom to care for. Moreover, this choice is itself correlated to experiences with pain and pleasure – concern for others must be physically embodied in the cognitive and emotional apparatus of the caring person. Thus, if past events lead a person to have a concern for others, then it is rational to be altruistic. Our definition of rationality requires only the feeling of pain and pleasure; it does not restrict the source of such feelings to material concerns for one's self. Also see Simon (1995).

[11]Even this "reflex" is learned. For example, young children react to their first "trial by fire" by crying out. Later, they figure out that avoiding or pulling away from fire leads to less pain.

[12]Kahneman and Tversky (1979, 1984) and Quattrone and Tversky (1988) are at the forefront of another population of scholars who argue that there are limits to rationality. Their experimental results are widely interpreted as providing a clear counterexample to the supposition that people are expected utility maximizers. We believe, however, that their experiments reveal more about the flaws in theories of information processing that do not account for framing effects. Our definition of rationality is perfectly consistent with their notion of framing and their experimental results. We interpret their results to show merely that there are nontrivial and systematic ways that people respond to complexity. Satz and Ferejohn (1994), Jones (1995), and Wittman (1995) also provide alternative critiques of what experiments such as these do and do not imply about rationality.

Survival requires rational choices of goods and services and rational allocations of our scarce cognitive resources.

Thus, in our definition of rational human behavior, we agree with Simon (1985) that a realistic model needs to take account of human limitations. We strongly disagree, however, that *bounded rationality* implies nonmaximizing behavior. We agree with Jensen and Meckling (1976: 307) that:

Simon's work has often been misinterpreted as a denial of maximizing behavior, and misused, especially in the marketing and behavioral science literature. His later use of the term "satisficing" (Simon 1959) has undoubtedly contributed to this confusion because it suggests rejection of maximizing behavior rather than maximization subject to costs of information and decision making.

Indeed, Simon (1995: 45) has recently clarified his view of rationality by proclaiming that "virtually all human behavior is rational. People usually have reasons for what they do."

Knowledge. The purpose of paying attention is to make reasoned choices. To make reasoned choices, people need to *know* something about the consequences of their actions. They need to know about relationships of the form "If A, then B." To gain this knowledge, they need not learn fundamental truths about the causal processes of our universe; they need only have beliefs that generate accurate predictions about the consequences of their actions. We define *knowledge* as the ability to make accurate predictions.[13] We say that a prediction of the form "If A, then B" is accurate if the *ex ante* belief "If A, then B" matches the *ex post* observation. So, if you can correctly predict the winner of the 1948 presidential election, then we say that you have knowledge about the topic. Similarly, the more accurate predictions you can make about the incentive effects of a new tax policy, then the more knowledgeable you are about that topic. We argue that the desired consequence of paying attention to a stimulus is to acquire knowledge sufficient for reasoned choice.

Note that having information and having knowledge are not the same thing. Knowledge is the ability to make accurate predictions; information is data. Knowledge requires information because accurate predictions require data – at a minimum you need some data to verbalize the prediction you are making. By contrast, you can know a long list of facts and fail to put them together in a way that allows you to make accurate

[13]Readers from cognitive science will note that our definition of knowledge closely approximates the modern definition of intelligent performance. We use the term *knowledge* here because it is far more common in social science parlance. For an extensive discussion of what constitutes knowledge, see Chapters 2, 3, and 6 of Newell (1990).

predictions. Thus, although you cannot have knowledge without having information, you can have information without having knowledge.

In sum, reasoned choice requires knowledge, knowledge requires information, and information requires attention. However, reasoned choice need not require either full information or unlimited attention. Instead, reasoned choice requires information that generates accurate predictions about the choice.

The Calculus of Attention

Because people usually lack the capacity to sort through all the stimuli in their environment, survival and prosperity require people to develop a calculus of attention. This calculus determines the return from attending to a given stimulus. Using $E(.)$ to define an expectation, we define the calculus as follows:

$$E(Return) = E(Benefit) - E(Opportunity\ Costs) - E(Transactions\ Costs).$$

$E(Return)$ refers to the expected return of paying attention to a given stimulus, $E(Benefit)$ refers to the expected benefit from paying attention, $E(Opportunity\ Costs)$ refers to the expected cognitive opportunity costs, and $E(Transactions\ Costs)$ refers to the expected cognitive transactions costs.[14] Thus, as the expected benefit from paying attention to a given stimulus increases, the expected return from paying attention also increases. Conversely, as the expected cognitive opportunity or transactions costs increase, the expected return from paying attention decreases.

Before we use the calculus to derive conclusions about attention, we take a moment to describe its components in greater detail. What we describe provides the intuition that underlies our model. The Appendix to Chapter 2 provides a more technical version of our model.

The Costs.   Some of the costs of paying attention to a given stimulus arise as a result of scarcity; that is, when we pay attention to one thing, we cannot attend to other things. For example, most of us cannot read a difficult book passage and carry on a conversation at the same time. If the stimuli we ignore prevent us from making costly mistakes, then our limited capacity for attention forces us to give up something of value. Let us define the cognitive *opportunity cost* of paying attention to a given stimulus as the returns forgone by not attending to other stimuli.

[14]The expected benefit can be thought of as either the short-run or long-run benefit of paying attention. That is, the knowledge gained from paying attention can have either an (expected) immediate payoff or a (expected and discounted) payoff sometime in the future.

Other costs of paying attention arise from the fact that some stimuli are harder to make sense of than are others. Let us define cognitive *transaction costs* as the energy needed to process a stimulus into a useful inference.[15] Differences in cognitive transaction costs can arise because of differences in the stimuli themselves. Some are familiar and easy to make sense of, such as your mother's voice, whereas others are not, such as the voice of someone speaking Sumerian. Interpersonal differences in cognitive transaction costs may also arise because of differences in our perceptual capabilities (some of us can see, hear, smell, or feel better than others).

The Benefits. The expected benefit from attending to a given stimulus comes from the new knowledge that the stimulus imparts. To be beneficial, a stimulus must help an individual make new and accurate predictions about the consequences of her actions. If a stimulus does not cause an individual to change her actions (i.e., take new or different actions), then the benefit derived from paying attention to the stimulus is zero. If a stimulus leads an individual to change her behavior, and this change prevents a painful mistake, then the benefit is positive. If, on the other hand, the stimulus leads an individual to change her behavior and this change causes the individual to make a painful mistake, then the benefit of paying attention to the stimulus is negative.

We define the expected benefit of paying attention to a given stimulus as: $E(Benefit) = \Sigma_M (P_{Prev}*E(Mistake) - P_{Cause}*E(Mistake))$. $E(Mistake)$ refers to the pain that a mistaken choice is expected to produce; P_{Prev} refers to the perceived probability that paying attention to the stimulus will prevent such a mistake; P_{Cause} refers to the perceived probability that paying attention to the stimulus will cause a costly mistake. The sign Σ_M denotes the summation over the set of all possible mistakes.

From this formula, we can see that if paying attention to a given stimulus reduces the likelihood of a costly mistake, then it increases the expected benefit of paying attention to that stimulus. Conversely, if paying attention to the stimulus increases the likelihood of a costly mistake, then it decreases the expected benefit of attention.

Conclusions. We now use the calculus of attention to identify the conditions under which a goal-oriented decision maker should attend to a particular stimulus. Our first conclusion challenges the view that more information is necessarily better. Remarkably, this conclusion can be

---

[15]On the general effect of transaction costs on decision making, see Coase (1937), Barzel (1989), North (1981), and Williamson (1975).

proven true in our model with or *without* reference to the costs of attention.[16]

Theorem 2.1:
- The benefit of more information can be zero or negative.
- The return from having more information can be zero or negative.
- More information is neither necessary nor sufficient for reasoned choice.

The actions we take on a daily basis belie the notion that more information is always better. For example, many expectant mothers undergo tests during pregnancy, some of which reveal the baby's sex. Many parents who know that this information is freely available ask that it not be revealed to them. Similarly, most people cannot name all of the ingredients in their toothpaste, nor can they explain why clouds produce rain. In each instance, people forget details they once knew or have chosen never to learn some details, even though these details were freely available and potentially relevant to their welfare. This selective ignorance implies that all of us, at some level, embrace the notion that *more information is not necessarily better.*[17]

Besides forgetting or never learning the seemingly mundane, we forget and ignore seemingly important facts. For instance, how many people actually read the warnings that come with most medication? These directions describe the conditions under which the medicine will be helpful and harmful, and how the medication interacts with other medications. This information is clearly important. Typically, however, we ignore it. As physicians know, patients often do not follow even strict instructions.[18] Again, it must be that people believe "more information is not always better."

Additional information is beneficial *only if it prevents a costly mistake (or, alternatively, if it causes a reasoned choice).* If people expend effort

[16]We call our conclusions Theorems 2.1 and 2.2, where the number before the period refers to the chapter number and distinguishes these results from those of subsequent chapters.

[17]Alternatively, those of us who grew up in urban areas (e.g., McCubbins) are considered smart for looking both ways before we cross the street (for this imparts greater knowledge about the likelihood of safe passage). While looking both ways before stepping into the street in remote rural areas could grant similar knowledge, most people choose not to (and those of us who grew up in remote, rural areas – e.g., Lupia – think that people who look twice before crossing a desolate road are rather peculiar).

[18]There is a large literature on the failure of patients to follow the orders of their health-care providers. In their review of this literature, Kaplan, Sallis, and Patterson (1993: 88) report, "Most studies indicate that at least 33 percent of all patients fail to adhere to the recommended therapeutic regimen." One explanation for this finding is that at least one-third of the patients judge the information contained in the regimen to be unworthy of attention.

acquiring information that does not ultimately prevent them from making some type of costly mistake, then, from the *ex post* perspective, they squandered a scarce resource.[19] Suppose, for example, that a person pays attention to stimulus X. If, as a consequence, she learns that she should make the same choice she was going to make before observing X, then she could have *ex post* regret about the acquisition – if she had known (*ex ante*) that the new information would not have affected her decision, then she would not have paid to learn.

Moreover, more information can actually be harmful. For example, say that you usually take the freeway to get to work. One day, before you start your commute, a neighbor informs you that the freeway is congested and suggests an alternative route. You take the alternate route. However, the alternate route is even slower than the freeway. In retrospect, you long for the freeway. In this case, more information made you worse off.

By contrast, the belief that more information is necessarily better is usually based on the assumption that information and knowledge are equivalent.[20] If this assumption is true, then more information cannot make you worse off. However, for most information, this assumption is clearly erroneous.

In sum, the benefits from attending to a particular stimulus need not derive from the untrue assumption that more information is necessarily better. Instead, information is valuable only if it prevents costly mistakes. This is why people reject so many opportunities to acquire political information. Even if people could acquire "complete information," the fact that information is valuable only if it prevents costly mistakes would dampen their desire to do so.

We now derive additional conclusions about attention by considering the costs as well as the benefits of attention. One consequence of this expanded view is three simple corollaries to Theorem 2.1:

- An increase in the expected cost of a mistake (that could be avoided by paying attention to a given stimulus) either induces attention to the stimulus or has no effect.
- An increase in the expected probability that paying attention to a given stimulus will prevent a painful mistake either induces attention to the stimulus or has no effect.

[19]For example, we may not know all the ingredients in asparagus pudding. However, reasonable people would never make the mistake of eating asparagus pudding. Therefore, we can prevent no costly errors by having more information about its makeup.

[20]This assumption is standard in economic information search models. When an actor in these models buys information, he often acquires complete knowledge of the consequences of his actions. In reality, however, political and economic actors seldom have such conjoined opportunities.

- An increase in the expected probability that paying attention to a given stimulus will cause a painful mistake either reduces attention to the stimulus or has no effect.

Adding two premises to the calculus of attention reveals more interesting consequences (in Theorem 2.2). First, we assume that there is substantial complexity in the environment. That is, we assume that there are thousands of stimuli to which a person could attend. Second, we assume that the opportunity cost of paying attention to a particular stimulus in this case is substantially higher than in the case where there are only one or two potentially relevant stimuli. Both premises are reasonable for a wide range of political contexts.

Theorem 2.2: People have an incentive to ignore many stimuli.

In fact, the normal response to a given stimulus is to ignore it. If we assume that the availability of many stimuli implies high enough opportunity costs, then Theorem 2.2 implies the following *corollary:*

- If a person can attend to only one stimulus, then he or she will attend to the stimulus for which the expected benefits are *extremely high* relative to the expected costs.

To put it another way, people pay attention only to those stimuli that are easy to process and strongly associated with the greatest avoidance of *pain* or the greatest production of *pleasure*.[21]

A concrete implication of Theorem 2.2 is that people should use simple and effective pieces of information when these are available. If cognitively cheap, pain-decreasing (or pleasure-enhancing) information is sufficient for reasoned choice, then people have little incentive to obtain more detailed information.[22] For example, drivers often rely on traffic signals

---

[21]That we pay attention to some stimuli and ignore most others implies that most of our decisions are based on very simple representations of the world that come from our past attempts to minimize pain and maximize pleasure. As Simon (1982: 306) argues, "The decision-maker's model of the world encompasses only a minute fraction of all the relevant characteristics of the real environment, and his inferences extract only a minute fraction of all the information that is present even in his model."

[22]The idea that individuals use shortcuts or cues is not new (e.g., Popkin 1991; Sniderman, Brody, and Tetlock 1991). We expand on this scholarship by deriving the conditions under which shortcuts will be used and the criteria that people use when they have many different shortcuts to choose from. That is, an individual (who does not already possess complete information) relies on an information shortcut when he or she perceives it to be cognitively cheap and correlated with an increase in pleasure or a decrease in pain. In this situation, an individual has no incentive to become completely informed. If there are more shortcuts available than a person can attend to, then he or she attends to the shortcut that is cheapest and most highly correlated with pleasure and pain. Our extension implies that the effectiveness of any shortcut, such as party, is not automatic or constant across situations. Instead, as we demonstrate in Chapter 3, a shortcut's effectiveness and usefulness vary across individuals and contexts.

for information about when they can safely navigate an intersection (as opposed to watching the actions of all other cars); on street signs for directions (as opposed to memorizing a map); and on dashboard warning lights to tell them about their car's health (as opposed to examining the engine). Of course, if they find that other cars routinely run red lights, that the street signs in a certain area are misleading (or are unfamiliar), or that their dashboard warning lights never turn off (or on), then these shortcuts cease to be useful.

The same dynamics justify voter decisions to attend to a candidate's party identification, work experience, involvement in scandals (if any), sound bites (e.g., tough on crime, tax cutter), interest group ratings, endorsements (e.g., supported by labor), or personal appearance instead of learning a candidate's complete legislative voting history, policy portfolio, or name. As with drivers' use of traffic lights, voters have an incentive to attend to stimuli that promise high returns. For example, a candidate's partisanship promises a higher return when candidates from different parties compete against each other than it does in nonpartisan or primary elections. The opposite is true for interest group and elite endorsements if such cues correlate with the schisms that divide party members.[23]

In sum, reasoned choice requires knowledge, but not necessarily detailed information; knowledge requires *some* information; information requires attention; and attention is scarce. Therefore, reasoned choice requires that people direct their attention in systematic ways. Cognitive science paradigms reveal that learning is active. When we combine the implications of this insight with the economist's insights about costs, benefits, and incentives, we find that people are wise to attend to certain types of stimuli while ignoring most other things.

Having presented an argument about the manner in which people gather information, we now direct our attention toward understanding how people use the information they gather.

THE COGNITIVE STOCK MARKET

Every human organism lives in an environment that generates millions of bits of new information each second, but the bottleneck of the perceptual apparatus certainly does not admit more than 1,000 bits per second, and probably much less. Equally significant omissions occur in the processing that takes place when information reaches the brain. As every mathematician knows, it is one thing to

[23]This claim is subject to the caveat that the endorsement is credible. We focus on the determinants of credibility in Chapter 3. Note also that voters may believe that all the issues they care about are correlated with the candidate's position on a single issue, such as abortion. Thus, they may rationally seek information about a candidate's position on the "hot button" issue and not bother with other information.

have a set of differential equations, and another thing to have their solutions. Yet the solutions are logically implied by the equations and exist simultaneously. All we have to do is figure out how to get them. By the same token, there are inferences that we don't draw from the information stored in our brains. The consequences implied by latent information in the memory become known only through active information-processing, and hence through active selection of particular problem-solving paths from the myriad that might have been followed.

– Simon (1982: 306)[24]

Like any useful commodity, our ability to process a new stimulus is scarce. When we hear a pane of glass shatter upstairs, it could mean that a robber is breaking into the house, that little Kenny threw a baseball through the window, or that a low-flying bird augured in beak first. Our dilemma is that we must regularly and quickly draw a single welfare-enhancing inference from the many theories that most stimuli render possible.

Consider the situation of a person on safari. Upon encountering a lion during an ill-advised sojourn alone into the savanna, he must decide, in the blink of a lion's eye, which of several nearby trees he should climb. He has no time for a close inspection of each tree, nor does he have the luxury of trying to experiment with alternative theories about the tree-climbing ability of lions. If his judgment is either incorrect or made with insufficient speed, he will become lion fodder. To satisfy the goal of pain minimization, he need not find the tallest tree; it is sufficient for him to find a safe one – quickly.

We do not have time to ruminate about every decision we make. Consequently, we must base a large number of decisions on a relatively small number of connections. Otherwise, we run the risk of being consumed by the lions of complexity.

People have an incentive to convert the information they have attended to into quickly retrievable plans for dealing with their environment. *We now argue that people can, and regularly do, generate a wide range of welfare-enhancing choices from a small store of information.* We explain this phenomenon by mixing a social science analogy (the stock market) with the cognitive science paradigm called connectionism.

Connectionism is a paradigm that explains how brains develop knowledge. Connectionist models are based on the premise that the anatomical representation of knowledge in living brains is connected networks of individual neurons. These anatomical neural networks develop in response to the body's reactions to environmental stimuli. Like muscles, neurons and networks can be strengthened by use. Like people who

[24]On the behavioral consequences of limited processing ability, also see Cyert and March (1963), March and Simon (1958), and Williamson (1975).

Theory

choose from a set of tools, the body relies on networks of neurons, favoring those that have proven useful in analogous situations. In short, connections that lead to successful ventures are used with increasing regularity, become stronger, and because they are stronger are even more likely to be used in the future.

For reasons that all can understand, most connectionist scholars do not examine actual brains. Instead, they use computer technology to simulate anatomical neural networks. As Holland et al. (1986: 25–6) describe,

> Connectionist models describe mental processes in terms of activation patterns defined over nodes in a highly connected network (Hinton and Anderson 1981; Rumelhart, McClelland, and the PDP Research Group 1986). . . . In a connectionist model the role of a unit in mental processing is defined by the *strength* of its connections – both excitatory and inhibitory – to other units. In this sense "the knowledge is in the connections," as connectionist theorists like to put it, rather than in static and monolithic representations of concepts. Learning, viewed within this framework, consists of the revision of connection strengths between units.

As social scientists, we are attracted to the connectionist paradigm because it treats knowledge as at least the partial product of active, goal-oriented behavior.

This brings us to a central modeling view in the cognitive sciences: *There is a competition among connections* (Fodor 1979, Greenwood 1991, Holland et al. 1986, Posner 1989). The connections we end up using are determined by the outcome of a mental tournament. This tournament is akin to a gigantic stock market, wherein each connection is like a stock, an asset whose value is based on the capitalized value of our experiences with the causal relations in our environment.

Within each of us, our experiences determine the value of connection-based "stocks." At the opening bell, perhaps an alarm clock in reality, our stocks start at a value determined by our previous activities. During the day, the stocks' relative values increase or decrease based on the new information that we attend to. On some days, one connection might be the winning "stock," because we perceive that it correlates highly with pleasure-inducing outcomes. On other days, this "stock" might lose value relative to other "stocks" because we learn that it correlates highly with costly mistakes that we do not want to repeat in the future.[25]

[25]To put it another way, stocks gain value by generating images that help us predict the consequences of our actions. Unfortunately, we cannot observe the consequence of an action until after we take it. Instead, *we must base all of our actions on imagined consequences.* Our images of the future are formed by the connections we hold. When these connections generate reliable predictions, they generate knowledge. For instance, when the ball leaves the hand of an expert bowler, its trajectory is based, in part, on what outcome the bowler imagines this trajectory will cause. The bowler does not know if his or her effort will lead to a strike until the final pin drops some seconds later. Such images must be the product of experience, of observed co-variations between actions (ours and others') and their consequences.

32

Virtually all people hold this tournament within themselves every day. To see how this is possible, note that the requirements for hosting a cognitive stock market are minimal. First, you must be able to observe outcomes and new information. Second, you must be able to remember some events that preceded the outcome. Third, for the connection to have any predictive value, you must believe that the future will resemble the past (a belief itself based on the winner of the "beliefs about the consistency of cause–effect relationships over time" tournament that each of us holds). If you can do these things, then the competition among connections can allow you to make a wide range of reasoned choices with a limited stock of encyclopedic knowledge.[26]

Which connections gain and retain value in cognitive stock markets? External regularities, the path of our life experiences, and our perceptive capabilities determine tournament winners. Although describing precise tournament dynamics is beyond the scope of our book, recent research in the cognitive sciences reveals what necessary characteristics tournament winners must have (e.g., Holland et al. 1986). Winning representations must be correlated with the experience of extreme pleasure or pain in a few trials or with some degree of pleasure or pain in multiple trials. Representations that do not associate with either pleasure or pain will be less useful, and we will rely on them less (these stocks pay lower dividends).

Some connections have high values regardless of whose brain hosts the cognitive stock market. If nature contains systematic characteristics that consistently produce pain and pleasure, then all people are likely to represent these characteristics in similar ways. For example, fire burns us all. Although we may have different thresholds of pain and different uses for fire, burning flesh induces pain in all parts of the world. Therefore, for all people, understanding the connection between fire and pain is a valuable asset and should be the basis of a highly valued cognitive stock.

The study of human language reveals many other connections that win a wide array of tournaments (Lakoff 1987). Indeed, the fact that humans can communicate with one another implies that we have many

[26]These tournaments are not specific to the human race. To see this, consider the classic T-maze and laboratory rat example. A rat is released into a maze with one capital T–shaped intersection. If the rat turns right, there is no food; if it turns left, it gets a pellet. Suppose that it first turns right. After a few trials, it goes left and finds food. If it is hungry, it continues to go left with increasing frequency for as long as pellets are there. Similar experiments have been administered with equivalent results on many other species, including bees. Variants of this experiment also suggest that hamsters employ probabilistic reasoning, in that they are quite sensitive to changes in the probability that different venues contain food. Descriptions of these experiments are contained in Churchland and Sejnowski (1992) and in Holland et al. (1986).

common beliefs (i.e., common portfolios of winning cognitive stocks). To see this, consider that metaphor and analogy are the basis of language, and if we shared no beliefs, then metaphor and analogy would be impossible. Therefore, the absence of common beliefs would leave each of us unable to relate to others. Furthermore, because we can train hamsters, dogs, pigeons, fish, and other animals (or they can train us), then we must share common representations of the world with these beings as well.

Commonalities in our environment and in our cognitive and perceptive abilities lead to *systematic* winners in our representational tournaments. Put simply, some stocks are always better investments than others, no matter who you are.[27] This implies another fundamental result from the cognitive sciences: *People should respond to some stimuli in systematic ways.*

For example, no one wakes up at 5:30 every morning to make sure the sun is going to rise. We all believe the sun will rise and set every day because it always has before. Everyone generalizes the same cause-and-effect relationship about night and day, even though no two people's experiences with Sol and Luna are the same. Learning is an active, goal-oriented process that integrates stimuli into a matrix of cause-and-effect correspondences. If enough of these correspondences are similar for all of us, then people should adapt to complexity in common and systematic ways.[28]

On the other hand, not all connections that have high values in one person's cognitive stock market will be valuable in another person's market. Either physical or circumstantial variance across individuals can lead different connections to have different values for different people. For example, people with different physical makeups (e.g., sex, height, weight, proclivity for allergies) may react to a single stimulus in different ways. To put it another way, what induces extreme physical pain in one person may have no effect on another person. These differences are sufficient to lead different people to hold different portfolios of "high-valued" cognitive stocks. Because differences in socialization can lead different people to have different experiences, these differences can have effects similar to those of varying physiques.[29] As long as multiple ways to

[27]Some aspects of the environment provide more effective cues about the consequences of our actions than do others.

[28]The emergence of systematic correspondences across a population can be thought of as the culture of that populace. Almond and Verba (1963: 13) define culture as "a set of orientations toward a special set of social objects and processes." These orientations arise largely from shared experiences (or lack thereof).

[29]Our theory implies that even clones of a single person could hold very different beliefs over time. That is, differences in socialization could lead them to find different connections valuable.

conceptualize the world permit survival, even people who share identical physiology (e.g., identical twins or clones) and many of the same experiences can draw different associations about cause and effect.

ATTENTION AND CONNECTIONS

When we connect the cognitive stock market to our theory of attention, we come to see how people with limited information can make reasoned choices in a wide range of complex circumstances. Through trial and error, people form simple attention strategies. As a rule, they ignore most of the information available to them. People diverge from this rule if they observe, or expect to observe, a string of sufficiently costly errors. In these cases, the most useful stimuli are those that lead to a pain-reducing or pleasure-inducing choice.

To see an example of how the unified attention–connection theory works, consider a simple parable. This parable is about the role of party identification on voting behavior in the United States. We know that most voters in presidential elections consistently vote along party lines. By contrast, partisanship is less of a factor in primary elections and in initiatives and referenda. Why might this be so?

In presidential elections, partisanship has strong connections to policy outcomes. Presidents, party organizations, and policy outcomes have strong and consistent historical associations. For example, every president elected in modern times has come from a political party with a well-established policy reputation. Therefore, in the context of presidential elections we should not be surprised to find that party-performance connections are highly valued, and often used, cognitive stocks. If people understand the differences between the parties, and if these differences correspond closely to factors that they believe cause pain and pleasure, then we should not be surprised that people stop looking for more information once they identify the candidate's party.

Party cues matter less in elections where parties do not compete against one another because they are not part of the same clarifying connections. So when candidates in primary elections or proponents of nonpartisan ballot initiatives claim partisan ties, the lack of a strong and consistent party-performance connection should make the cues less effective and less often attended to.

Similar logic provides a foundation for understanding the limits of brand names and party labels as judgmental shortcuts in economic choices. For example, people pay a premium for Mercedes-Benz automobiles and frequent McDonald's restaurants because the brand names imply reliability. If any of these companies attempted to be the sole sponsor of political candidates, would they have the same success? Similarly, if the Republican Party attempted to run an automotive plant by itself, would people believe that they were buying top-quality products? Probably not, because brand names and party labels are valuable to consumers and voters only if the brands have strong and consistent connections to particular outcomes. In contexts where these associations break down, so does the value of the brand name.

In sum, people pay attention, and connect the information they attend to, in ways that are likely to minimize costly mistakes. These attention and connection strategies allow people to substitute simple cues for detailed information. When simple substitutes for detailed information are available, then people who have limited information can make reasoned choices. When no such substitutes are available, the informational requirements for reasoned choice increase. As a result, judging a person's capacity for reasoned choice requires more than just asking political trivia questions.

CONCLUSION

The fact that humans are able to communicate linguistically with one another provides perhaps the clearest and most certain evidence that reliable and accurate judgment is possible. Such communication requires, for example, that I be able to interpret accurately the meaning of your utterances and hence to subsume correctly the particular words that you are using under conceptual categories that we share. It is impossible to claim that communication of this sort does not occur, for the meaningful expression of such a claim would itself presuppose precisely the possibility that is being denied.

– Steinberger (1993: 157)

In this chapter, we argue that people have neither the ability nor the incentive to pay attention to most things. For the moment, at least, we assert that politics falls into the "most things" category. Thus, it should come as no surprise to find that they pay little or no attention to the great political debates that animate the denizens of Washington, the writers of political commentary, and social scientists.[30]

We presume that most people *choose* to have very little information about most political issues. However, we conclude that their attention strategies *do not necessarily prevent* them from making reasoned

[30]Dye and Zeigler (1984: 162) explain, "Many people have no opinion about political issues debated vigorously in the mass media. In general, no more than a third of the public recognizes legislative proposals that have been the center of public debate for months, and sometimes years. Even among that third, few would be able to describe the proposal accurately or in detail, and fewer still would successfully describe the intricacies and alternatives available to policy makers."

choices.[31] Asserting that limited information precludes reasoned choice is equivalent to requiring that people who want to brush their teeth recall the ingredients of their toothpaste.

Of course, we are not the first analysts to conclude that political actors can use simple pieces of information to make complex decisions. Throughout the 1980s and 1990s it was commonly argued that voters could use simple cues to make reasoned choices on complex decisions (e.g., see Popkin 1991; Sniderman, Brody, and Tetlock 1991). We concur with the basic insight of these studies – people can find effective substitutes for encyclopedic information.

To these studies we add an explanation of when simple substitutes for a particular set of political facts are sufficient for reasoned choice. We also explain why people choose to use the few cues they use while simultaneously ignoring the many cues they ignore. We find that the cues most likely to be attended to are the cues that are likely to prevent costly mistakes in the future because similar cues have prevented costly mistakes in analogous circumstances in the past. So, besides demonstrating that something like party identification is a cue that helps people make reasoned decisions, our theory explains the conditions under which the party cue is likely to be relevant as well as the contexts in which people are likely to ignore it.

In politics as elsewhere, people respond to the bounds that the twin scourges of scarcity and complexity impose upon them. Is the complexity and scarcity that lead people to lack detailed information sufficient to prevent them from making reasoned choices? Undoubtedly, people do make mistakes in many of the decisions that a democracy calls upon them to make, just as consumers make mistakes in their purchasing decisions. However, people also lack detailed information about the cars they buy, the airlines they fly, and the medical treatments they receive. Few would claim that these people regularly fail in these decisions. More generally, people lack detailed information about almost everything, yet they do not regret most of the numerous choices they make each day. It is wrong to conclude that people who lack detailed political information cannot make reasoned choices.

In Chapter 3, we focus on how people learn from others. We go in this direction because political decision makers tend to acquire informa-

---

[31]Iyengar (1990: 161) explains, "political attention is discretionary" and continues, "information about public affairs is, therefore, likely to be domain-specific; how much one knows . . . depends on the particular subject-matter domain. The more relevant some domain is to the individual, the higher the level of information concerning that domain. In sum, rather than acquiring information about all things political, individuals specialize in particular domains." Also see Hinich and Munger (1994).

tion from the oral or written testimony of others. Learning from others is no trivial task, especially when both the decision maker and the person supplying the testimony are goal-oriented, strategic, and possibly at cross-purposes. As in this chapter, we examine the relationship between information and choice and draw some unusual conclusions.

3

How People Learn from Others

Reasoned choice requires knowledge – that is, people must be able to predict the consequences of their actions. To obtain this knowledge, people have two options. First, they can draw knowledge from personal experience. Second, they can draw knowledge from what other people say, write, or do.

In many political settings, only the second option is available. This is true because politics generates problems that are unfamiliar to peoples' "own experience and uncorrected by trial and error" (Lane 1995: 117). In these settings, personal experience does not provide sufficient knowledge for reasoned choice. Therefore, in many political settings, a person who wants to make a reasoned choice must have the opportunity and the ability to learn from others.[1]

In this chapter and the next, we explain how people make choices in settings where personal experience is insufficient for reasoned choice *and* where people have opportunities to learn from one another. We focus on these settings because we believe that they best describe the situations that confront many voters, jurors, and legislators.

Can people gain knowledge from others? We take two steps to answer this question. In this chapter, we take the first step by offering a unique explanation of *how* people learn from others. This explanation answers

---

[1]Political settings vary in the number of opportunities they offer. At one extreme, voters in major elections have opportunities to learn from newspaper articles, news broadcasts, television advertisements, direct mail, speeches, rallies, interest group endorsements, voter information pamphlets, workplace conversations, and family debates. Members of Congress have opportunities to learn from party leaders, the votes cast in committee, lobbyists, staff, colleagues, and experts in the executive branch. Jurors have opportunities to learn from eyewitnesses, expert witnesses, attorneys, and the presiding judge. At the other extreme, some political settings offer no opportunities to learn. For people in these settings, only personal experience can generate reasoned choice.

questions such as "Who can learn from whom?" and "How do people decide whose advice to follow and whose advice to ignore?" In Chapter 4, we take the second step and explain *what* people learn from others. This explanation answers the question "When is learning from others a sufficient substitute for personal experience as the basis of reasoned choice?"

Returning to the focus of this chapter, *how* people learn from others, we begin by noting that many answers to this question already exist. It is widely believed, for example, that people learn from others only if these others possess characteristics such as a particular racial identity, gender, age, or education. Social scientists offer other explanations. Some scholars argue that people rely on factors such as party identification (Downs 1957), known issue biases (Calvert 1985), likability (Brady and Sniderman 1985), certain histories of observed behaviors (Sobel 1985), being in a competitive situation (Milgrom and Roberts 1986), shared policy interests (Krehbiel 1991), or elite status (Zaller 1992). Other scholars argue that people learn from the aggregate actions of others such as are contained in history (Downs 1957, Fiorina 1981, Key 1966), polls (McKelvey and Ordeshook 1986), the media (Iyengar and Kinder 1987; Page, Shapiro, and Dempsey 1987), levels of campaign expenditure (Lupia 1992), the size of public protests (Lohmann 1993), certain campaign events (Lodge, Steenbergen, and Brau 1995; Popkin 1991), and public mood (Rahn, Kroeger, and Kite 1996).

Individually, each of these explanations of how we learn from others is valuable and enlightening. Each reveals a judgmental shortcut that people undoubtedly use as a substitute for the personal experience that they lack. We agree with Sniderman, Brody, and Tetlock (1991: 70), however, who argue, "The most serious risk is that . . . every correlation between independent and dependent variables [is] taken as evidence of a new judgmental shortcut." No person can use all shortcuts all the time. Each person must choose what and whom to believe.

The study of how people choose whom to believe is often referred to as the study of persuasion. In what follows, we first review existing explanations of persuasion. Then, we offer an explanation of our own.

THE ARISTOTELIAN THEORIES OF PERSUASION

Learning from others requires *persuasion*. We define persuasion as *one person's successful attempt to change the beliefs of another*. In settings where reasoned choice requires learning from others, *persuasion is a necessary condition for reasoned choice*.[2]

---

[2]For example, suppose that person A's ability to make a reasoned choice depends on what he or she can learn from person B. If B can persuade A, then reasoned choice is possible. By contrast, if B cannot persuade A, then A cannot make a reasoned choice.

The question "How do people choose whom to believe?" is equivalent to the question "Who can persuade whom?" An early answer to these questions is found in Book I of Aristotle's *Rhetoric:*

Of the modes of persuasion furnished by the spoken word there are three kinds. The first kind depends on the personal character of the speaker; the second on putting the audience into a certain frame of mind; the third on proof, or apparent proof, provided by the words of the speech itself. Persuasion is achieved by the speaker's personal character when the speech is so spoken as to make us think him credible. We believe good men more fully and more readily than others: this is true generally whatever the question is, and absolutely true where exact certainty is impossible and opinions are divided. This kind of persuasion, like the others, should be achieved by what the speaker says, not by what people think of his character before he begins to speak. It is not true, as some writers assume in their treatises in rhetoric, that the personal goodness revealed by the speaker contributes nothing to his power of persuasion; on the contrary, his character may almost be called the most effective means of persuasion he possesses. (translation from Barnes 1984: 2155)

For many modern political issues, "exact certainty" is impossible and "opinions are divided." Therefore, most modern political interaction clearly falls into the category where Aristotle expects people to base their decisions about whom to believe on their assessments of a speaker's *personal character.* In Book II of *Rhetoric,* Aristotle reveals what he means by personal character:

There are three things that inspire confidence in the orator's own character – the three, namely, that induce us to believe a thing apart from a proof of it: good sense, excellence, and good will. False statements and bad advice are due to one or more of three causes. Men either form a false opinion through want of good sense; or they form a true opinion, but because of their moral badness do not say what they really think; or finally, they are both sensible and upright, but not well disposed to their hearers, and may fail in consequence to recommend what they know to be the best course. These are the only possible cases. It follows that anyone who is thought to have all these good qualities will inspire trust in his audience. (translation from Barnes 1984: 2194)[3]

Aristotle concludes that a speaker's personal character, along with the content of his statement, determines who can persuade whom. By contrast, we argue that persuasion need not depend on assessments of personal character.

---

[3]The foremost virtues a speaker can exhibit are wanting what is good for the person to whom he is speaking (good will), the internal moral fortitude required to act on the basis of what is good for the other person (excellence), and germane knowledge that makes statements from a speaker who has good will and excellence convincing (good sense). We thank Mark Turner for advice on translating Aristotle. However, he bears no responsibility for whatever errors may underlie our use of the Aristotelian passages.

Theory

Two premises drive the wedge between Aristotle's conclusion and our own. First, Aristotle bases his conclusion on the assumption that all situations are identical to the Athenian situation. To Aristotle, society is a small city-state where *citizens know one another well.* In this society, people know who has good sense, good will, and excellence, and they know who lacks these characteristics. In our society, however, we do not always know one another well. We are often uncertain about what other people know and are leery of their underlying motives. Therefore, it may be impossible for us to know much about another person's character. Aristotle concludes that persuasion requires such knowledge. We disagree. For example, many people are influenced by what they read in the *New York Times* or see on CNN while knowing little about the character of those who write or speak for these organizations. By contrast to Aristotle, we base our explanation of persuasion on the premise that *people need not know one another well.*

We also differ from Aristotle in concluding that persuasion does not require positive or affective character assessments of any kind. Instead, we argue that *incentive-altering external forces offer alternate means for assessing credibility.* These forces are present in culture, norms, markets, political institutions, and legal institutions. They affect what people *choose* to say and what people *choose* to believe. How these forces work should be familiar to any member of an advanced industrial economy. For example, every day, millions of people buy goods from, and sell goods to, people about whom they know little or nothing. Each of these transactions requires some degree of trust (e.g., that the currency offered as payment is legitimate and that a good has its advertised characteristics). Because buyers and sellers do not know each other well, they must have an alternate and effective means for evaluating credibility. One such means is an external force that substitutes for unobservable personal characteristics. For example, laws and customs realign strangers' incentives, giving people a basis for trust in billions of situations where it would not otherwise exist. These external forces are the substitutes that make advanced economies possible. We argue that analogous substitutes make advanced democracies possible because they allow people to learn from others.[4]

We recall the Aristotelian view because it pervades contemporary studies of social, economic, and political communication. Contemporary so-

[4]This type of argument has a well-established lineage in certain subfields of political science and economics. For example, economists in the industrial organization (e.g., Williamson 1975) and mechanism design (e.g., Baron 1989; Myerson 1979, 1983, 1989) subfields have demonstrated an important set of relationships between external forces, individual incentives, and collective outcomes. In addition, political scientists such as McKelvey and Ordeshook (1986) show how voters can substitute simple poll results for more complex information.

42

cial scientists commonly assume that people know one another well, ignore the role of incentive-altering external forces, and conclude that personal character is the key to persuasion. For example, widely cited game theoretic treatments of communication assume that actors *know* one another's ideal points (a game theoretic analogy to Aristotle's personal character) and conclude that listeners believe speakers only if speakers and listeners have ideal points that are close to one another.[5] Psychologists use subject responses to speaker attribute questions (a social psychological analogy to Aristotle's personal character) to conclude that persuasion requires characteristics such as "honesty" and "fairness."[6] In addition, many of the answers suggested by political scientists to the question "How do people learn from others?" are also Aristotelian – ideology, likability, partisanship, known biases, and elite status are all based on personal characteristics.[7]

By contrast, we offer a theory of persuasion based on the premise "people may not know one another well" and the premise "incentives matter." We use the theory to derive necessary and sufficient conditions for persuasion in a simple setting. These conditions explain how peoples' interests, their cognitive limitations, and external forces affect how they choose whom to believe. Our theory reveals the conditions under which people can and cannot gain from others the knowledge that reasoned choice requires.

OUR THEORY OF PERSUASION

Our theory is unique in that it consists of a novel combination of assumptions, results in a novel set of findings, and produces important and *testable* implications about the political consequences of limited information. Like all theories, ours builds from scholarship of the past. Its lineage is most directly traced to economic games of incomplete information

[5]In fact, the explicit claim of models such as Crawford and Sobel (1982), Gilligan and Krehbiel (1987), and Gilligan and Krehbiel (1989) is that proximate interests are both necessary and sufficient for persuasion and for communication to lead to an increase in knowledge.

[6]Classic psychological treatises on persuasion include Eagly and Chaiken (1993), McGuire (1969), Petty and Cacioppo (1986), and Sherif, Sherif, and Nebergall (1965). The incorporation of these insights into political science is a recent growth industry. Examples of this research, broadly construed, are described in Iyengar (1991), Iyengar and McGuire (1993), Lodge and McGraw (1995), Mutz, Sniderman, and Brody (1995), Popkin (1991), Sniderman, Brody, and Tetlock (1991), and Zaller (1992).

[7]Similarly, scholars who argue that people learn from interest group endorsements (Grofman and Norrander 1990, Lupia 1994), the opinions of "fire alarms" – extralegislative actors who "go off" when they see a problem (McCubbins and Schwartz 1984) – and the actions of large groups (Lohmann 1993) are also Aristotelian as they all assume that people know important things about other peoples' character.

Theory

(e.g., Harsanyi 1967, 1968a,b), signaling models (e.g., Banks 1991, Spence 1973, McKelvey and Ordeshook, 1986), and strategic communication models (e.g., Calvert 1986, Crawford and Sobel 1982, Farrell and Gibbons 1989).[8] Our theory also contains premises that are common to studies of communication and learning in cognitive science (Churchland and Sejnowski 1992; Holland et al. 1986; Lakoff 1987; Simon 1979, 1985) and psychology (Hovland, Janis, and Kelley 1953; Eagly and Chaiken 1993; Petty and Cacioppo 1986).[9] To enhance the readability of the text, we relegate technical arguments and proofs of our conclusions to the Appendix to Chapter 3.

We build our explanation of how people choose whom to believe from a central theme of Chapter 2 – learning is active. Moreover, whether a

[8]To the extent that our theory represents a quarrel with existing formal models of communication, it is not a quarrel with efforts such as Crawford and Sobel (1982) or Spence (1973). These scholars studied bargaining situations where it was reasonable to assume that communicants knew a great deal about one another. Our quarrel is with the importation of these models into political science debates where people do not know one another well. In fact, our efforts closely follow Crawford and Sobel's (1982: 1450) final admonition:

> Some worthwhile extensions of the model are suggested by the fact that the structure of our model interacts with the rational-expectations character of our solution concept in such a way that concepts like lying, credibility, and credulity – all essential features of strategic communication – do not have fully satisfactory operational meanings within the model. Generalizations that would test the robustness of our results and to help remedy this defect include allowing lying to have costs for [the speaker], uncertain to [the principal], in addition to those inherent in its effect on [the principal's] choice of action; allowing [the principal] to be uncertain about [the speaker's] preferences, and therefore about his incentives to communicate truthfully, and allowing [the speaker] to be uncertain about [the principal's] ability to check the accuracy of what he is told.

[9]We have not compared our explanation of persuasion with that of the dual process models of persuasion offered by Petty and Cacioppo (1986) and Eagly and Chaiken (1993). That is because they are, in our view, quite difficult to compare. The main thrust of the dual process theories is the identification of two routes to persuasion: the central/systematic route and the peripheral/heuristic route. These scholars claim, and demonstrate empirically, that people use the central/systematic route (i.e., they put great effort into incorporating the new information into their current set of beliefs) when the receiver faces a very important and complex decision. They claim that people use the peripheral/heuristic route (i.e., they put little effort into incorporating new information) when the receiver faces a less important or complex decision. The source of the incomparability between the dual process thesis and our Chapter 3 theory is that the dual theories focus on the amount of *attention* that a person will give to a stimulus. The dual process theories do not focus on how people choose among potential heuristics. Our theory of persuasion does focus on how people make these choices.

We regard the decision to pay attention as a *prerequisite* for filtering good advice from bad. The dual process theories and our Chapter 2 model of attention are, therefore, comparable. In the cases where these explanations of attention overlap, they are consistent.

thousand people are offering advice to one person, or one person is offering advice to thousands, persuasion depends on *individual* decisions about whom to believe. Therefore, our theory of persuasion focuses on individual decisions about what to say and whom to believe.

We examine a situation where an otherwise badly informed person who wants to make a reasoned choice is offered another person's advice. As we are interested in politics, we focus on the case where the person seeking advice lacks information about the intentions and expertise of the advice giver. Thus, the decision maker lacks not one but two relevant types of information.

In what follows, we first introduce a basic model of communication. Our basic model modifies Crawford and Sobel's seminal cheap talk model. Our modification allows us to answer the question "Who can persuade whom when people do not know one another well?" Then, we extend our basic model to answer the question "How do external forces affect who can persuade whom when people do not know one another well?" The basic model and the extensions, together, make up our theory of persuasion.

The Basic Model: Communication When People Do Not Know One Another Well

We model communication as an interaction between two players, a *principal* and a *speaker*. At the conclusion of this interaction, the *principal* chooses one of two alternatives, called x and y. You can think of the principal as someone who must decide which candidate to vote for, which applicant to select for a post in the bureaucracy, whether to vote for or against a bill, or whether to conclude that a defendant is guilty or not guilty.[10] Before the principal makes this choice, the *speaker* provides information about the relative attributes of x and y. Speakers common to political contexts include friends, relatives, co-workers, media organizations, interest groups, political candidates, political parties, bureau-

---

[10]We focus on the case where the principal chooses one of two alternatives because it is simple and common to politics. To see how common this case is, consider the following facts. All legislative agendas are binary choice agendas. Most jury decisions are a choice between one of two litigants or one of two legal points of view. Regulatory decisions often entail simple acceptance or rejection of a single proposal to changes in the regulatory status quo (for surveys, see Joskow and Noll 1981, Kahn 1988). Moreover, presidents either accept or veto bills. Many candidate-centered elections are explicitly, or implicitly, two-candidate affairs. Of course, voters sometimes choose from three or more alternatives. However, even here binary choice is a good analogy as even in these situations voters could characterize their choice as that between "candidate A" and "the other candidates," or "the incumbent" and "any alternative" (see Simon 1955, March and Simon 1958).

crats, prosecuting attorneys, defense attorneys, and witnesses. Unless otherwise stated, and we will state otherwise, we assume that all elements of this interaction are common knowledge. For clarity, we refer to the principal as a "she" and to the agent as a "he."

The basic model we present modifies the standard cheap talk model (Crawford and Sobel 1982) by adding three substantively relevant types of uncertainty. We depict the basic model's sequence of events in Figure 3.1. The bold portions of Figure 3.1 indicate differences between our basic model and the standard cheap talk model.

The sequence of events begins with the potential for uncertainty. We follow game theoretic custom and model this potential uncertainty as three probabilistic moves by nature.[11] The order of these moves is irrelevant to our results.

One of nature's three moves determines whether x is *better* or *worse* than y for the principal. If nature chooses *better* and the principal chooses x, then she earns positive utility $(U \geq 0)$. If nature chooses *worse* and the principal chooses x, then she earns negative utility $(\underline{U} \leq 0)$. We assume, without a loss of generality, that if the principal chooses y, then she earns utility 0.[12]

Nature chooses *better* with probability $b \in [0, 1]$ and chooses *worse* with probability $1-b$.[13] The most important assumption in the model is that the principal is uncertain about whether x or y is better for her. The probability b represents the principal's prior beliefs about which alternative is better for her.

Another of nature's moves determines whether or not the speaker has the knowledge that the principal desires. Nature chooses "speaker knows whether x is better or worse than y" with probability $k \in [0, 1]$ and

[11]In games of incomplete information, a player's "type" is a summary of the personal attributes about which other players are uncertain (e.g., Harsanyi 1968a,b). For our purposes, the conventional use of the term "type" is insufficient. We are interested in the distinct effects of experimentally separable attributes about which political actors are often uncertain. For example, we gain considerable insight by treating as separable the principal's uncertainty about the speaker's interests and the principal's uncertainty about the speaker's knowledge. So, while the conventional use of "type" collapses these attributes into a single measure (as the extensive form reveals, the speaker in the basic model can be one of six types), we do not. Therefore, to avoid confusion with that usage, we do not use the term "type."
[12]Note that U need not equal $-\underline{U}$.
[13]This assumption is without a loss of generality to the case where x and y are points in finite-dimensional space; where both the speaker and the principal have ideal points and quasi-concave utility functions over this space; and where a player's prior beliefs about the origins of x, y, and the speaker's ideal point are representable as independent distributions over the space. The representation in the text is offered for its simplicity.

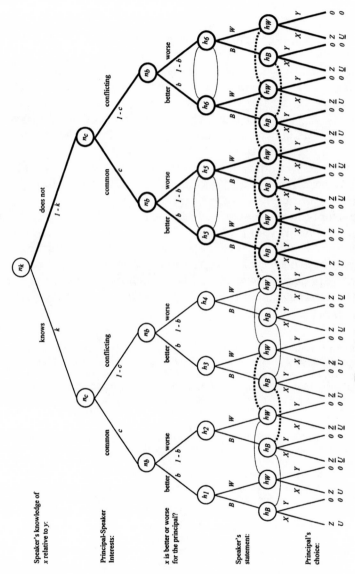

Figure 3.1. Our basic model of persuasion.

Theory

"speaker does not know whether x is better or worse than y" with probability $1-k$. This assumption allows us to represent the principal as uncertain about how much the speaker knows. We represent this uncertainty as follows: The principal knows the probability k, but not how much the speaker actually knows.[14] In the standard cheap talk model, by contrast, it is common knowledge that $k = 1$.

Another of nature's moves determines the relationship between the speaker's and the principal's interests. If nature chooses *common* interests, then the speaker benefits when the principal makes a utility-maximizing decision – the speaker receives utility $Z \geq 0$ when the principal receives utility $U \geq 0$ and receives utility $\underline{Z} \leq 0$ when the principal receives utility $\underline{U} \leq 0$. If nature chooses *conflicting* interests, then the speaker benefits when the principal *does not* make a utility-maximizing choice – the speaker receives utility $\underline{Z} \leq 0$ when the principal receives utility $U \geq 0$ and receives utility $Z \geq 0$ when the principal receives utility $\underline{U} \leq 0$. The speaker earns utility 0 when the principal chooses y.

Nature chooses *common* interests with probability $c \in [0, 1]$ and *conflicting* interests with probability $1-c$.[15] We assume that the principal is uncertain about the speaker's interests. We represent her prior beliefs about these interests as the probability c. Aristotelian theories assume that the principal knows the speaker's interests. However, the complexity and uncertainty that politics engenders makes it likely that political principals lack such knowledge.

---

[14]This assumption differs from the classic economic signaling and strategic communication theories in two ways. First, the classic models assume that the speaker is knowledgeable (i.e., they assume $k = 1$). We assume that the speaker does not necessarily know what he is talking about. Second, the classic models assume that the principal knows how much the speaker knows. We assume that the principal may be uncertain about this because it represents one common way in which modern decision makers do not know one another well.

Austen-Smith (1994) offers an alternative conception of speaker knowledge as a variable, rather than a constant, within models of strategic communication. The Austen-Smith model differs from Crawford-Sobel in that the sender has an opportunity to acquire knowledge that the receiver cannot observe. Moreover, when the sender chooses to be knowledgeable, he can prove as much to the principal. The difference between our basic model and Austen-Smith 1994 is that in our model the sender and receiver need not know each other's ideal points, and the sender cannot prove to the principal that he is knowledgeable.

[15]It is the possibility of conflicting interests that transforms our analysis into a study of what Goffman (1967: 10) defined as *strategic communication*:

> There will be situations where an observer is dependent on what he can learn from a subject, there being no sufficient alternate sources of information, and the subject will be oriented to frustrate this assessment or facilitate it under difficult circumstances. Under these conditions gamelike considerations develop even though very serious matters may be at stake. A contest over assessment occurs. Information becomes strategic.

48

After nature's three moves, the *game* begins. First, the speaker sends a signal of "better" or "worse" to the principal. The signal "better" means: "I assert that x is better than y for the principal." The signal "worse" means: "I assert that x is worse than y for the principal."[16] The speaker selects which signal to send and *need not tell the truth*. Second, the principal chooses x or y. After she does so, the game ends and both players receive a utility payoff.

We now explain persuasion in the basic model. We find two equilibrium sets of behaviors.[17] In one, the principal bases her choice on what the speaker says, and the speaker tells the truth only if he knows or believes himself to have common interests with the principal. Otherwise, the speaker lies.

In the standard cheap talk model, people cannot deceive one another *in equilibrium*. This result follows from their assumption that people know one another well enough to see lies coming in advance. Deception occurs in the first equilibrium of our model because people do not know one another well. We will have more to say about this later in the chapter.

In the second equilibrium, the principal ignores the speaker, and persuasion does not take place. The principal's prior beliefs about the speaker's interests and knowledge determine which of these two equilibria occur. When the principal's prior beliefs lead her to assess a high probability that she and the speaker have common interests and the speaker is knowledgeable, then the persuasive equilibrium can occur. Otherwise, the nonpersuasive equilibrium occurs.

[16]We make this assumption for simplicity. However, both statements contain knowledge sufficient for reasoned choice in the game. More precise statements, if true, would not cause the principal to choose differently. Ongoing research in linguistics and the cognitive sciences also motivates this assumption (see Lakoff 1987, Holland et al. 1986). These scholars argue that there are many more ideas than ways to express them. Rather than provide a full description of an idea, language merely "prompts" a mental image or mental space. This is referred to as the access principle (Fauconnier 1985). Also see Turner (1991) for a discussion of mental images and the use of metaphors and conceptual blends in conveying images. However, not any metaphors will do; people who want to be understood need to use metaphors that are *easy to* understand. These metaphors must be simple and direct. Again, Simon's research informs our own:

> The oil gauge on the dashboard of an automobile is an example of the use of classification in program-evoking. For most drivers, the oil pressure is either "all right" or "low." In the first case, no action is taken; in the second case a remedial program is initiated (e.g., taking the automobile to a repair shop). Some auto manufacturers have substituted a red light, which turns on when the oil pressure is not in the proper range, for the traditional gauge. This example also illustrates how substituting standards of satisfactory performance for criteria of optimization simplifies communication. (March and Simon 1958: 163)

[17]See Proposition 3.1 in the Appendix to Chapter 3.

Theory

We state this relationship with the following theorem:

Theorem 3.1: Absent external forces, perceived common interests are a necessary condition for persuasion. Perceived common interests, however, are not sufficient for persuasion.

In Chapter 2, we argued that people *ignore* stimuli that they do not expect to facilitate reasoned choices. Here too, persuasion requires the principal to believe that the speaker's statement will help her avoid costly mistakes. That is, persuasion does not occur if the principal believes that the speaker is likely to have conflicting interests. If, however, the principal believes that common interests are more likely, then persuasion is possible. Theorem 3.2 tells us why having perceived common interests is not sufficient for persuasion in our model.

Theorem 3.2: Absent external forces, perceived speaker knowledge (k > 0) is a necessary condition for persuasion. Perceived speaker knowledge, however, is not sufficient for persuasion.

So, if the principal is *certain* that the speaker does not have the knowledge she desires, then persuasion will not occur. By contrast, if the principal believes that the speaker might possess the knowledge she requires, then persuasion is possible. So, even in the case where the principal is certain that the speaker has common interests, her belief that the speaker lacks knowledge leads her to ignore the speaker's statement.

The necessity of perceived speaker knowledge highlights an important limitation of scholarly and popular explanations of persuasion. For example, some people hold the view that conservatives are necessarily more persuasive to other conservatives, that African-Americans are necessarily more persuasive to other African-Americans, and so on. We find that the reliability of these explanations is conditional. Regardless of which personal attributes a speaker has, if he is perceived to lack knowledge, then he cannot persuade.[18]

---

[18]As noted earlier, the seminal model on strategic information transmission makes a similar argument. Crawford and Sobel (1982, 1431) claim that "equilibrium signaling is more informative when agents' preferences are more similar." In their model, all equilibria are partition equilibria, which means that all equilibria can be stated in terms that describe how accurate the speaker's statements are (i.e., the message space is partitioned and the more segments a message space contains, the more persuasive and enlightening the speaker's statement is). They later (1441) conclude that "the more nearly [the speaker's and receiver's] interests coincide – the finer partition there can be. . . . As [the distance in their interests goes to infinity], [the number of partitions] eventually falls to unity and only the completely uninformative equilibrium remains." In fact, however, they prove in Corollary 1 that this number goes to unity (the speaker's statement is totally uninformative) for even relatively small interest conflicts (i.e., the result is "cheap talk"). Similar conclusions are drawn in Gilligan and Krehbiel (1987, 1989) and in Austen-Smith (1990a,b, 1993). Note that a similar result is achieved in our model by restricting c to equal 0 or 1.

Perceived speaker knowledge, although necessary, is not a sufficient condition for persuasion, for even a seemingly knowledgeable speaker can persuade only when trusted. For example, many people believed that Richard Nixon knew about the Watergate break-in and that Bill Clinton was knowledgeable about the extent of his marijuana use, but a lack of trust diminished the persuasiveness of their statements about these topics.

While we have pointed out limits to the relationship among knowledge, interests, and persuasion, we have revealed only the tip of the iceberg. Two corollaries reveal more cold realities about persuasion in our model.

Corollary to Theorem 3.1: Actual common interests are neither necessary nor sufficient for persuasion.

Corollary to Theorem 3.2: Actual speaker knowledge is neither necessary nor sufficient for persuasion.

When people do not know one another well, it is *perceived* speaker knowledge and interests, not *actual* speaker knowledge or interests, that drive persuasion. Therefore, a speaker who has common interests and the knowledge that the principal desires can fail to persuade. Moreover, a speaker can persuade even if he knows nothing and his interests conflict with those of the principal.

Numerical Examples

To highlight the implications of our basic model, we provide two numerical examples. In each of the examples, we present an initial case where persuasion occurs in equilibrium. Then, we show how a change in one of three factors affects persuasion. Table 3.1 contains the examples. For simplicity, we set $U = |U| = |Z| = 1$ and $Z = 2$. So, in each of the examples, the speaker earns more when he and the principal have common interests than he loses when they have conflicting interests.

In example 1: case 1, the principal believes that the speaker is more likely to be knowledgeable than not and more likely to share common interests with her than not. In addition, her prior belief about the probability that x is better is .35. Absent a persuasive statement from the speaker, the principal's expected utility from choosing x is $-.3$. Because this is less than the utility of 0 that she will earn for choosing y, she chooses y. In equilibrium, however, the speaker's statement, better, changes the principal's beliefs about which alternative is better for her. Her posterior belief about the probability that x is better grows to approximately .51.[19]

[19]We calculated this belief from the equilibrium stated in Proposition 3-1 (see Appendix). In the cases described in the numerical example, the posterior beliefs are calculated as follows: *(b × (ck + ((1-k)(1-c)) + c(1-k))/[(b × (ck + ((1-k)(1-c)) + c(1-k)) + ((1-b) × ((1-c)(1-k) + c(1-k)))].*

Theory

Table 3.1. *Numerical examples.*

Example	c = prior probability of common interests	k = prior probability that the speaker is knowledgeable	b = prior probability that x is better	Persuasion if the speaker says better, in equilibrium
Example 1				
case 1	.8	.7	.35	Yes
case 2	.49	.7	.35	No
case 3	.8	0	.35	No
case 4	.8	.7	.35	No
Example 2				
case 1	1	.5	.4	Yes
case 2	.49	.5	.4	No
case 3	1	0	.4	No
case 4	1	.5	.1	No

After the principal hears the statement, her expected utility from choosing x is approximately .03, which is greater than the utility of 0 she would get for choosing y.[20] Therefore, the speaker persuades the principal to choose x.

The same is not true of the remaining cases in example 1, each of which differs from case 1 in only one way. In case 2, the principal's prior belief about the probability of common interests drops. In this case, her posterior belief about the probability that x is better remains virtually unchanged. In case 3, the principal's beliefs about the speaker's knowledge are less optimistic. In this case, her posterior beliefs about x are identical to her prior beliefs. In case 4, the principal's prior beliefs make her more certain about which alternative is better (i.e., b is closer to 0 or 1 and further from .5). *In all three cases, the speaker is no longer sufficiently credible to change the principal's beliefs in equilibrium.* Therefore, the principal ignores the speaker, and persuasion does not occur.

The structure of example 2 is similar to that of example 1. The difference is that in the initial case of example 2, the principal is now certain that she and the speaker have common interests, and persuasion occurs. In addition, her prior belief about the probability that x is better is .4. Absent a persuasive statement from the speaker, the principal's expected

---

[20]In this example, the numerator of the expected utility of choosing x conditional on having heard better is $kcbU + k(1-c)(1-b)\underline{U} + (1-k)(1-c)bU + (1-k)(1-c)(1-b)\underline{U} + (1-k)cbU + (1-k)c(1-b)\underline{U}$.

utility from choosing x is $-.2$. Because this is less than the utility of 0 that she will earn for choosing y, she chooses y. In equilibrium, however, the speaker's statement, better, changes the principal's beliefs about which alternative is better for her. Her posterior belief about the probability that x is better grows to approximately $.57$. After the principal hears this statement, her expected utility from choosing x is approximately $.14$, which is greater than the utility of 0 she would get for choosing y. Therefore, the speaker persuades the principal to choose x in case 1. In cases 2 and 3, the principal's decreased confidence in the speaker's interests or knowledge renders her no longer willing to base her choice on the speaker's advice. In case 4, the principal is relatively certain about which alternative is better. As a result, the speaker can no longer persuade.

Note also that of all the cases provided in Table 3.1, deception is possible only in the initial case of example 1. Deception is possible here because the speaker is persuasive and because we did not specify the speaker's *actual* interests. So, while the probability of common interests in this case is high $(.8)$, if nature draws the low probability event (conflicting interests) then the outcome of the game is that the speaker lies to and successfully deceives the principal. If, by contrast, nature draws the high probability event (common interests), then the speaker tells the truth and the principal chooses the alternative that is better for her.

Three Extensions: The Effects of External Forces

We now turn our attention to how people do (and do not) learn from one another in the presence of external forces. These forces dramatically change what persuasion requires and, by providing substitutes for knowledge and interest, weaken further the validity of the Aristotelian view. Each of the three forces we examine is common to politics and represents a broad class of forces that can affect speaker and principal incentives.

The first force is *verification*. We represent verification as follows – after the speaker speaks but before the principal chooses, nature reveals to the principal whether x is better or worse for her. Verification occurs with probability $0 < v < 1$.[21] In words, we examine the case where speaker statements can be verified as true or false before the principal makes a choice.

The second force is *penalties for lying*. We represent these penalties as a cost, $pen \geq 0$, that the speaker must pay when sending a false signal. This penalty directly affects the speaker's utility. If the principal and the speaker have *common* interests and if the speaker *lies*, then the speaker

[21]Note that the case where $v = 0$ is the basic model and that the case where $v = 1$ is trivial.

Theory

receives utility $Z\text{-}pen$ when the principal receives utility $U \geq 0$ and receives utility $\underline{Z}\text{-}pen \leq 0$ when the principal receives utility $\underline{U} \leq 0$. If the principal and the speaker have *conflicting* interests and if the speaker *lies,* then the speaker receives utility $\underline{Z}\text{-}pen \leq 0$ when the principal receives utility $U \geq 0$ and receives utility $Z\text{-}pen$ when the principal receives utility $\underline{U} \leq 0$. If the speaker tells the truth, then the speaker's utility is the same as in the basic model. Penalties for lying are a common example of statement-specific costs.[22] Our motivation for focusing on penalties for lying are the explicit fines levied on people who lie (e.g., in cases of perjury) and the losses in valued reputations for honesty that result from being caught making false statements.[23]

We call the third force *observable costly effort.* We represent costly effort as a cost, $cost \geq 0$, that the speaker must pay to send any signal. If he does not pay, then the principal does not receive a signal. Intuitively, there is a cost for almost any cognitive task, and speaking is no exception.[24]

Verification, penalties for lying, and costly effort cover the range of effects that external forces can have on communication. Verification affects the manner in which the principal receives the speaker's statement. It is independent of any costs associated with making statements. Both penalties for lying and costly effort affect the speaker's costs and are independent of the manner in which the signal is received. Penalties for lying are a simple example of statement-specific costs. Costly effort is an example of communication costs that are independent of what is said.

We now present our main conclusion.

Theorem 3.3 (The Conditions for Persuasion): The following conditions are individually necessary and collectively sufficient for per-

---

[22] We focus on penalties for lying because of the role that fear of deception plays in critiques of the democracy. Another example of statement-specific costs was illuminated during the O.J. Simpson criminal trial. Late in the trial it was revealed that detective Mark Fuhrman, in a series of taped interviews, had used the "N-word" to describe African-Americans. In the contemporary idiom, the "N-word" is but one of many words, most of them less offensive, available to describe African-Americans. It is singular, however, in the malicious intent associated with its use. It is fair to say that words like this bring about statement-specific costs. Given the availability of other relatively "costless" descriptions of African-Americans, our model would predict that these words would be used by either a speaker who believed that the cost would never be assessed or a speaker who believed that it would be assessed with some non-zero probability but felt so strongly about the value of associating his views with the "N-word" that it justified the cost's payment.

[23] Although we focus on the case where these costs are common knowledge, our results are robust to the assumption that the principal is uncertain about them. Note also that other statement-specific costs, such as rewards or penalties for telling the truth, have similar dynamics.

[24] In watching politics or a faculty meeting at a university, it is easy to forget that although talk may be cheap, it is not free.

54

suasion: The principal must perceive the speaker to be trustworthy and the principal must perceive the speaker to have the knowledge she desires.

Absent external forces, persuasion requires perceived common interests and perceived speaker knowledge. In the presence of external forces, these requirements can be reduced. As the likelihood of verification, the magnitude of the penalty for lying, or the magnitude of costly effort increases, the extent to which perceived common interests are required decreases. In other words, with respect to persuasion, external forces can be substitutes for common interests (and for each other).

So, persuasion occurs *only if* the principal is initially uncertain about which alternative is better for her, believes that the speaker may have the knowledge she desires, and believes that the speaker has an incentive to reveal what he knows. If even one of these three conditions is unsatisfied, then persuasion cannot occur.

In the parlance of psychology, Theorem 3.3 implies that the principal's perceptions of the speaker's incentives and knowledge are *the fundamental source effects* – they determine whether or not a speaker can persuade a principal. From this theorem it follows that other well-known source effects (such as those based on the speaker's party, ideology, or reputation) work when they do *because* they influence an audience's perceptions of a speaker's knowledge or incentives.

Unlike Aristotelian theories of persuasion, Theorem 3.3 implies that persuasion may be independent of the principal's perception of the speaker's interests. So, when incentive-altering external forces are present, speaker attributes (such as ideology, partisanship, reputation, actual level of knowledge, or affective relationship to the principal) may have no bearing whatsoever on his ability to persuade the principal. Theorem 3.3, thus, amends explanations of persuasion based exclusively on personal character. This point is summarized in the corollary to Theorem 3.3:

Corollary to Theorem 3.3: Perceived common interests are not necessary for persuasion.

For example, it is widely taken for granted that an elite conservative speaker can more effectively persuade a conservative than a liberal, or a Democrat should find another Democrat's opinion to be more credible, or an African-American should readily believe another African-American. By contrast, we conclude that when external forces substitute for a speaker's character, no particular characteristic is a necessary condition for trust. To see such a substitution in action, consider that some contexts affect a speaker's incentives in ways that make clear to speakers and principals alike that certain statements are more costly than others (e.g., a court of law where the threat of perjury and cross-examination are implemented to affect witnesses' incentives). As a result, if we put a speaker with conflicting interests (i.e., who absent external forces would want the alternative that is worse for the principal) in a context where certain false statements are extremely costly, then the *context* supplies the principal with a rationale for believing the speaker. Alternatively, Theorem 3.3 implies that a principal may regard a speaker as perfectly disgusting and as having interests that conflict with her own, but if external forces induce the speaker to tell the truth (e.g., the speaker is subject to a penalty for lying) and if the principal perceives the speaker to be knowledgeable, then the principal has a basis for believing the speaker. So while it is true that the principal does require a basis for believing that the speaker will reveal the knowledge he has, such a basis need not come from speaker attributes; it can come just as effectively from the external forces in whose presence the speaker and principal interact. In Chapters 4, 5, and 10, we will use this knowledge to describe how political institutions affect persuasion and reasoned choice. In what follows, we briefly describe how each of the external forces affects persuasion.

Verification. When we add verification to the basic model, we achieve the same two equilibria as in the basic model.[25] In one equilibrium, the principal bases her choice on what the speaker says. The speaker tells the truth in this equilibrium only if he knows or believes himself to have common interests with the principal. Otherwise, the speaker lies. In the other equilibrium, the principal ignores the speaker, and persuasion does not take place.

Verification works by posing the threat that the principal can discern true signals from false ones.[26] This threat changes the speaker's incentives in the following way: As the probability of verification increases, the probability that the speaker can benefit from sending a false signal decreases.[27] Because only a speaker with conflicting interests could ever gain by sending false signals, verification has a direct effect on the speaker only if he and the principal have conflicting interests. By contrast, when the speaker and principal have common interests, verification is not much of a threat. In this case, the speaker wants the principal to make a reasoned choice and is indifferent as to whether the principal learns what she needs to know directly from the speaker or through a verification.

[25]See Proposition 3.2.
[26]See Corollary 1 to Proposition 3.2.
[27]See Corollary 2 to Proposition 3.2.

The limit of verification, when introduced on its own, is that it cannot induce the speaker to tell the truth when he would otherwise lie. Verification merely induces the principal to ignore the speaker's signal if it is false; it does not penalize the speaker for lying. So, on its own, verification's threat to the speaker is that his signal will be ineffective. Therefore, *verification decreases the expected value of communication for speakers who can gain from making false statements.* By contrast, verification does not have the same effect on a speaker who has common interests.

When contemplating the relationship between verification and persuasion, it is important to be cautious about confounding verification and competition. By contrast, we conclude that competition is neither necessary nor sufficient for persuasion. Competition is not necessary because it is not the only way to induce trust. Moreover, competition is not sufficient for persuasion, because "added competitors" need not be knowledgeable and trustworthy. Therefore, adding a competitor would be like attempting to change a speaker's incentives by threatening that he will be verified with probability 0. Competition in our model induces persuasion only if the added competitor induces one of the conditions we describe in Theorem 3.3.

Penalties for Lying. To foreshadow the effect of penalties for lying, we first describe how lying occurs in the equilibrium of the basic model. In equilibrium, the principal does not follow the advice of a speaker who she knows will lie in equilibrium. However, the speaker lies in equilibrium when he expects the principal to mistake him for a truth teller.

Our result lies in contrast to the standard cheap talk model, where people *cannot deceive one another in equilibrium.* Underlying this result is the assumption in the standard cheap talk model that people know one another well enough to see lies coming in advance (i.e., all players have rational expectations about the truth value of signals). The reason that deception occurs in reality and in our model is that people do not always see lies coming.

Returning to penalties for lying, note that they facilitate persuasion when they give the principal, who otherwise expects lies, a reason to believe that she can distinguish truth tellers from liars.[28] If penalties are small, then the game's equilibrium is as before – if the principal perceives the speaker to be knowledgeable and to have common interests, then the principal bases a choice on what the speaker says, and the speaker tells the truth only if he knows or believes himself to have common interests with the principal – otherwise, the speaker deceives. If the principal

[28]See Proposition 3.3.

57

does not have these priors, then the principal ignores the speaker, and persuasion does not take place.

With larger penalties, however, the speaker lies only if the expected benefit of lying is greater than the penalty. If penalties for lying are large enough, then the speaker never deceives, and the principal can trust the speaker. However, penalties for lying do not have to be so large to induce persuasion. To see why, consider the following example.

Suppose that the speaker knows, but the principal is uncertain about, whether *x* is *better* or *worse* than *y* for the principal. Suppose further that the principal and the speaker have conflicting interests. Specifically, if *x* is *better* for the principal, then the speaker loses $20 when the principal chooses *x;* if *x* is *worse* for the principal, then the speaker earns $75 when the principal chooses *x*. Suppose further that if the principal chooses *y,* then the speaker earns nothing, and that the penalty for lying is $50. In this situation, the penalty is big enough to dissuade the speaker from lying when *x* is *better* for the principal – that is, the speaker has to pay $50 to avoid losing $20. It is not big enough to do so when *x* is *worse* for the principal – that is, the speaker can pay $50 to earn $75. So if *x* is *better,* then the speaker will say *better,* and if *x* is *worse,* then the speaker may say *better* or *worse*. Therefore, if the principal hears the statement *worse,* then the penalty for lying allows her to infer that the statement must be true.

In general, a principal who believes that the speaker faces a penalty for lying can make one of the following two inferences upon hearing a statement from the speaker: (1) the statement is true; or (2) the statement is false and the value to the speaker of lying is greater than the expected penalty. When penalties for lying have this effect, they provide a new window from the principal's perceptions to the speaker's incentives and can provide a basis for trust.[29]

Observable and Costly Effort. The logic underlying this effect closely follows the adage "actions speak louder than words."[30] Someone who takes a costly action (i.e., exerts effort) reveals something to others about how much a particular outcome is worth to him or her. For example, if a knowledgeable speaker pays $100 for the opportunity to persuade us, then we can infer that the difference in expected value to the speaker between what the speaker expects us to do after hearing his statement and what the speaker expects us to do if we do not hear the statement is at least $100. Therefore, even if the speaker ultimately delivers his

[29]See Corollary 1 to Proposition 3.3.
[30]See Proposition 3.4. The logic underlying this external force is equivalent to the logic of Spence (1973), the seminal paper on costly signaling in economics. For simplicity, we describe the case where the cost of effort is known. It is trivial, however, to extend our results to the case where the principal does not know, but can form beliefs about, both the magnitude of the effort required for the speaker's speech and the exact shape of the speaker's utility function.

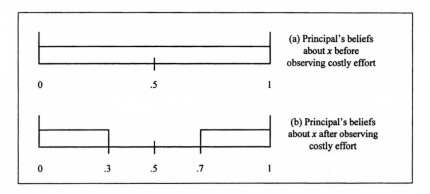

Figure 3.2. The effect of costly action.

statement in a language that we do not understand, the speaker's payment informs us that our choice is important to him.

Observable costly effort can allow the principal to make a new inference about the speaker's interests. Specifically, the principal can infer how much the speaker's preferred alternative differs from the one that she would have chosen otherwise. In Figure 3.2, we depict a spatial example of how a speaker's costly and observable effort can affect a principal's beliefs. At the top of Figure 3.2, we display a set of prior beliefs that the principal could hold about the location of x. Now, let $y = .5$ and let C be the cost to the speaker of having an opportunity to say "better" or "worse" to the principal. Suppose further that the speaker knows the location of x when he decides to pay C, that the principal knows that the speaker knows this, and that only a policy change of distance .2 or greater makes an expenditure of C worthwhile. Then, upon observing payment of C, and before the speaker says a word, the principal can correctly infer that x is not within distance .2 of y. As we depict in the bottom of Figure 3.2, the principal learns from the speaker's payment of C that x is not between .3 and .7. This new information alone can provide the principal with a clearer window to the speaker's incentives and greater knowledge about the location of x.

DYNAMIC IMPLICATIONS

In addition to being substitutes for common interests, external forces are also substitutes for one another. In the same way that the threat of verification lowers the degree of perceived common interests and perceived knowledge necessary for persuasion, it also lowers the magnitude of the penalty for lying or costly effort required for persuasion. This substitutability is possible because each external force has a similar effect on the speaker and the principal – they give the speaker an incentive to take certain actions and they give the principal a window to the speaker's incentives. As a result, external forces, if present together, work in complementary ways to induce persuasion where it would not otherwise exist.

Theorems 3.1, 3.2, and 3.3 specify the *minimum* levels of perceived common interests and perceived knowledge that persuasion requires. In some cases, the requirements are more stringent. For example, suppose that, before a speaker speaks, the principal is quite certain that she knows that x is *better* for her (e.g., $b = .98$). Then, the principal cannot be talked out of her belief unless she is also quite certain that the speaker is knowledgeable *and* trustworthy (i.e., *c and k* must be very high).

There is a similar relationship between the requirements of persuasion and the effect of external forces. All else constant, as b approaches 0 or 1, the magnitude of verification, costly effort, or penalties for lying required to make a speaker persuasive is nondecreasing. That is, an external force will be more effective at generating persuasion when the principal lacks strong prior beliefs about which alternative is better for her. At the extreme, if the principal believes that she is very unlikely to make a costly mistake, then only the strongest external force will be sufficient to make the principal believe the speaker.

What Happens When There Is More Than One Principal? (or, How to Be Persuaded by People with Whom You Disagree)

In our model, a principal who perceives a speaker to have conflicting interests with her own can be persuaded by the speaker only if external forces are present. However, this claim seems to contradict an experience that all of us have had. Specifically, sometimes we seem to be persuaded by other people *because* they have conflicting interests. For example, suppose that Mr. Colin ardently opposes any sort of environmental regulation. We can imagine a case where Mr. Colin can be persuaded by the endorsement of a pro-environmental group. He may, for example, take what they say and do the opposite.

In our basic model, where there are no external forces, this type of persuasion cannot occur. The same is true for the Aristotelian theories. For when a principal either knows or believes a speaker to have conflicting interests, the principal has an incentive to *ignore* the speaker and has no incentive to do the opposite of what the speaker says. The reason these conclusions do not square with Mr. Colin's behavior is that, in reality, Mr. Colin is in a situation where another premise is true. To explain Mr. Colin's behavior, we now extend our model to account for that premise.

The extension consists of adding further principals to the basic model. We call these players *observers* and refer to each observer as a "she." The only difference between observers and the principal is that the observers cannot directly affect the speaker's utility. Examples of observers include individuals at a mass rally, or people watching a nationally televised political speech.

Our theory implies that persuasion requires an observer to perceive a basis for trusting what the speaker says. In this extension of our model, the following factors can provide sufficient bases for trust: "the observer believes that the speaker has an incentive to make truthful statements to her," "the observer believes that her interests conflict with both the principal's and the speaker's, and that the speaker has an incentive to make truthful statements to the principal."

So, a speaker's statements can persuade an observer when the observer believes the speaker to be knowledgeable and truthful in what he says to the principal. So, if some observer perceives a common interest with *both* a speaker and a principal whose interaction she observes, then the observer can be persuaded by the speaker, as a spillover from the original communication. If, by contrast, an observer believes herself to have conflicting interests with both the speaker and the principal, then the speaker will again be persuasive, but in a different direction. In this case, observers should take the speaker's advice and do the opposite. For example, suppose that you are a Democrat who observes Newt Gingrich addressing an important group of Republican supporters. If you believe that Gingrich is knowledgeable, that he is attempting to win the favor of the group he is addressing, that he and the group perceive themselves to have common interests, and that your interests conflict with both, then you ought to take Newt's advice but do the opposite of what he recommends. In sum, *observers* can be persuaded by speakers who are perceived to have conflicting interests only if either the speakers are subject to the external forces described previously or the speakers have common interests with the principal they are addressing.[31]

What Happens When There Is More Than One Speaker?

Extending our model by increasing the number of speakers can affect persuasion in one of two ways. First, additional speakers may be different from the original speaker. For example, additional speakers may have personal characteristics that the original speaker did not. Moreover, additional

[31]Calvert (1985) and Farrell and Gibbons (1989) describe instances of this type of persuasion. Our modification to this scholarship lies in our definition of when this type of persuasion can occur.

speakers may be subject to external forces that the original speaker did not face. So, while the original speaker may not have been persuasive, additional speakers might be. In this way, additional speakers would affect when persuasion occurs. Second, additional speakers can affect persuasion if their presence generates external forces that alter the incentives of the original speaker. For example, if an additional speaker makes the original speaker easier to "verify," easier to penalize for lying, or easier to impose observable costly effort requirements upon, then the additional speaker can give a principal a reason to trust the original speaker.

PERSUASIVE IMPLICATIONS

Our conditions for persuasion clarify how people choose whom to believe. These conditions have the following implications about who can persuade whom: All statements are not equally informative, all speakers are not equally persuasive, and you do not necessarily learn more from people who are like you.

All statements are not equally informative. The obvious reason for this inequality is that statements vary in content. A second reason that should now be apparent is that statements also vary in *context*. For example, the same person making the same statement to the same *audience under different sets of external forces* need not be equally persuasive in each.

All speakers are not equally persuasive. A person's ability to persuade depends on how he or she is perceived by others. Some recent theories of economic and political decisions, such as the many variations of the Condorcet Jury Theorem, include the assumption that people believe everything they hear (Feddersen and Pesendorfer 1995, Grofman and Feld 1988). These theories' main conclusion is that when group decisions are made by some form of majority rule, the groups can make a reasoned choice even if many members of the group lack seemingly crucial information. Although the theme of this conclusion resembles our conclusions, the arguments underlying these conclusions are potentially at odds. In the political contexts that most people care about – elections, legislatures, and courtrooms – it is unreasonable to assume that people believe everything they hear. In fact, Theorem 3.3 implies that people should believe everything they hear only under extraordinary circumstances. Therefore, the relevance of jury theorem results to the political contexts that most people care about is tenuous at best.[32] Our claim that all speakers are

[32]Ladha's variations on the jury theorem are an exception. Ladha (1992, 1993) evaluates the robustness of the jury theorem in cases where individuals makes errors. Our preference is for such models to go further in this direction, showing the robustness of the jury theorems when people do not know one another well, have potentially conflicting interests, and, as a result, may attempt to deceive one another.

not equally persuasive also contradicts the belief that knowledge is power. Knowledge cannot be power unless the knowledgeable person can persuade the person over whom he or she would have power.[33]

You do not necessarily learn more from people who are like you, nor do you necessarily learn more from people you like. This is why you feed your children what a pediatrician recommends instead of what they want. Conversely, if the penalties for lying are high enough, people can be persuaded by speakers whom they know to have conflicting interests.

Our explanation of how people choose whom to believe can be used to amend popular Aristotelian theories. That is, it is easy to demonstrate that explanations of who can persuade based on the concepts of reputation, credibility, trust, honesty, affect, ideology, or partisanship are conditional. Consider, for example, the claim that reputation is a prerequisite for persuasion, as is sometimes done in institutional economics. In our model, *reputation is neither a necessary nor a sufficient condition for persuasion.* Were reputation a sufficient condition for persuasion, then two interactions between the same principal and speaker would necessarily make the speaker trustworthy (a simple extension of our model shows this to be false). Were reputation a necessary condition for persuasion, then the principal in the model we present would never believe the speaker.[34] We conclude that reputation generates persuasiveness only if it generates the conditions for persuasion. Therefore, although it is true that certain reputations can help a speaker persuade, not all can.

Explanations of persuasion based on *ideology, affect,* and *partisanship* suffer the same fate as reputation. None of these factors is necessary or sufficient for persuasion in our model. To see why, consider the following example. You might really *like* Mr. A or know him to be a conservative like yourself but believe that he knows nothing whatsoever about policy B. In this case, you should not follow Mr. A's advice. Alternatively, you might believe Mr. A to be a knowledgeable, nonconservative, and unlikable person who nevertheless faces a strong incentive to reveal what he knows. In this case, you should follow his advice.

---

[33]If it seems counter-intuitive or wrong that the speaker's actual knowledge has nothing to do with his persuasive power, consider your own experience. You do not know much about the people from whom you receive most of your political information. (How much do you know about the people who speak on CNN or write for the *New York Times*?) You do not have access to detailed information about the extent of most other people's knowledge. Therefore, you must base your choice of whom to believe on your subjective beliefs. If you believe that a speaker knows nothing, then you have no grounds for following his advice. This is true even if (unknown to you) the speaker actually possesses the knowledge you desire.

[34]The same logic exposes the flawed logic of the methodological critique that a repeated play format is required to construct a model of learning. Even if the folk theorem did not call into question the robustness of all of these analyses, the preceding argument makes clear that learning from others does not require repeated interactions.

Theory

Theorem 3.3 implies that persuasion based on personal character is possible in the following case.

When an analyst encounters a persuasive attempt and is considering the hypothesis "Factor F causes the listener to change her mind about topic T," she should ask herself the following questions: "Is it reasonable to assume that the listener perceives factor F to be correlated with the speaker's knowledge of T?" and "Is it reasonable to assume that the listener perceives factor F to be correlated with either the speaker's interests or his incentives to reveal what he knows about T?" If the answer to both questions is "No," then factor F cannot be a cause of persuasion, in the sense of our model, and the hypothesis should be discarded. If the answer to either question is "Yes," then she has a basis for continuing the analysis. If the answer to both questions is "Yes" then she has an even stronger reason to continue.

The conditions for persuasion reveal when personal attributes (e.g., partisan cues, ideology, affective relationships, and the like) are most useful for understanding persuasion. To see this, consider ideology. In cases where there is a high correlation between ideology and the factors underlying the conditions for persuasion (such as common interests or penalties for telling certain lies), then knowing a speaker's ideology can be a good indicator of whether he should be trusted. In cases where there is no clear correlation, concepts such as ideology and party are useless cues. To put it another way: *Concepts like reputation, party, or ideology are useful heuristics only if they convey information about knowledge and trust. The converse of this statement is not true.*

CONCLUSION

The political consequences of limited information can be very serious. However, our theorems suggest that people do not suffer these consequences nearly as often as many scholars and pundits proclaim. Politics often forces people to learn what they need to know from the oral and written testimony of other people. In these cases, limited information precludes a principal from making a reasoned choice if the conditions for persuasion do not apply. Therefore, if a principal has access to the testimony of at least one speaker whom she perceives as knowledgeable and trustworthy, then limited information need not preclude reasoned choice. However, and unlike prior explanations of persuasion, we conclude that trust need not be derived from a principal's assessment of a speaker's personal character. Instead, we argue that external forces that alter and clarify a speaker's incentives can serve as the basis for trust. When people can learn from others, reasoned choice requires neither encyclopedic information nor relevant personal experience.

Other critics look at how most modern citizens obtain information and conclude that people are regularly and easily deceived. What many of these critics fail to realize, however, is that learning is active. If learning were passive, as is often assumed, then every heavily advertised product or program would garner much attention and universally rave reviews. Of course this does not happen. People have incentives to be, and in fact are, quite selective about whom they choose to believe.

Food for Thought

We argue that persuasion is a function of perception, context, and choice. We also assert that the explanation of persuasion that we offer can help clarify many questions about political interaction. In Parts II and III of this book, we describe a wide variety of experiments and case studies that support our assertion. Because some readers may not want to wait that long, we end this chapter with two simple parables.

Gritz. Because government deals with scarcity and requires collective action to get anything done, the product of government is often a product of compromise. Compromise can be easy or hard to obtain. When it is hard to obtain, it requires negotiation.

In recent years, the U.S. government has had to engage in negotiations with a new set of actors. We follow convention and refer to these actors as *militias* – domestic paramilitary groups whose basis for existence is a claim of government illegitimacy. In the early and mid-1990s, standoffs between militias and government law-enforcement agencies became increasingly common. For example, prolonged negotiations at Ruby Ridge, Waco, and with the Montana Freemen lasted for weeks. Each conflict also gained wide national attention.

The government had a great deal at stake in these negotiations. In addition to the lives of those involved in the standoff, the government's handling of these situations would send a powerful signal to other existing or nascent militias about how future conflicts would be settled.

The U.S. government is arguably the most powerful organization in the country, if not the world. One reason for its power is its access to capital. Given the importance of the negotiations just mentioned, it is reasonable to believe that the government had an interest in hiring the most skilled negotiator it could find. The government's ability to access resources suggests that it could have brought in just about anyone.

At Ruby Ridge and in Montana, the U.S. government brought in retired Colonel Bo Gritz. Was Col. Gritz the best negotiator that the United States could find? A couple of facts about Gritz might persuade you that he was not.[35] Bo Gritz is a former Green Beret, a highly decorated Vietnam veteran, and former Special Forces agent. In 1988, he was, for a time, former Ku Klux Klansman David Duke's running mate on the Populist Party's presidential ticket. In 1992, he was the Populist Party's presidential candidate. He won about 100,000 votes on a platform that called for an end to income taxes, foreign aid, and the Federal Reserve. He conducted a program called SPIKE (Specially Prepared Individuals for Key Events) that trained ordinary citizens in weapons use and survival skills. He also wrote a book entitled *Called to Serve* that the Anti-Defamation League characterized as peddling "the anti-Semitic myth that Jewish families control the Federal Reserve System."

Many prominent people were available to be the government's negotiator. Why did the government choose government-hostile Bo Gritz over someone more like retired generals Norman Schwarzkopf or Colin Powell? Our theory offers a suggestion. Compromise requires negotiation, and negotiation requires persuasion. As we have argued, persuasion requires knowledge and trust. Therefore, a necessary condition for effective negotiations with militias was the introduction of negotiators whom the militias would perceive as both knowledgeable and trustworthy. Because the militia's fundamental operating premise is the illegitimacy of government, government-friendly negotiators, such as Powell or Schwarzkopf, were less likely to be trusted. By contrast, the government could reasonably expect Gritz to be persuasive to militia members. Moreover, it is not at all clear that the government could get another person whom they could trust who had Gritz's "militia credentials."

The Ruby Ridge and Montana standoffs ended with the government achieving results it desired. In both cases, Gritz was widely credited with playing a role. Quoting the Associated Press, "Gritz helped end a 1992 standoff in Ruby Ridge, Idaho, between the FBI and white separatist Randy Weaver, whom he persuaded to surrender."[36] To many people, Gritz was a dangerous extremist, but, for a government that needed to establish credibility in order to achieve a settlement, he was an "effective extremist." At some level, the government understood that militia members would make choices about whom to believe. This understanding was essential for the success it had.

---

[35]See "Freemen Make Their Case on Paper, in Video" by the Associated Press and located at the *Salt Lake Tribune*'s internet archives at http://205.218.36.7:80/96/APR/29/TWR/00281116.htm; "Gritz Says Feds Must Move Rapidly" by the Associated Press and also located at the *Salt Lake Tribune*'s internet archives; and "ADL Report: Armed & Dangerous: Idaho" by the Anti-Defamation League and located at www.adl.org.

[36]See "Freemen Make Their Case on Paper, in Video."

Tamales. Another example where understanding the conditions for persuasion that we derive is beneficial comes from the presidential election of 1976. Samuel Popkin began his 1991 book *The Reasoning Voter* with a parable from that election (1).

Predictably enough, the San Antonio rally for President Ford featured Mexican food, and so the President of the United States was served his first tamale, a food not common in Grand Rapids, Michigan, or even in Washington, D.C. While reporters and television cameras recorded the scene, Ford proceeded with gusto to bite into the tamale, corn husk and all.

At this point in Popkin's book, there are two types of readers. One group of readers recognizes Ford's "gastronomic gaffe" because they themselves have had the similar experience of eating a hot tamale. The other type of reader waits for something interesting to happen in this anecdote. Such a reader waits until page 2 and learns that "The snack was interrupted after the first bite so that his hosts could remove the corn shucks which serve as a wrapper and are not supposed to be consumed."

Popkin's anecdote is a clever way to demonstrate how simple pieces of information can convey knowledge. However, the likely existence of readers who do and do not initially get the point of the story again points to the limits of persuasion. For people familiar with Mexican food, Ford's gaffe suggests ignorance. To the extent that ignorance of tamale shucking is connected to ignorance on more important issues, the news footage may lead viewers to think differently about Ford's issue positions. However, for many people, the shucking–issue connection does not exist. So viewers watching this event could recognize Ford's gaffe and not consider him any less credible about any issue. Moreover, for the many people untrained in the art of tamale shucking, our Chapter 2 argument suggests that they would likely ignore this story altogether, as they would not recognize Ford's gustatory gambit as a gaffe.

The lesson we draw from our use of Popkin's tamale parable is that it is unwise to discuss the effect of simple cues like party, ideology, or reputation as affecting a populace in a uniform way. As Popkin himself points out as he concludes his book (page 236), "Ask not for more sobriety and piety from citizens, for they are voters, not judges; offer them instead cues and signals which connect their world with the world of politics." Persuasion is a function of perception, context, and choice. Understanding this can help us better describe how people use the information they are offered.

4

What People Learn from Others

In politics, reasoned choice can be difficult. It can be difficult because politics and government present problems that are unfamiliar to most people. As a result, people often turn to others to acquire the knowledge that reasoned choice requires.

In the previous chapter, we presented a theory of how people learn from others. We found that persuasion requires a perception of knowledge and a basis for trust. We also showed that a basis for trust can be derived, in turn, from the incentive effects of external forces or from a listener's perception that he or she and a speaker have common interests.

To explain the relationship between limited information and reasoned choice, it remains to be explained *what* people learn from others. Under what conditions can someone else provide us with the knowledge we need in order to make a reasoned choice? There are three simple, mutually exclusive, and collectively exhaustive categories describing what can happen when one person attempts to learn from another.

- The first category is *enlightenment*. Enlightenment is the process by which, as a result of observing the actions or hearing the statements of someone else, we increase our ability to make an accurate prediction about the consequences of our actions. If we initially lack the knowledge sufficient for reasoned choice and we can obtain this knowledge only from others, then we can make a reasoned choice only if we become enlightened by these others.[1]
- The second category is *deception*. Deception is the process by which, as a result of the actions or statements of someone else, there is a reduction in our ability to make an accurate prediction about the

[1]Enlightenment need not imply that someone learns the truth, nor does deception imply that someone is lied to. Rather, enlightenment occurs when one person furnishes another with knowledge. Recalling our Chapter 2 definition of knowledge (i.e., the ability to make accurate predictions), we argue that enlightenment requires only an improvement in knowledge, not knowledge of truth.

consequences of our actions. We are deceived when someone lies to us *and* we believe that person.

- The third category is that we *learn nothing*. When we learn nothing, our ability to make an accurate prediction goes unchanged.

There is a vigorous debate about whether political communications, such as presidential election campaigns, enlighten or deceive voters (see, for recent examples, Ansolabehere and Iyengar 1995; Greider 1992; Lodge, Steenbergen, and Brau 1995; and Popkin 1991). At stake in this debate is what we can say about most citizens' ability to make reasoned choices. If these communications enlighten, then citizens can make reasoned choices. If these communications regularly fail (i.e., they are either deceptive or uninformative), then citizens will be less capable.

In this chapter, we use our theory of communication to derive necessary and sufficient conditions for enlightenment and deception. Understanding these conditions is the key to making more accurate judgments about who is, and is not, capable of reasoned choice.

THE CONDITIONS FOR ENLIGHTENMENT

Theorem 4.1 describes the necessary and sufficient conditions for enlightenment in our model:[2]

Theorem 4.1: Communication leads to enlightenment if and only if:

1. the speaker is persuasive,
2. only the speaker initially possesses the knowledge that the speaker needs, and
3. common interests or external forces induce the speaker to reveal what he knows.

Theorem 4.1 shows enlightenment to have three requirements. First, enlightenment requires persuasion. This, in turn, requires that the principal perceive the speaker to be both knowledgeable and trustworthy. Recall that the source of these perceptions can come from beliefs about the speaker's personal character or from knowledge of external forces. Second, the speaker must possess the knowledge that the principal needs. These two requirements together imply that both *actual knowledge* and *perceived knowledge* are necessary conditions for enlightenment. Third, the speaker must either have common interests or face external forces that induce him to reveal what he knows. This requirement together with the first requirement implies that both an *actual incentive* to reveal what

---

[2]We focus on the case where enlightenment, and later deception, is purposeful. That is, our conditions for enlightenment describe the case where the speaker intends to enlighten.

the speaker knows and the *principal's perception* of this incentive are necessary conditions for enlightenment. Figure 4.1 depicts the relationship between the conditions for persuasion and the conditions for enlightenment.

The implications of Theorem 4.1 contradict Aristotelian explanations of social, economic, or political learning. These explanations focus solely on incentive compatibility, between speaker and principal, as the most important determinant of who learns from whom, and they rely on the premise that the principal can distinguish speakers who are knowledgeable and trustworthy from those who are not. In many social, political, and economic contexts, however, people do not know which speakers are knowledgeable and trustworthy. This is why even incentive-altering contracts or institutions need not be sufficient for enlightenment. This is true because enlightenment requires a speaker who has an incentive to reveal what he knows *and* a principal who has the ability to perceive the speaker's incentives accurately. Therefore, even if a speaker's incentives are compatible with the principal's interests, enlightenment will not occur unless the principal's beliefs about these incentives are accurate. It follows that contractual or institutional solutions to information problems must introduce external forces that act on *both* the speaker's incentives and the principal's beliefs.

THE CONDITIONS FOR DECEPTION

Perhaps the greatest internal threat to democracy arises from the possibility that those who exercise power can deceive those upon whose authority they act. This threat, however, requires the possibility of deception – you cannot *lead* a person to act against her interests if you are incapable of deceiving her. The most nefarious form of deception is willful deception – where the speaker lies not by accident but with the intent to cause the principal harm. We focus on the case of willful deception (henceforth called deception) here. Theorem 4.2 describes the necessary and sufficient conditions for deception in our model:

Theorem 4.2: Communication leads to deception if and only if:

1. the speaker is persuasive,
2. only the speaker initially possesses the knowledge that the principal needs, and
3. neither common interests nor external forces induce the speaker to reveal what he knows.

Deception requires that the speaker be both persuasive and knowledgeable. These requirements are precisely the same as the first two requirements in the conditions for enlightenment. Thus, the conditions for en-

70

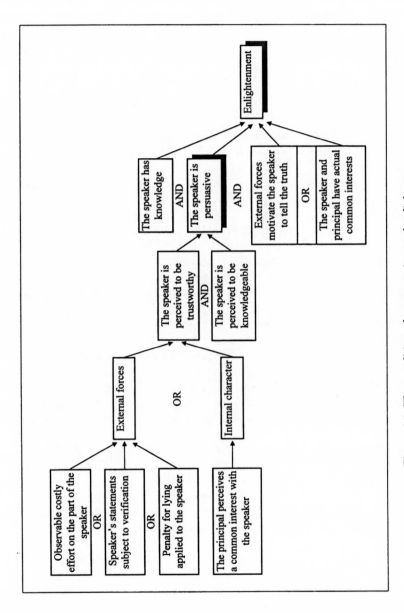

Figure 4.1. The conditions for persuasion and enlightenment.

lightenment and the conditions for deception differ in only one way. In the former, either actual common interests or external forces induce the speaker to reveal what he knows. In the latter, no such forces act on the speaker. Therefore, the factor that determines whether persuasive testimony enlightens or deceives is whether the basis for trust that the principal perceives actually does or does not exist. If the basis exists, then persuasive testimony enlightens. Otherwise, persuasive testimony deceives.

Theorem 4.2 implies that the speaker can deceive the principal only if he is correct in his belief that his deception will not be anticipated or discovered. For if the principal either anticipates or discovers deception, then she has an incentive to disregard the speaker's advice. Thus, *willful deception requires a principal who does not have and cannot obtain knowledge about the speaker's incentives.* These conditions are depicted in Figure 4.2.

Of course, and despite our best efforts, we are deceived by others. Sometimes we are accidentally deceived by people who lack the knowledge we thought they had; other times we are willfully deceived by people who lack the common interests we thought they had. Both types of deception require a misperception on our part.

One of the clearest examples of misperception resulting in deception is the Gulf of Tonkin Resolution (August 7, 1964), which formed the basis for U.S. military expansion in Vietnam. The resolution allowed the president "to take all necessary measures to repel any armed attack against the forces of the United States and to prevent further aggression" (Stone and Barke 1989: 481). The Democratic majorities in the House and Senate, in passing the resolution, relied on the information given them by President Lyndon Johnson. But the president lacked knowledge about the Gulf of Tonkin incident. Consequently, after passing the resolution, many members of Congress felt misled by the president's statements regarding the incidents in the Gulf of Tonkin. Senator J. William Fulbright (D.-Ark.), for example, stated, "Throughout this whole affair, it has . . . been characterized by a lack of candor" (quoted in Goulden 1969: 167). In short, the Congress's misperception about the administration's knowledge enabled the president to obtain extraordinary powers that were "out of proportion with the incident" in the Gulf (Stone and Barke 1989: 481).[3]

Our conditions for persuasion and deception, however, reveal a rigid limit to the claim that political decision makers are regularly or easily deceived. The first limit derives from the fact that *not everyone is persua-*

[3]Congress attempted to remedy this situation by passing the War Powers Act in 1973.

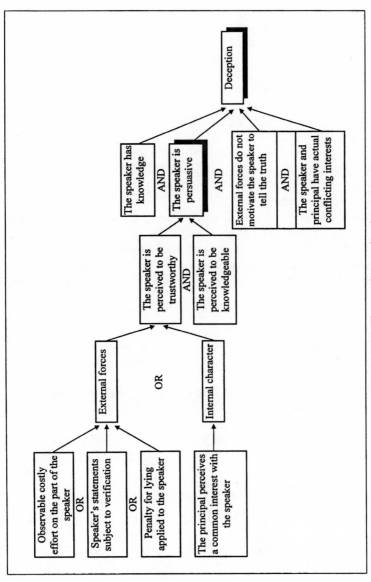

Figure 4.2. The conditions for deception.

sive. People listen to some radio talk show hosts and not others; they watch some news programs and not others; they follow the endorsements of some interest groups and not others; and they listen to some of their friends and not others. Similarly, people read some books and not others, and they buy some products with very little advertising while declining to buy others even though the airwaves repeatedly sing their praises.

The second limit is that not everyone who can persuade can deceive. A persuasive speaker can deceive only if he faces a principal who cannot see deceptions coming. For principals who receive advice in contexts that threaten verification or penalties for lying, or that require costly and observable effort, likely liars can be branded as such and deception becomes more difficult.

Theorems 4.1 and 4.2 also reveal the danger of basing conclusions about what people can learn from one another on the premise that people know one another well. For if people know enough about one another, then deception is impossible.

Of course, people who study politics or care about democracy know that deception is possible and believe that it occurs. What these observers want to know is *the conditions under which deception can occur*. A theory which assumes that people need not know one another well can generate these conditions. A theory in which deception is impossible cannot.

Aristotelian theories of communication are based on the assumption that people know one another well. The combined effect of these theories has been to reinforce two mistaken impressions. First, these theories reinforce the impression that persuasion and enlightenment are equivalent. They are not. Persuasion is a necessary condition for enlightenment and enlightenment is a sufficient condition for persuasion, but the converse of these statements is not true. Therefore, persuasion and enlightenment are not equivalent. Second, because deception is impossible, these theories reinforce the impression that more information is necessarily better, a point that we have refuted in each of the preceding chapters.

DISCUSSION: HOW WE CHOOSE WHOM TO BELIEVE

Our conditions for enlightenment and deception reveal a set of simple strategies that people can use to learn from others more effectively. For example, people readily ignore speakers who they believe lack the knowledge they need. People also use knowledge of others' backgrounds and knowledge of their circumstances to evaluate their character and incentives. These strategies lead all of us to rely more on the testimony of family, friends, and colleagues and less on the testimony of strangers. Indeed, you are likely to be reading this book on the recommendation of a colleague whom you perceived as knowledgeable and trustworthy. Similarly, people who shop for cars are far more likely to seek advice from *Consumer Reports* or *Road and Track* than they are from *Mad* magazine.

Political elites also choose strategies that are consistent with the conditions for enlightenment. When political candidates take positions, for example, or make promises, they do so knowing that their rivals and political commentators are waiting in anticipation to expose any disingenuous statements. For many of them, verification of false statements entails potentially career-ending costs. Likewise, in deciding how to vote on a bill or in deciding whether to approve an agency's actions, legislators draw on numerous competing information sources. Constituents, interest groups, members of the executive branch, and their colleagues all provide advice. Some of these sources are perceived to possess common interests.[4] Others pay substantial costs to bring this advice, or face a penalty for lying (e.g., the loss of their reputation). Competition-induced verification together with observable costly effort and penalties for lying give legislators effective substitutes for the detailed policy information they often lack.

Our explanation of how and what people learn from one another provides one more critical advantage – it provides insight into how the design of political institutions can help people make reasoned choices. To see this insight, consider two arguments. The first argument is familiar: Reasoned political choice requires political knowledge, this knowledge usually requires the testimony of others, and learning from others requires persuasion; therefore, reasoned choice usually requires persuasion. The second argument is as follows: People can design political institutions, institutions can contain incentive-altering external forces, external forces can affect what speakers say and help listeners evaluate a speaker's credibility; affecting what speakers say and helping listeners evaluate credibility can stack the deck in favor of the conditions for enlightenment and against the conditions for deception; therefore, people can design political institutions that make enlightenment possible in contexts where it would not otherwise occur.

Combining these two arguments produces the conclusion that *people can design institutions to facilitate reasoned choice.* This outcome is possible when people can structure institutions to impose verification threats, costly effort requirements, or statement-specific costs, such as penalties for lying, that provide speakers with incentives to reveal what they know and principals with the ability to perceive speaker incentives accurately. By contrast, when reasoned choice requires enlightenment

---

[4]See Matthews and Stimson (1970, 1975) and Kingdon (1977) on learning in Congress.

and these structures cannot be created, then people may be hard pressed to make reasoned choices.

Perhaps the clearest example of an institutional design that generates the conditions for persuasion and enlightenment in a context where neither would otherwise exist is found in courtrooms. Jurors face an environment where personal experience is usually insufficient for reasoned choice; they cannot go back in time, for example, to be at a crime scene. The witnesses and attorneys who attempt to persuade them are people whom they have never met and whom they likely will never encounter again. Jurors are, therefore, unlikely to know these speakers well. Further, they know that the prosecution and defense have interests that conflict with each other's. In this environment, they are likely to be uncertain about which speakers have common interests with them.[5] However, jurors can rely on the fact that all testimony is subject to immediate verification (through cross-examination and the collection of evidence) and penalties for lying (e.g., perjury).

CONCLUSION

We lack detailed information about most of the decisions we make. In Part I of this book, we have identified the conditions under which limited information prevents reasoned choice. In Chapter 2, we explained that reasoned choice rarely requires detailed information and that people have incentives to be very selective about what information to attend to. In Chapter 3, we explained that politics often forces people who want to make reasoned choices to rely on the testimony of others. In Chapters 3 and 4, we explained how people sort through the testimony that others offer them. In so doing, we identified the strategic foundations of enlightenment and deception in political contexts. We revealed that institutions matter for politics not only because they can shape people's incentives but also because they can affect who can learn from whom.

Our ultimate goal is the ability to make more accurate judgments about the political consequences of limited information. We want more reliable predictions about whether or not a particular democratic principal who has limited information is capable of reasoned choice. If we want to avoid a hasty rush to judgment, our analysis suggests that we ask the following questions about the people we study:

---

[5]Of course, the presiding judge may have common interests with the jurors, but it is unclear that he or she is knowledgeable about the evidence. Also, the presiding judge is often more concerned with procedure than with justice.

What People Learn from Others

1. *What choice does the person need to make?*
2. *What information is sufficient for the person to make a reasoned choice?*

The answers to the first two questions focus attention on whether the person possesses the knowledge sufficient for reasoned choice. These questions should dissuade us from using a set of *ad hoc* questions about political trivia, or casual observation of another person's inability to recall a set of detailed facts, as the basis for judging a person incapable of reasoned choice. People do not often need encyclopedic recall to make reasoned choices.

3. *Does the person already possess the information described in question 2?*
   If so, **STOP.**   Reasoned choice is possible and does not require learning from others.

   If not, ask the following:
4. *Is there a cost-effective way for the person to acquire this information without relying on others?*
   If so, **STOP.**   Reasoned choice is possible and does not require learning from others.

   If not, ask the following:
5. *Is there someone who can provide the person with the information required?*
   If so, continue.
   If not, **STOP.**   Reasoned choice is impossible.
6. *Does the person ignore all others who can provide the required information?*
   If so, **STOP.**   Reasoned choice is impossible.
   If not, continue.
7. *Does the person perceive the speaker to be knowledgeable?*
   If so, continue.
   If not, **STOP.**   Reasoned choice is impossible.
8. *Does the person perceive the speaker to have either common interests or an incentive to reveal what he knows?*
   If so, continue.
   If not, **STOP.**   Reasoned choice is impossible.
9. *Do the conditions for enlightenment exist?*
   If so, **STOP.**   Reasoned choice is possible.
   If not, **STOP.**   Reasoned choice is impossible.

Our theory of communication challenges the many critiques of democracy that are based on the assumption that ordinary people cannot make reasoned choices. We argue that democracy need not be threatened by the fact that relatively few Americans have memorized such information as the names of their U.S. senators, or that few can recall, without looking, the content of the U.S. Constitution's seventh amendment. Unless knowledge of these facts is a necessary condition for reasoned choice, the fact that people lack such information is insufficient justification for concluding that they are incapable of basing their choices on reason. Therefore, it is wrong to assume that citizens who cannot recite central passages from a civics text are less competent to vote than those who can.

5

Delegation and Democracy

Democracy requires delegation. The people, through elections, delegate their authority to representatives. Elected representatives, in turn, delegate some of their authority to the leadership of their assembly and to the bureaucracy. The people, through constitutions and statutes, also delegate their authority to judges and jurors. Each of these delegations involves a *principal*, the person or persons delegating, and an *agent*, the person or persons to whom authority has been delegated.

In a democracy, the people and their representatives, at different times and in different capacities, can be either principals or agents. In a courtroom, for example, jurors serve both as agents of the people and as principals for the attorneys who present them with evidence. Elected representatives are, of course, both agent and principal in their various relations – agents of the people in one respect, but, collectively, they are the principal with respect to their leadership and to the bureaucracy.

The central dilemmas of delegation are that agents often do not have common interests with their principals and that agents may have information about the delegation that their principals lack. In studying democracy, we are interested in when these dilemmas do and do not cause delegation to fail. We say that delegation *succeeds* when an agent's actions *improve* a principal's welfare. We say that delegation *fails* when an agent's actions *reduce* a principal's welfare.

Many scholars and political observers conclude that modern democracy's delegations fail. For instance, public opinion, voting behavior, and elections scholars argue that the principal democratic delegation, from the people to their government, is ripe for systematic failure. They claim that unprincipled officeholders, who have conflicting interests with the electorate, and voters, who lack information about politics, cause this failure. Observers of the U.S. Congress conclude that legislator ignorance has similar effects. Niskanen (1971) and Lowi (1979), for example, argue that public officials, from every level of government, are at the mercy of

79

self-serving special interests, lobbyists, and bureaucrats.[1] These arguments portray legislators as the slaves, rather than the masters, of the bureaucracy they oversee.[2]

In this chapter, we identify the conditions under which conflicting interests and information asymmetry cause delegation to fail. In the process, we argue that common claims about the failure of delegation must be reevaluated. Although we agree with the premise that democratic agents and principals may have conflicting interests, and the premise that agents have information advantages that principals do not, we challenge the claim that democratic principals lack the means for coping with these dilemmas. Instead, we find that if a principal has access to the testimony of others and either the ability to identify enlightening testimony or access to institutions that give her this ability, then delegation can succeed even if the dilemmas of delegation are present.

We organize the chapter as follows. First, we discuss the dilemma of delegation. Next, we introduce a new theory of delegation that incorporates lessons from our previous chapters. We then identify conditions under which democracy's most important delegations succeed and fail.

THE DILEMMA OF DELEGATION

In the most general terms, delegation requires at least two people: a principal, the person or persons who initially hold the authority to take certain actions, and an agent, the person or persons to whom the principal delegates authority.[3] In Figure 5.1, we depict a basic model of delegation. For clarity, we refer to the principal as a "she" and to the agent as a "he."

In a basic delegation model, Nature first provides both players with information about the game (this move is not depicted in Figure 5.1). Unless otherwise stated, we assume that all aspects of this interaction are common knowledge. Next, the agent proposes a single alternative to a preexisting policy status quo. Then, the principal either accepts the proposal (i.e., chooses x) or rejects it in favor of the status quo (i.e., the outcome or policy is the same as it was before the agent offered a pro-

---

[1]Also see Dodd and Schott (1979), Ogul (1976), and Schick (1976).

[2]Other scholars argue that the authority the legislature once held has been usurped by congressional committees in the United States and by parliamentary leaders in other countries. See Dodd and Oppenheimer (1977), Ripley (1983), and Shepsle and Weingast (1987).

[3]While the Greeks and Romans recognized many of the problems associated with delegation (Magagna and Mares, forthcoming), modern agency theory has greatly advanced our understanding of delegation (Ross 1973). Our basic model of delegation echoes many classic treatments, including Niskanen (1971) and Romer and Rosenthal (1978).

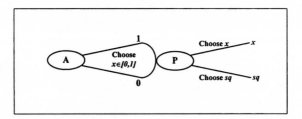

Figure 5.1. The basic model of delegation.

posal).[4] The only exception to the common knowledge assumption is that *the principal is uncertain about whether the agent's proposal is better or worse for her than the status quo.*

When democratic critics such as Lowi (1979), Schumpeter (1942), and Weber (1946) proclaim that important delegations fail, they argue that principals cannot adapt to their limited information. However, it is important to recognize that the critics reach their conclusions by *assuming* that principals are incapable of adaptation. Like the basic delegation model, their arguments assume that principals have no alternatives to ignorance. Therefore, their conclusions about the frequency of failed delegation are not surprising.

Is this assumption warranted? Do democratic principals lack the means for adapting to their limited information? To answer these questions, we step outside of the basic model and inventory alternatives to ignorance.

The principal has three ways of obtaining information about her agent's actions. They are: *direct monitoring* of an agent's activities (the principal gathers information herself), attending to the *agent's self-report* of his activities, or attending to *third-party testimony* about the agent's actions. Although each of these options can provide an alternative to ignorance, each option also has serious drawbacks.

The problem with *direct monitoring* is that it can be very expensive. For instance, it might take years for a legislative principal to understand all of the nuances of a tax policy or the military's grand strategy. The opportunity cost of this effort is enormous. Because voters, legislators, and jurors have many responsibilities to attend to, direct monitoring of

[4]We model delegation as a sequential game that begins when an agent offers a take-it-or-leave-it policy proposal to the principal and ends when the principal either accepts it (perhaps by doing nothing) or rejects it in favor of the status quo policy (i.e., policy on that issue is left as it was before the agent's offer). While we and most analysts focus on a single act of delegation, the consequences of delegation over a long period of time can be understood by allowing the principal and the agent to play the game we describe over and over again.

any or all of their agents is prohibitively costly. Therefore, a principal who wants greater knowledge has a strong incentive to rely on the oral or written testimony of others.

The drawback of *relying on the agent's self-report* is that the agent may be reluctant to reveal what he knows (see Lupia and McCubbins 1994a). For example, if an agent and principal have conflicting interests, then the agent has no incentive to share his expertise with the principal.

If agents have no incentive to share expertise and if direct monitoring is prohibitively costly, then a principal who wants greater knowledge can get it only from the testimony of a third party. When a principal relies on *third-party testimony* (e.g., that of a speaker), she does not have to pay (directly) the cost associated with direct monitoring. In addition, the principal may not face the same interest conflicts that keep an agent from revealing what he knows. However, third-party testimony is not a panacea. Third parties and principals may also have conflicting interests (e.g., the principal is a liberal and the third party is a conservative). To put it another way, relying on a third party for knowledge is itself an act of delegation. If the third party and principal have conflicting interests, if the third party has expertise that the principal does not, and if the principal cannot adapt to the third party's advantages, then the principal cannot obtain knowledge from the third party.

If it is indeed true that principals and agents have conflicting interests, that principals know too little about their agent's activities, that direct monitoring is prohibitively costly, and that principals cannot learn from others, then failed delegation is inevitable. However, the consequences of delegation need not be so bleak. In what follows, we will identify the conditions under which delegation can succeed despite conflicting interests, knowledge asymmetry, and the dangers of learning from others.

A THEORY OF DELEGATION WITH COMMUNICATION

We begin by extending the basic delegation model to include a speaker.[5] Therefore, our model of delegation requires three people. We call these

[5]An insight from McCubbins and Schwartz (1984) motivates this choice. McCubbins and Schwartz argue that when there is something substantial at stake in a democratic delegation, numerous knowledgeable individuals will find it in their interest to come forth and provide testimony in an effort to affect the principal's decision. Speakers who can affect a principal's decision, so that it more closely aligns with what they want, can serve their own interests by speaking up. In these cases, the problem for the principal is not the common assumption that she is bereft of sources of knowledge. The problem is that the principal needs to know whose advice to follow and whose to ignore. Note that the case we describe is without a loss of generality to the case where the agent makes statements about his own proposal. In this case, the agent and the speaker are the same player.

people the *principal,* the *speaker,* and the *agent.* The agent can propose a single alternative, $x \in [0, 1]$, to the commonly known status quo policy, $sq \in [0, 1]$. The alternative x is an analogy, for example, to a bureaucratic agent's formal proposal to change a particular policy, a candidate's policy platform, or a legislative agent's unspoken plan of action. The principal either accepts the agent's proposal or rejects it in favor of the status quo. As in our model of persuasion, the speaker attempts to influence the principal's choice by sending a signal to her about the agent's proposal, and the principal's choice affects all players' welfare. Unless otherwise stated, we assume that all elements of the model are common knowledge.

Our model consists of five basic assumptions. We sketch these assumptions here and provide technical descriptions in the Appendix to Chapter 5.

Assumption 5.1: The agent, speaker, and the principal are goal oriented.

Each player has an ideal point on $[0, 1]$ and a single-peaked utility function.[6] We assume that each player prefers that the principal choose the alternative, x or $sq,$ that is closest to his or her own ideal point.

Assumption 5.2: The principal is uncertain about which alternative is better for her.

We assume that the principal has beliefs about, but may not know, whether x or sq is closest to her ideal point. Specifically, the principal knows the location of sq and her own ideal point, $p.$ However, the principal is uncertain about the location of $x.$

Assumption 5.3: The speaker makes a statement and can lie.

As in Chapters 3 and 4, the speaker can make one of two statements to the principal – "the agent's proposal is *better* for you than the status quo" and "the agent's proposal is *worse* for you than the status quo." As in previous chapters, the speaker need not make a truthful statement.

Assumption 5.4: The sequence of events is as follows.

Figure 5.2 depicts the five steps in the sequence of events. First, nature provides each player with the common knowledge (this move is not depicted in the figure). Second, the agent can propose a single alternative, $x,$ to the status quo. Proposing is costly. To make a proposal, the agent must pay the exogenously determined cost, $C \geq 0$ (e.g., the signatures required for placing a candidate or referendum on the ballot, or the

---

[6]Because any two points in space determine a line, it is trivial to show that our conclusions hold for binary choice between points in N-dimensional space. In addition, all of our conclusions are robust to the class of utility functions whose value is monotonically decreasing in distance from an ideal point.

Theory

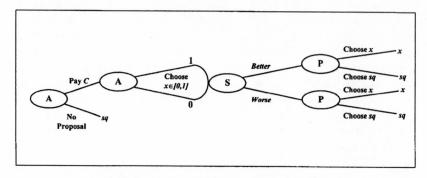

Figure 5.2. Delegation with communication.

collective action required to place a bill on a legislative agenda). If the agent does not pay C, then the game ends and each player's payoff is determined by the spatial distance between sq and the player's own ideal point – the bigger the distance, the smaller the payoff. If the agent pays C, then he proposes x and the game continues.[7] Third, the speaker makes his statement (depicted as *Better or Worse* in Figure 5.2). Fourth, the principal chooses x or sq. Then, the game ends. Each player's payoff is then determined by the distance between the alternative that the principal chooses, x or sq, and each player's own ideal point. The agent's payoff is reduced by C if he makes a proposal.

Assumption 5.5: The speaker is one of two types.[8]

We use the lessons of previous chapters to define two speaker types, called *persuasive* and *not persuasive*. When the speaker is persuasive, the principal believes her signal and may be able to learn what she needs to know about the agent's proposal. When the speaker is not persuasive, the principal ignores the signal. In this case, our model of delegation is equivalent to a model of delegation with no speaker at all (as depicted in Figure 5.1).

---

[7]Our results are without a loss of generality to the case where the agent is uncertain about the consequences of his actions. That is, the effect of communication has the same type of effect on the agent's incentives regardless of whether the agent knows or is uncertain about the consequences of his actions.

[8]Recall that in games of incomplete information, a player's "type" is a summary of the personal attributes about which other players are uncertain (e.g., Harsanyi 1968a,b). In Chapter 3, we were interested in the distinct effects of experimentally separable attributes about which political actors are often uncertain. There, the conventional use of the term "type" was insufficient. In this chapter, we are interested in the effect of uncertainty on delegation and uninterested in rederiving the previous chapter's results. Therefore, in this chapter, we use the term "type" in the conventional way.

84

Delegation and Democracy

Underlying this definition of the speaker's type, of course, are the conditions for persuasion from Chapter 3 – the perceived relationship between speaker and principal interests, the principal's perception of the speaker's knowledge, penalties for lying, verification, and observable costly effort. Assumption 5.5 allows us to bring our previous conclusions to bear on the topic of delegation while keeping our model's complexity to a minimum.

We now present our conclusions about delegation. We first present two general conditions that determine the outcome of delegation. We then present a set of more precise conditions that determine when each of the two general conditions is satisfied.

The General Conditions

The first general condition for successful delegation is the *knowledge condition*. The knowledge condition is fulfilled if and only if the principal can correctly infer whether the agent's proposal is better or worse for her than the status quo. The second general condition is the *incentive condition*. To satisfy the incentive condition, the agent must have an incentive to make a proposal that is better for the principal than the status quo. This second requirement is satisfied either if the agent and principal have common interests or if external forces motivate the agent to propose an alternative that is better than the status quo both for him and for the principal. The relationship between delegation and these two general conditions in our model is as follows:

Theorem 5.1: If both the knowledge and the incentive conditions are satisfied, then delegation succeeds. If neither condition is satisfied, then delegation fails.

If both conditions are satisfied, then the agent makes a proposal that enhances the principal's welfare and the principal knows enough to accept it. In this case, the outcome of delegation is better for the principal than the status quo – delegation succeeds. When neither condition is satisfied, the principal cannot hold the agent accountable for his actions and the agent has no incentive to increase the principal's welfare – delegation fails.

If *only one* of the two conditions is satisfied, then the worst that can happen, from the principal's perspective, is the retention of the status quo. To see this, consider two cases. First, if only the knowledge condition is satisfied, the principal knows enough about the agent's proposal to base her decision on whether the proposal is better or worse for her than the status quo. In this case, the principal can reject any welfare-reducing proposal. Therefore, the worst outcome the principal can obtain is the status quo. Alternatively, if only the incentive condition is satisfied, then

85

the agent makes a proposal that improves the principal's welfare. In this case, if the principal rejects the proposal, she gets the status quo; otherwise, the principal does better.

How to Satisfy the Knowledge Condition. The knowledge condition requires that the principal distinguish whether the agent's proposal is better or worse for her than the status quo. There are two ways to satisfy this condition:

Theorem 5.2: The knowledge condition is satisfied only if:
- *the principal's prior knowledge is sufficient for her to distinguish proposals that are better for her than is the status quo from proposals that are worse for her or*
- *the principal can learn enough to make the same distinctions. When the principal initially lacks knowledge, the conditions for persuasion and enlightenment are necessary for the satisfaction of the knowledge condition.*

Recall that delegation succeeds if both the knowledge and the incentive conditions are satisfied and fails if neither is satisfied. Therefore, Theorems 5.1 and 5.2 imply the following: If the incentive condition *and both* of Theorem 5.2's two conditions fail, then delegation fails. By contrast, the consequence of delegation is no worse than the status quo for the principal if *either* of the two conditions in Theorem 5.2 *or* the incentive condition is satisfied. Moreover, if the incentive condition *and either* of the two conditions in Theorem 5.2 is satisfied, then delegation succeeds.

These two theorems also imply that *the principal need not know very much about what her agents are doing in order to ensure successful delegation.* For example, if the incentive condition is satisfied and either the principal has sufficient prior knowledge about the consequences of the agent's proposal *or* gains enough knowledge by observing the agent's costly effort *or* is sufficiently enlightened by the speaker's testimony, then delegation can succeed.

How to Satisfy the Incentive Condition. The incentive condition requires that the agent offer a proposal that makes the principal better off than does the status quo. There are two ways to satisfy this condition in our model.

Theorem 5.3: The incentive condition is satisfied only if:
- *the principal's ideal point is closer to the agent's ideal point than it is to the status quo and the agent gains more than C if the principal chooses his proposal instead of the status quo, or*
- *the knowledge condition is satisfied and there exists a point that both the principal and the agent (after paying C) prefer to the status quo.*

86

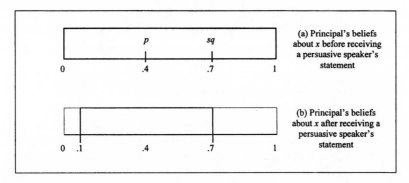

Figure 5.3. The incentive condition with the persuasive speaker as a verifier.

(If the principal initially lacks the knowledge, then the conditions for persuasion and the conditions for enlightenment are the keys to satisfaction of the knowledge condition.)

To see why Theorem 5.3 is true, consider the following. In our model, the agent must weigh the costless option of making no proposal against the costly option of making a proposal. Therefore, it is always better for the agent to propose nothing than to propose something that is worse for him than the status quo. To put it another way, a necessary condition for the satisfaction of the incentive condition is that there be at least one alternative that is better for the principal than the status quo and that the agent prefers to the status quo so much that he is willing to pay C to achieve it. If no such alternative exists, then any proposal that is better than the status quo for the agent leaves the principal worse off than the status quo and vice versa.

If the agent's ideal point is better for the principal than the status quo and allows the agent to recover the costs of proposing it, then, in equilibrium, the agent proposes it when he makes a proposal. If the agent's ideal point does not fit this description, then satisfaction of the incentive condition requires a knowledgeable principal. This can be achieved when the principal learns from a persuasive speaker.

To see an example of how this works, consider Figure 5.3. Figure 5.3a depicts a set of prior beliefs that the principal could hold about the agent's proposal. In this example, $sq = .7$, the principal's ideal point is .4, the agent's ideal point is located at 0 (although the principal does not know this), $C = 0$, and the principal has uniform prior beliefs (i.e., she believes that x is equally likely to be located at any point in [0, 1].) In the absence of a signal from a persuasive speaker, the principal's equilibrium response

87

is to accept the agent's proposal, and the agent's equilibrium response is to propose his ideal point. Because the agent's ideal point is actually worse for the principal than the status quo, the incentive condition is not satisfied. And, because the knowledge condition is not satisfied, delegation fails.

We now reexamine the example after introducing a new stimulus: A persuasive speaker states that x is *better* than the sq for the principal. Figure 5.3b depicts the principal's updated beliefs after she receives this signal. Because the conditions for enlightenment hold, the speaker signals *better* if and only if the agent's proposal is in fact better for the principal than is the status quo. Therefore, the principal's best response is to accept the agent's proposal only if the speaker signals *better*. Because the agent's ideal point is not better for the principal, the agent knows that the status quo will be the outcome if he proposes his ideal point. However, if the agent proposes a point between .1 and .7, then the speaker will signal *better* and the principal will accept the agent's proposal. Therefore, when the knowledge condition is satisfied, the agent has an incentive to propose an alternative that is better for the principal. Thus, in this example, the presence of a knowledgeable and persuasive speaker causes delegation to succeed.

Conversely, if the conditions for deception hold instead of the conditions for enlightenment, then the agent will propose his ideal point, and the principal will accept it. The speaker's ability to deceive leads the principal to accept a proposal that she would have rejected had she been enlightened, and delegation fails.

The principal's knowledge of the agent's proposal cost, C, can have a similar effect. That is, the fact that an agent either had to pay $1 million or risk a prolonged filibuster to make a proposal can provide the principal with greater knowledge of the proposal's consequences. Specifically, the principal can infer that the proposal and the status quo are so different that the agent found the payment of this cost worthwhile. The effect of the agent's costly effort on the principal's knowledge in this example parallels the effect of the speaker's costly effort, as described in Chapter 3.

More generally, when the agent faces a principal who can distinguish better proposals from worse proposals, then he knows that proposing any point that is worse for the principal than the status quo, including his own ideal point, leads to the status quo as the outcome of delegation. In these conditions, the agent should make only a proposal that makes both him and the principal better off relative to the status quo. By contrast, if the same agent faces a principal who is incapable of distinguishing worse from better proposals, then the agent has no incentive to make a proposal that benefits the principal. Therefore, when there exists a proposal that both the principal and agent (after paying C) prefer to the status quo, satisfaction of the knowledge condition is also sufficient for satisfaction of the incentive condition.

Delegation succeeds if the knowledge and the incentive conditions are satisfied and fails if neither is satisfied. It follows that if the knowledge condition *and both* of Theorem 5.3's conditions fail, then delegation fails. By contrast, the consequence of delegation is no worse than the status quo if *at least one of the two* conditions in Theorem 5.3 *or* the knowledge condition is satisfied. Moreover, if the knowledge condition *and any* of the conditions in Theorem 5.3 are satisfied, then delegation succeeds.

WHAT IT ALL MEANS

In Figure 5.4, we diagram our conclusions about the relationship between persuasion, enlightenment, and delegation. The direction of causality in Figure 5.4 is from left to right. For example, we can trace the relationship between penalties for lying and successful delegation as follows: "Penalties for lying applied to the speaker" causes (is to the left of and has an arrow pointing to) "The speaker is perceived to be trustworthy"; "The speaker is perceived to be trustworthy" causes "The speaker is persuasive"; "The speaker is persuasive" has an arrow pointing to "Enlightenment," which, in turn, has an arrow pointing to the "Knowledge Condition," which then has an arrow pointing to "Delegation Succeeds." The moral of following this particular path is that penalties for lying can cause successful delegation.

A more general moral is as follows – we can compare the likelihood of successful delegation in two or more institutions by comparing the extent to which the concepts at the terminal branches on the left side of Figure 5.4 characterize each setting. That is, if we could enumerate the extent of factors such as "observable costly effort" and "speaker has knowledge," then we could describe these institutions in terms of their conduciveness to successful delegation. We, in fact, conduct such an exercise in Chapter 10.

Together, Theorems 5.1 through 5.3 imply that there are many routes to successful delegation. Many of them provide the principal with ways to adapt to her limited information. For example, delegation fails *only* if all of Theorem 5.2's conditions and Theorem 5.3's conditions fail. By contrast, delegation succeeds if *any* of the conditions in Theorem 5.2 and any of the conditions in Theorem 5.3 are satisfied. Theorems 5.1, 5.2, and 5.3 reveal myriad ways to make delegation succeed, some of which require the principal to have very little information. Thus, it is the possibility by any number of means, and not necessarily principals who have

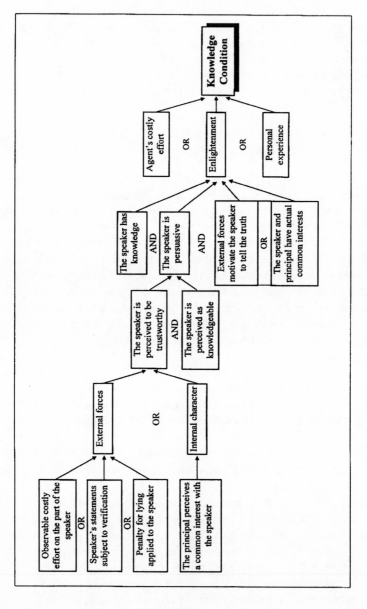

Figure 5.4a. Steps to the satisfaction of knowledge condition.

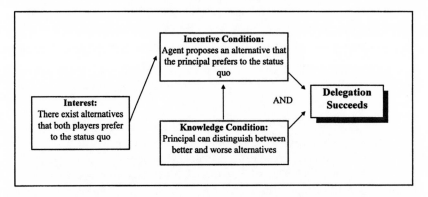

Figure 5.4b. Conditions for successful delegation.

expertise, that provides the sturdy ground upon which successful delegation can be constructed.

A Tougher Standard for Evaluating the Consequences of Delegation

Throughout the chapter, we have said that delegation *succeeds* when the agent takes actions that improve the principal's welfare and that delegation *fails* when agent actions reduce the principal's welfare. However, it is possible to argue that successful delegation should do more than just increase the principal's welfare. After all, delegation can be a costly endeavor for the principal (Alchian and Demsetz 1972, Jensen and Meckling 1976). Finding an agent, and dealing with that person, can impose heavy opportunity or transactions costs (e.g., Spence 1974, Kiewiet and McCubbins, 1991, Laffont and Tirole 1993). Therefore, it is possible to argue that delegation should be called successful only if it increases the principal's utility by more than a trivial amount.

We now take these arguments into account and offer a second, tougher, and more complex definition of successful delegation. Let the opportunity and transaction costs of setting up and maintaining delegation be represented by the constant $K > 0$. Our tougher definition of successful delegation is one in which the agent's actions enhance the principal's welfare by more than K.[9] All other outcomes constitute failed delegation. Unlike

[9] As Kiewiet and McCubbins (1991) describe, the costs to the principal of employing agency control mechanisms can yield a negative net benefit. Spence (1974) further notes that, even before agency control mechanisms become necessary, there are sunk costs involved in the initial process of delegation, as the agents are selected by the principal.

the previous definition, if an agent takes an action that enhances the principal's welfare by less than K, then we say that delegation fails.

This tougher definition affects our results in the following way:

Theorem 5.1': If both the knowledge and the incentive conditions are satisfied, then delegation can succeed. If either condition is not satisfied, then delegation fails.

This tougher definition does not affect Theorems 5.2 and 5.3. Therefore, our conclusion that there are multiple paths to successful delegation continues to hold. For example, under the new, tougher definition, delegation fails only if either *both* of Theorem 5.2's two conditions or *both* of Theorem 5.3's two conditions fail. By contrast, delegation can succeed if any of the Theorem 5.2 conditions and any of the Theorem 5.3 conditions is satisfied.[10] Thus, even with this tougher definition, successful delegation does not seem as improbable as we have often been led to believe.

CONCLUSION

Delegation is a necessary component of modern democracy. Many people believe that the efficacy of modern democracy depends on the answer to the question "When can delegation succeed?" We have shown that the consequence of delegation depends on two conditions: the incentive condition and the knowledge condition. The satisfaction of both conditions turns on whether or not the principal can become enlightened, which itself depends on the conditions for persuasion and the conditions for enlightenment. Only when these latter conditions fail does the principal's limited information and the strong tendency of democratic principals and agents to have conflicting interests imply that delegation must fail. Otherwise, delegation can succeed.

In the first five chapters of this book, we have argued that limited information is not sufficient to strip the reason from our choices or to turn asunder our democratic delegations. In Chapter 2, we argued that the manner by which people direct their attention and the manner in which they draw connections allow them to use a small array of facts to make a broad range of reasoned choices. In Chapter 3, we argued that if people can learn from others, then reasoned choice does not require extensive personal information. In Chapter 4, we identified the conditions under which people learn what they need to know from the testimony of others. We also identified the characteristics that political institutions

[10]In these cases success depends on the size of K – the larger it is, the more difficult it is for delegation to succeed.

92

must have if they are to promote persuasion, enlightenment, and reasoned choice. In this chapter, we combine all of these lessons in an effort to explain why neither complexity nor conflicts of interest are sufficient to cause democracy's delegations to fail. We find that if political actors cannot or do not adapt to their limited information, then they will fail to make reasoned choices and cannot delegate successfully. However, lessons from both the cognitive and social sciences reveal many ways in which people can adapt to limited information. By identifying these ways and describing the conditions under which they are viable, we have identified a surprisingly broad set of conditions under which seemingly ill-informed people are capable of reasoned self-governance.

PART II

Experiments

6

Theory, Predictions, and the Scientific Method

In Part I, we concluded that limited information does not preclude either reasoned choice or successful delegation. If these conclusions are to be compelling, then we ourselves must be persuasive. The persuasiveness of our argument depends on two things. First, our conclusions must follow from our premises. Second, the premises and conclusions we offer must be suitable representations of real decision making. The point of Part I of the book, and the proofs in our Appendices, is to convince our readers that our conclusions do indeed follow from our premises. The point of Part II is to persuade our audience that our theories are, indeed, suitable representations of how people reason and make choices.

In Part II, we treat our theories of communication and delegation as *explanations* rather than as *arguments*. In an argument, the goal is to *show* that a conclusion is true. In an explanation, the goal is to *explain why* a conclusion is true (Schwartz 1980: 202). To put it another way, the premises of an argument are the observable starting points from which one builds to get to an unobservable conclusion. By contrast, an explanation builds from unobservable premises to an observable conclusion.

When some of an explanation's premises are unobservable, it is impossible to provide *direct* evidence that *all* of them are suitable representations of the situation about which the explanation is directed. This is a common scientific dilemma. For example, the basic premises of quantum mechanics, a set of beliefs about how unseen and unseeable forces work within atoms, are (at present) unobservable. Similarly, our theories here rely, in part, on systematic features of physical and chemical processes in the human brain. As social scientists, we are (at present) unable to observe such processes ourselves.

We, therefore, attempt to persuade our readers to believe that our explanations are suitable representations of real decision making in the following way. First, we convert our theoretical conclusions into empirical predictions. Table 6.1 lists these predictions and indicates the theorems

Table 6.1. *Predictions.*

Theorem	Predictions
	Persuasion
3.1	If the principal believes that the speaker is knowledgeable, then an increase in the principal's assessment of the probability that the speaker has *common interests* leads to an increase in the incidence of persuasion.
3.2	If the principal believes that she and the speaker have common interests, then an increase in the principal's assessment of the probability that the speaker is *knowledgeable* leads to an increase in the incidence of persuasion.
3.3	If the principal believes that the speaker is knowledgeable, then an increase in the speaker's observable *costly effort* leads to an increase in the incidence of persuasion.
3.3	If the principal believes that the speaker is knowledgeable, then an increase in the *penalty for lying* leads to an increase in the incidence of persuasion.
3.3	If the principal believes that the speaker is knowledgeable, then an increase in the probability of *verification* leads to an increase in the incidence of persuasion.
	Enlightenment
4.1	In the presence of common interests or external forces that induce truth telling, an increase in the incidence of persuasion leads to an increase in the incidence of enlightenment.
	Deception
4.2	In the absence of common interests or external forces that induce truth telling, an increase in the incidence of persuasion leads to an increase in the incidence of deception.
	Delegation
5.1 and 3.1	If the speaker is knowledgeable and there are no external forces, then giving the speaker and principal *common interests* will induce an agent who has common interests with the principal to make proposals that are favorable to the principal.
5.1 and 3.2	If the principal and speaker have common interests, then making the speaker *knowledgeable* will induce an agent to make proposals that are favorable to the principal.
5.1 and 3.3	If the speaker is knowledgeable and has interests that conflict with those of the principal, then introducing a sufficient *penalty for lying* on the speaker will induce an agent who has common interests with the principal to make proposals that are favorable to the principal.
5.1 and 3.3	If the speaker is knowledgeable and has interests that conflict with those of the principal, then introducing a sufficient threat of *verification* will induce an agent who has common interests with the principal to make proposals that are favorable to the principal.

from which each prediction is derived. In the chapters to follow, we test the eleven predictions listed in Table 6.1.

Second, we evaluate these predictions using a series of laboratory and survey experiments. In Chapter 7, we describe our laboratory experiments on persuasion. In Chapter 8, we present our laboratory experiments on delegation. In Chapter 9, we describe our survey experiment on persuasion.

The design of our laboratory experiments draws from lessons of experimental psychology (e.g., Campbell and Stanley 1966; Cook and Campbell 1979; Hovland, Janis, and Kelley 1953; O'Keefe 1990; Petty and Cacioppo 1986) and experimental economics (e.g., Fiorina and Plott 1978, Forsythe et al. 1992, Friedman and Sunder 1994, Frolich and Oppenheimer 1992, Herzberg and Wilson 1990, Kinder and Palfrey 1993, McKelvey and Ordeshook 1990, Miller and Oppenheimer 1982, Morton 1993, Palfrey 1991, Plott 1991, Roth 1987, Williams 1991).

Like all empirical science, our laboratory experiments require an *inductive leap*. This leap is the assumption that our method of experimental observation is a faithful analogy to our theory. Though many social scientists do not realize it, *all* scientists make this leap when they use empirical research to evaluate theoretical explanations.[1]

---

[1]A frequent problem with social science empirical work is that researchers often fail to state, question, or discuss these assumptions, despite the fact that they are often false. For example, to be compelled by an analysis that evaluates the null hypothesis "A person's level of education does not affect his or her racial tolerance," you must believe that the analyst's measures of education and tolerance are reasonable analogies of these abstract concepts. Typically, the measure of education used in the survey literature is a respondent's self-reported years of schooling, whereas common measures of tolerance include responses to questions about school integration and public accommodation. However, it is plain to see that neither construction *actually* measures the abstract concept to which it is related. Furthermore, researchers almost never discuss the plausibility of their implicit assumptions. For example, reliance on the self-reported years of schooling as a proxy for education fails to account for differences in actual hours spent in the classroom, level of classes taken, school quality, and individual performance. Indeed, such a measure would lead us to believe that college attendee and former Washington Redskins lineman Dexter Manley (who admitted to being illiterate) is at least as educated as Microsoft chairman Bill Gates.

If social scientists want people to be compelled by their claims, they must use suitable analogies to connect their theories and empirical instruments. Similarly, the use of any statistical technique also requires a number of assumptions (e.g., the Gauss-Markov assumptions) that should be discussed in connection to one's data. Social scientists often gloss over the assumptions they make despite the fact that they are often false within the domains they study. For example, political scientists often use seven-point scales to assess the impact of factors such as party and ideology. Many scholars who use these measures in their regressions implicitly assume that the scale is linear (e.g., that a "strong democrat," usually represented by the number 3, is three times as partisan as a "weak democrat," usually represented by the number 1). This is an extremely strong assumption and is likely to be a bad analogy for most peoples' relative degree of partisanship. Depending on the type of regression technique used, derived coefficients can depend heavily on this particular assumption. If the assumption is not a good analogy, then the analysis should not be compelling.

Experiments

Because our laboratory allows us to control important aspects of the experimental environment, we can use it to generate faithful empirical analogies to our theories. For example, we replicate the assumption that the principal makes a binary choice by having subjects predict the outcomes of coin tosses. To replicate the assumption that the principal can learn from a speaker's statement, some subjects (i.e., speakers) sent messages about coin-toss outcomes to other subjects (i.e., principals). We argue that our experimental analogies are indeed faithful representations of our theory and are sufficient for us to make powerful claims about our predictions' reliability.

Our second type of test is a survey experiment. Since the 1930s, when survey methodology became popular, "considerable advances have been made in all aspects of survey methodology" (Kalton 1983: 6).[2] These advances include sampling design, data analysis, and instrumentation. A recent innovation called computer-assisted telephone interviewing (or CATI) allows new types of interactions with survey respondents. We used the technology to present more than 1,400 subjects with complex binary choices. We then provided the subjects with messages from speakers. We drew inferences about persuasion by varying the speakers' attributes and measuring the subjects' perceptions of the speakers' attributes and incentives. The relationships between the subjects' issue positions and perceptions of the speakers allowed us to draw powerful inferences about who can persuade whom.

In Chapter 10, we turn from controlled experiments to an examination of the central institutions of modern democracy. Specifically, by investigating the incentives created by electoral, legislative, bureaucratic, and judicial institutions, we demonstrate that the institutions of democracy can also be the institutions of knowledge. That is, we show that the incentive effects of democratic institutions can also forge the conditions for enlightenment, reasoned choice, and successful delegation.

[2]Some prominent examples of the use of surveys in political science include Campbell et al. (1960), Johnston et al. (1992), Nie, Verba, and Petrocik (1976), Sniderman, Brody, and Tetlock (1991), and the contributions to Weisberg (1995).

7

Laboratory Experiments on Information, Persuasion, and Choice

In Part I, we used our theories of attention and communication to clarify the relationship between information and choice. We began in Chapter 2 by arguing that reasoned choice does not require complete information. We continued in Chapter 3, where we argued that many people must gain from others the knowledge that reasoned choice requires. We then explained *how* people learn from others. In contrast to Aristotelian theories, we focused on the case where people need not know one another well. We found the roots of persuasion in external forces and in a principal's perceptions of certain speaker characteristics. In Chapter 4, we explained that communication *enlightens* only if a principal accurately assesses a persuasive speaker's incentives and knowledge. We then concluded that reasoned choice is possible in a far wider range of cases than many critics claim.

We now put our conclusions to the test. In this chapter, we use laboratory experiments to evaluate our expectations about persuasion, enlightenment, deception, and reasoned choice. We designed our experiments to be a close analogy to our theory. Therefore, our experiments had a principal and a speaker. As in our model, the principal's job was to choose one of two alternatives, while the speaker's job was to make one of two statements to the principal about her choice. Specifically, we asked the principal to predict the outcome of a coin toss, about which she was uncertain (i.e., we asked the principal to predict whether an unobserved coin landed on heads or tails). We asked the speaker to make a statement to the principal about whether heads or tails would be a better prediction.

To make subjects' incentives analogous to the principal's and speaker's incentives in our model, we paid the principal and speaker for their actions. We paid the principal a fixed amount, usually $1.00, for a correct prediction. We tested some of our theory's hypotheses by varying the ways in which we compensated the speaker. In some cases, the principal knew that the speaker also earned $1.00 when the principal predicted correctly (i.e., the speaker and principal had common interests). In other cases, the principal knew that the speaker earned $1.00 when the principal made an *incorrect* prediction (i.e., the principal and speaker had conflicting interests). In still other cases, we made the principal uncertain about how the speaker earned money and, in particular, whether she and the speaker had common or conflicting interests.

More generally, we tested our theory's hypotheses by varying perceived speaker attributes, actual speaker attributes, and external forces. The reason for varying these parameters is that in our model, external forces and perceived speaker attributes determine whether or not the speaker's statement is persuasive (Theorem 3.3), while external forces and actual speaker attributes determine whether a persuasive statement enlightens (Theorem 4.1) or deceives (Theorem 4.2). Simply put, we established conditions in the experiments where we expected the speaker to be *persuasive and enlightening, persuasive and deceptive,* or *unpersuasive.*

For example, we expected the speaker to *persuade and enlighten* when he saw the coin-toss outcome before making his statement (i.e., the speaker was knowledgeable) and had an incentive, from either common interests or external forces, to reveal what he knew (i.e., the speaker was trustworthy). By contrast, we expected the speaker to *persuade and deceive* when the speaker was knowledgeable and the principal had mistaken beliefs about the speaker's motives (i.e., the principal believed that she had common interests with the speaker, but in actuality they had conflicting interests). An example of where we expected the speaker to be *unpersuasive* is in cases where the principal knew that the speaker did not see the coin-toss outcome before making a statement.[1]

Table 7.1 presents a summary of the principal's behavior in our persuasion experiments. The top portion of the table describes the principal's behavior in trials where we expected the speaker to be persuasive and enlightening. The middle portion of the table summarizes the principal's behavior when we expected no persuasion. The bottom portion of the table describes the results when we expected persuasion, but not necessarily enlightenment.

Our measure of persuasion in Table 7.1 is the number of times that the principal's prediction matched the speaker's statement. When the number of matches was significantly greater than the number of matches that would occur by chance (which, in most cases, was 50 percent), then

---

[1]In running the experiments, we were very careful to state the rules of the experiment and nothing more. For example, we told the subjects how the principal and the speaker earned money and whether or not the speaker saw the outcome of the coin toss, but we did not tell the subjects how they should behave in order to maximize their payoff.

Table 7.1. *Summary of results.*

	Persuasion	Enlightenment	Deception	Reasoned choice
	Behaviors When the Conditions for Persuasion and Enlightenment Were Satisfied			
Observed	89	93	7	83
	1,136/1,280	1,057/1,136	79/1,136	1,067/1,280
Predicted	100	100	0	100
	Behaviors When the Conditions for Persuasion Were Not Satisfied			
Observed	58	57	43	52
	668/1,161	383/668	285/668	600/1,161
Predicted	50	50	50	50
	Behaviors When the Conditions for Persuasion Were Satisfied and the Conditions for Enlightenment Were Not Satisfied			
Observed	90	50	50	53
	104/116	52/104	52/104	62/116
Predicted	100	N/A	N/A	50

we have strong evidence of persuasion. Our measures of enlightenment and deception refer only to persuasive statements and depend on whether or not the principal made a correct prediction about the coin toss. If the principal's prediction matched the speaker's statement and was correct, then we say that the principal was enlightened. When the statement was persuasive and the principal's prediction was incorrect, then we say that the principal was deceived.

Table 7.1 reveals that our theory provided a powerful forecast of the observed experimental behaviors. The top section of the table summarizes behavior for the cases where the conditions for persuasion and enlightenment were satisfied by the experimental design. In these cases, our theory predicts that the speaker should *persuade* and *enlighten* the principal. The top of Table 7.1 shows that this outcome was a regular occurrence: Persuasion occurred in almost 90 percent of these cases and enlightenment occurred in more than 90 percent percent of these cases.

The middle section of Table 7.1 summarizes behavior for cases where the conditions for persuasion were not satisfied. In these cases, we expected that the principal's predictions should be *independent* of the speaker's statement and that the principal should make a correct prediction approximately half the time (the rate expected by chance for predicting

103

a coin toss).[2] The middle section of Table 7.1 shows that our expectations were again fulfilled: Persuasion, enlightenment, and reasoned choice (correctly predicting the coin-toss outcome) occurred at approximately the level of chance.

The bottom section of Table 7.1 summarizes behavior for cases where the conditions for persuasion were satisfied but the conditions for enlightenment were not. In these cases, our theory predicts that the speaker *persuade* the principal, but because the conditions for enlightenment were not satisfied, there should also be a high incidence of deception, far greater than the 7 percent deception observed in the trials of Table 7.1's top section. The bottom section of Table 7.1 shows that persuasion was, as expected, a common occurrence; it occurred in almost 90 percent of these cases. However, in stark contrast to the results reported in the top section of the table, in half of these trials the principal was deceived by the speaker.

Overall, when we set experimental parameters to satisfy our theory's conditions for persuasion, the speaker was persuasive about 90 percent of the time. Otherwise, the speaker "persuaded" only at a rate equal to chance (approximately 50 percent). Similarly, when the conditions for enlightenment existed in the experiment, then enlightenment did indeed occur – greater than 90 percent of persuasive statements enlightened, while only 7 percent deceived. Thus, our theory provides a powerful and efficient way of understanding how people in our experiment learned what they needed to know and when they could be deceived.

In what follows, we describe our experimental design. We then review our five types of persuasion experiments. We conclude with an overview of these experiments and a more detailed summary of our results.

EXPERIMENTAL DESIGN

In 1996, we ran a series of experiments on information, persuasion, and choice. Our subjects were undergraduates at the University of California, San Diego. We recruited these subjects by posting flyers on the UCSD

---

[2]To see why we predict "independence" and reasoned choice at the rate of chance, rather than 0 percent persuasion and 0 percent reasoned choice, recall that the conditions for persuasion are not satisfied when the principal *has no reason to base her actions on the speaker's statement.* To achieve 0 percent persuasion, the principal would have systematically to do the opposite of what the speaker recommends. However, to take such an action implies that the principal *is conditioning her action on the speaker's statement,* which is contrary to the prediction of the model in the case described. Instead, we expect the "principal" to guess the coin-toss outcomes without systematic regard to whether her prediction matches or contradicts the speaker's statement.

campus. These signs told prospective subjects how to make an appointment for an experimental session.[3]

When subjects came for their appointments, we paid them a nominal amount (usually $2.00) just for showing up. We then asked subjects to read and sign a standard consent form. The form told them that they would be in an experiment on "decision making" and notified them of their right to leave at any time. All subjects signed the form and none left the experiment early.

We designed our experiments to be analogous to the situations faced by the speaker and the principal in our theory. Our experiments provide valid tests of our hypotheses only if these analogies are faithful to our theory. We present our experimental design by describing these analogies, the most important of which are listed in Table 7.2 and described below.[4] In the table's left column, we list our theory's premises. In the right column, we list the experimental analogy that corresponds to each premise.

At the top of Table 7.2, we list premise–analogy pairs that were *constant* within and across our experiments. We call these analogies constant because we used them in all of our experiments. In the rest of Table 7.2, we list premise–analogy pairs that *varied* across our experiments. We tested our hypotheses by using different versions of the varying analogies across experimental conditions. That is, we used our varying analogies to create the conditions for persuasion and the conditions for enlightenment in some experimental situations and not in others.

The Constants

The first constant analogy concerns the participants. In our theory, we model communication as an interaction between a *principal* and a *speaker*. In our experiment, we assigned each subject to be either a principal or a speaker.

---

[3]Our flyers gave prospective subjects a number to call for an appointment. Our research assistants fielded these calls, verified the callers' ages (eighteen years or older) and undergraduate standing, and assigned experiment appointment times to eligible callers. Typically, we scheduled more subjects than we needed in a given experiment because of an expected 20 percent no-show rate. When extra subjects arrived, we admitted only the number needed for the experiment into the laboratory on a first-come, first-admitted basis. We then paid the extras $5.00 and invited them to sign up for another experiment. No person was a subject in our experiments more than once.

[4]To enhance this chapter's readability, we omit some details of our experimental design. These details include such things as slight variations in the payoff scheme and where the experiments took place. We found no evidence that these variations affected the results. More information is available at: http:\\polisciexplab.ucsd.edu. This web site also explains how to acquire a videotape about our experiments.

Table 7.2. *Theoretical premises and experimental analogies.*

Theoretical premise	Experimental analogy
Constants	
1. "We model communication as an interaction between two players, a *principal* and a *speaker*."	Each subject was a principal or a speaker.
2. "The *principal* chooses one of two alternatives called x and y."	The principal predicted "heads" or "tails."
3. "If nature chooses *better* and the principal chooses x, then she earns positive utility. If nature chooses *worse* and the principal chooses x, then she earns negative utility. If the principal chooses y, then she earns 0."	The experimenters paid the principal a fixed positive amount for every *correct* prediction that he or she made. The experimenters paid the principal nothing for every *incorrect* prediction that he or she made.
4. "The speaker sends a signal of "better" or "worse" to the principal . . . and need not tell the truth."	The speaker signaled "heads" or "tails" to the principal. The speaker did not have to tell the truth.
Principal Characteristic Variables	
1. "Nature chooses *better* with probability b $\epsilon[0, 1]$ and chooses worse with probability 1-b."	The experimenters tossed fair coins.
1a. The principal knows which alternative is better.	1a. The principal observed the coin toss.
1b. The principal is uncertain about which alternative is better.	1b. The principal did not observe the coin toss but knew that the experimenters tossed fair coins.
Speaker Characteristic Variables	
2. "Nature chooses whether the speaker and principal have *common* or *conflicting* interests."	The experimenters chose whether the speaker and the principal had common or conflicting interests.
2a. The speaker and principal have *common* interests.	2a. The principal and speaker earned money only if the principal made a *correct* prediction.
2b. The speaker and principal have *conflicting* interests.	2b. If the principal made a *correct* prediction, then only the principal earned money. If the principal made an *incorrect* prediction, then only the speaker earned money.
2c. Nature chooses *common* with probability $c\epsilon[0, 1]$ and *conflicting* with probability 1-c.	2c. The experimenters rolled a die to determine whether the speaker and principal had common or conflicting interests.

106

Table 7.2. (*cont.*)

Theoretical premise	Experimental analogy
	Only the speaker knew the outcome of the die roll.
3. "The speaker knows whether x is better or worse than y with probability $k\epsilon[0, 1]$ and does not know whether x is better or worse than y with probability $1-k$."	The experimenters chose whether or not the speaker observed the coin toss.
3a. The speaker has complete information.	3a. The speaker observed the coin toss.
3b. The speaker has incomplete information.	3b. The speaker did not observe the coin toss.
3c. The principal is uncertain about how much the speaker knows.	3c. The experimenters rolled a die to determine whether the speaker did or did not observe the coin toss. Only the speaker knew the outcome of the die roll.
External Force Variables	
4. "Verification: After the speaker speaks, but before the principal chooses, nature reveals to the principal whether x is better or worse for her.	
4a. No verification.	4a. No verification.
4b. Verification.	4b. The experimenters revealed the true coin-toss outcome with probability v.
5. "We represent [penalties for lying] as a cost, *pen* ≥ 0, that the speaker must pay when he sends a false signal."	
5a. No penalties for lying.	5a. No penalties for lying.
5b. Penalties for lying.	5b. The speaker paid a penalty if he or she made a false statement.
6. "We represent costly effort as a cost, *cost* ≥ 0, that the speaker must pay to send a signal."	
6a. No costly effort required.	6a. No costly effort required.
6b. Costly effort required.	6b. The speaker had to pay a fixed amount in order to make a statement.

Experiments

The second constant analogy concerns the principal's choice. In our theory, the *principal* chooses one of two alternatives, called x and y. In our experiments, the principal also chose one of two alternatives, *heads* and *tails*. That is, we framed the principal's choice as an opportunity to predict the outcome of a coin toss. The random nature of the coin toss further allowed us a simple way to introduce uncertainty into the principal's decisions.

The third constant analogy concerns the consequences of the principal's choice. In our theory, the principal receives a higher payoff for choosing the alternative that was better for her. In our experiments, the principal earned more money when she made a *correct prediction*. For example, when the coin-toss outcome was heads, we paid the principal $1.00 for correctly predicting heads. If the principal incorrectly predicted tails, however, we paid her nothing.[5]

The fourth constant analogy concerns the speaker's choices. In our theory, the speaker signals "better" or "worse" and is not required to tell the truth. In our experiments, the speaker signaled "heads" or "tails" and also did not have to tell the truth. Moreover, the experimental signals, "heads" and "tails," were good analogies of the theoretical signals "better" and "worse." To see why, consider the case where the coin-toss outcome was tails. Because we paid the principal for a correct prediction, the signal "tails" was akin to the signal "better," while the signal "heads" was analogous to the signal "worse."

The Variables

We varied the remaining analogies to test our hypotheses. Our general idea was to establish one condition in which we did not expect the principal to be persuaded by the speaker's statement or action. We refer to this condition as the *control*. We tested hypotheses by establishing another condition where we expected different, and often persuasive, outcomes. We refer to this condition as the *treatment*.

Treatment and control conditions differed from each other in only one respect: In the treatment condition we usually introduced a stimulus that we expected to lead to persuasion. To cite a simple example, recall our conclusion that perceived speaker knowledge is a necessary condition

---

[5]We implemented these and subsequent payment schemes to satisfy the requirements of *induced value theory*. Induced value theory describes the conditions that enable the experimenter to influence the subjects' incentives; this is done by linking the subjects' rewards to their actions (Smith 1976, 1982). Induced value theory requires that each subject's reward depend on his or her actions, that the subjects prefer more reward (e.g., money) to less, that the subjects base their utility predominantly on the reward, and that each subject have private information about his or her reward.

for persuasion. To test a hypothesis based on this conclusion, we varied the speaker's knowledge across experimental conditions. In the control condition, the speaker was not shown the coin-toss outcome before he sent a signal to the principal. The treatment differed from the control only in that the speaker observed the coin toss.

Our first variable analogy concerns the principal's information. In our theory, the principal has either complete or incomplete information about the consequences of her actions. In our experiment, we varied what the principal knew about coin-toss outcomes. In some conditions, we revealed the coin-toss outcome before asking the principal to make a prediction. In other conditions, the principal had to make predictions without knowing the correct prediction in advance.

Three variables define the speaker's characteristics. The first of these three concerns the relationship between the principal's and speaker's interests. In our theory, both the principal's and speaker's payoffs depend on the principal's choice. In our experiments, the same relationship existed. In some cases, we paid the speaker only if the principal made a *correct* prediction. In these cases, the speaker and principal had a common interest in having the principal make a correct prediction. In other cases, we paid the speaker only if the principal made an *incorrect* prediction. In these cases, the speaker and principal had conflicting interests – the principal benefited when she made a correct prediction, and the speaker benefited when the principal made an incorrect prediction.

The second variable analogy concerns what the principal knows about the speaker's interests. In our theory, the principal need not know the speaker's interests. In our experiment, we sometimes did not tell the principal whether she and the speaker had common or conflicting interests. Instead, we rolled a die to determine whether the speaker and principal had common or conflicting interests. While we told all players that we determined the speaker's interests by the roll of the die, only the speaker knew the actual outcome of the die roll. Therefore, only the speaker knew what his true interests actually were; the principal merely had beliefs about these interests.

The third speaker characteristic variable concerns the speaker's knowledge. In our theory, we assume that the principal need not know how much the speaker knows. In our experiment, we sometimes did not tell the principal whether or not the speaker knew the coin-toss outcome. Instead, we rolled a die to determine whether or not the speaker would see the coin toss. While we told all players that we determined the speaker's knowledge by the roll of the die, only the speaker knew the outcome of the roll. Therefore, only the speaker knew whether or not he had been shown the coin-toss outcome.

Experiments

The three remaining variable analogies concern the external forces from our theory of persuasion. In some treatment conditions, we introduced a penalty for lying. In these conditions, all subjects were told that if the speaker lied about the coin-toss outcome, then the speaker would be penalized. In other treatments, we subjected the speaker's statements to random verification. In yet other treatments, we forced the speaker to exert an observable, costly effort (i.e., pay a fixed cost) before sending a signal.

The ten analogies in Table 7.2 constitute our basic experimental design. In addition to emulating our theory, this design also has the virtue of presenting subjects with simple and familiar situations. To ensure that subjects saw these situations as simple and familiar, we began each experimental session with simple explanations and examples of the experiment's sequence of events, what information subjects would have, and how subjects would earn money. We were extremely careful not to suggest particular behaviors to subjects – we simply explained to them what their options were and did not tell them which options to choose. After we gave a set of instructions, we administered a brief quiz *on the instructions*. Most subjects achieved perfect scores on these quizzes. That subjects understood the instructions so well gives us confidence that they, like the speaker and principal in our model, understood the situation they were in. As a result, we are confident about our ability to use the results from our experiments to draw meaningful inferences about our hypotheses.[6]

---

[6]The quizzes primarily served as a pedagogical device to familiarize the subjects with the experiment. Secondarily, we used the quizzes to identify subjects who could and could not answer questions about the experimental *instructions*. (We paid the subjects a small amount – e.g., 10 cents – for each correct quiz answer in order to motivate them to pay attention to the instructions.) If a subject incorrectly answered a predetermined number of questions, then his or her responses were omitted from the data for the set of trials on which the quiz was based. While we corrected each subject's quiz in his or her presence, we never informed a subject if he or she failed a quiz. Inclusion in the data of responses from subjects who failed the quizzes does not alter the results.

Note that we differ from many economic experiments in that we did not implement "rationality tests," wherein subjects who participate in a preliminary experiment must behave as predicted in order to participate in the main experiment. An example of such a test is described by Cooper et al. (1993: 1309), who state, "We require that players pass a 'rationality' test in session I and that any cohort must choose the dominant strategy 85 percent of the time before we pool this with the rest of the data. We have required this for all of our published experiments." This procedure is analogous to excluding outliers in a regression analysis and is of questionable scientific value. In designing and conducting our experiments, we never selected subjects on the basis of *behavior* in previous experiments.

Other Design Elements

To make our experiments even more like our theory, we took two precautions to limit what the subjects could learn about one another. First, we used partitions to prevent visual contact. Subjects in our experiments could not see one another. Second, we prevented subjects from speaking to one another. This second precaution was somewhat ironic given the critical role of communication in our theory. However, there was a problem with letting subjects speak to one another. Permitting this form of communication decreased our ability to control the communication environment. Therefore, it decreased our ability to control whether the conditions for persuasion and the conditions for enlightenment were satisfied or violated. Without this control, we could not have used the experiments to test our hypotheses. Therefore, to simulate our theory while simultaneously controlling the communication environment, we asked the speaker to signal "heads" or "tails" by checking an appropriately labeled box on a sheet of paper. Then, an experimenter, and not the speaker, read this message. These controls prevented subjects from identifying one another by either sight or sound.

Two additional elements of our experimental design allowed us to conduct our experiments in a cost-effective way. First, we allowed the principal and speaker to interact multiple times. In our theory, the principal and speaker interact only once. Ideally, we would have liked to have the principal and speaker in our experiments interact just once. However, setting up our experiments required significant labor, time, and expense. It was impractical to invite subjects to come to our laboratory for the purpose of making just one decision. Therefore, we had the principal and speaker interact many times.

However, we took precautions to make each interaction seem as though it was the only one (i.e., we took a number of steps to reduce repeated play effects). Specifically, in all of our experiments, we did not provide subjects with any information about the past actions of any other subject. So, subjects learned how much they earned during the experiment *only after the experiment was completed.* Moreover, subjects learned only the sum total of their earnings; we did not give them detailed information about particular choices. Therefore, our subjects never learned which of their predictions were correct and which were incorrect. The principal also never learned when the speaker told the truth and when he lied. During the experiment, our subjects had absolutely no information about what other subjects did in the past. Thus, they had an incentive to treat every interaction with the speaker (or the principal) as though it were the only interaction.

111

Experiments

Second, we ran experiments with one speaker and seven to eleven principals.[7] In our theory, by contrast, we study the interaction between a single speaker and a single principal. Our decision to use multiple principals was motivated by our desire to generate experimental data on *how people choose whom to believe.* Specifically, while we were interested in gathering data on speaker behavior, we were more interested in gathering data about principal behavior. Our design allowed us to gather the data we desired at a much lower price than running with one principal per speaker.

Again, we took precautions to ensure that principals and the speaker had the same incentives they would have had if there had been only one speaker and one principal. First, we prevented principals from affecting one another's payoffs by paying them for only their own predictions. Second, and as we described previously, we prevented principals from affecting one another's payoffs *indirectly* by either seeing one another, hearing one another, or receiving information about the previous actions of other players. Therefore, the principals' payoffs were neither directly nor indirectly affected by the actions of the other principals. As a result, from each *principal's* perspective, it was as though the experiment were between only him- or herself and the speaker. We also presented all principals with exactly the same set of incentives. Because the speaker knew this and could not receive feedback about previous principal actions, the speaker had no basis upon which to discriminate among principals. Therefore, from the speaker's perspective, it was as if he were interacting with just one principal.[8]

EXPERIMENTS ON PERSUASION AND REASONED CHOICE

Each experimental session involved two experimenters, two to four assistants, and eight to twelve subjects. Each session consisted of two sets of benchmark trials and one to four different experimental conditions.[9]

[7]At the outset of each new experimental condition, we selected one subject to be the speaker. All of the other subjects acted as principals. To make the experiment less abstract, we referred to principals as "predictors" and the speaker as the "reporter" during the experiment.
[8]For example, in some treatments we paid the speaker $1.00 every time a principal made a correct prediction. So, if ten principals made correct predictions, then the speaker earned $10.00. If we had just one principal and paid the speaker $10.00 for every correct prediction, then our expectations about the speaker's incentives (and expected earnings) would be identical.
[9]At the conclusion of the last trial, we asked all subjects to fill out post-experimental questionnaires; then we paid them and ended the session.

Benchmarks

We used the first five trials of every experimental session to establish two important benchmarks. The first benchmark was: *What choices would principals make if they knew the consequences of their actions?* The answer to this question allows us to make plausible claims about which experimental behaviors are equivalent to reasoned choices.

We expect that *if principals know the consequence of their actions, then they will choose the alternative that gives them the highest payoff.* All of our subsequent hypotheses (see Table 6.1) depend on this proposition's being true. We tested this proposition by beginning each experiment with two *complete information* benchmark trials. In these trials, all subjects were principals and we showed the coin-toss outcome to everyone before asking them to make predictions. Because our experiments' principals earned money only if they made correct predictions (e.g., $1.00 for each correct prediction and $0.00 for each incorrect prediction), we expected that they would make correct predictions. In fact, subjects in the complete information benchmark trials made correct predictions 376 of 389 times (97 percent). Therefore, we have strong support for the proposition that principals who have complete information *choose the highest valued alternative and that such decisions constitute reasoned choices.*

The second benchmark was: *What choices would a principal make if she lacked knowledge about the consequences of her actions and had no opportunity to learn from a speaker?* The answer to this question allows us to make plausible claims about what subjects choose absent a speaker. Certain variations from this behavior in the presence of a speaker constitute evidence of persuasion.

In the third through sixth trials of all of our experiments, all subjects were still principals. In these trials, we asked the principals to make predictions without seeing the coin-toss result in advance. Under these circumstances, we expected *the principals' predictions to appear random* (i.e., equally likely to be heads or tails). This follows because, for a flip of a fair coin, *the expected payoff from predicting heads equals the expected payoff from predicting tails.* If principals chose randomly, then we should have observed correct predictions approximately 50 percent of the time. In fact, we observed correct predictions approximately 48 percent of the time (377 of 780) in our incomplete information benchmark trials. Therefore, we have strong support for the proposition that principals who have incomplete information and choose among alternatives of equal expected value choose randomly.[10]

---

[10]In some trials, we paid the subjects a small fee for predicting heads, regardless of if the prediction was correct or not. In these trials, we found that the subjects predicted heads 124 out of 144 times (86 percent). While this was below the expected 100 percent, it differs significantly from random behavior.

Experiments

We ran five experiments – two in which we varied the speaker's character-istics, including a knowledge experiment and an interest experiment, and three in which we introduced external forces, including a penalty-for-lying experiment, a verification experiment, and a costly effort experiment. To simplify the exposition, we describe these experiments' implications for persuasion and reasoned choice. Later, we will discuss these experiments' implications for enlightenment and deception.

Each of the conditions consisted of multiple trials (i.e., four to ten coin tosses). We conducted every trial within a condition under identical circumstances (except for the coin-toss outcomes, which we determined by actually tossing the coin once for each trial). We varied experimental parameters only across conditions. In all of the control and treatment conditions that follow, *principals did not observe coin-toss outcomes.*

How We Use the Data.   For every principal, each condition generated a *string* of observations. For example, over five trials within a condition, we observed a principal predicting the *string:* "heads, heads, tails, heads, tails." We use these strings to evaluate our hypotheses. Our test statistic for our hypotheses about persuasion is simply the number of times that principals' predictions matched the speakers' signals. The strongest evi-dence of persuasion is a string of consistent matches, as the likelihood of such a string's resulting from random behavior approaches zero as the number of trials increases. We also use the strings to evaluate null hypotheses of the form "the principal makes random predictions" (as was the case in the incomplete information benchmark trials). If the test statistic deviates significantly from random behavior and most of the principals' predictions match the speaker's advice, then we have strong evidence of persuasion.

In what follows, we present the data in two ways. In the text, we provide summary statistics about the incidence of persuasion and rea-soned choice. In a series of figures, we use the strings mentioned previously to create bar graphs that depict trends in behavior. Each figure contains one or more bar graphs, and each bar graph pertains to a specific control or treatment condition.

Each graph's horizontal axis plots the number of times a principal's prediction matched a speaker's signal. The vertical axis of each graph measures the number of principals whose behavior fell into each category. For example, Figure 7.1a shows that seven principals made predictions that matched the speaker's signal two of five times.

Information, Persuasion, and Choice

To make our claims about variations from random behavior easier to follow, each figure also contains a line that conveys the distribution of principal behavior strings that would most likely have occurred had all principals chosen randomly.[11] For example, in Figure 7.1a, if eleven principals had chosen randomly, we would most likely have observed three principals whose choices agreed with those of the speaker two of five times (i.e., 31 percent of the strings would fall into category 2 in the figure). Moreover, graphs in which observations stack to the right depict conditions where principal predictions consistently matched speaker signals. These graphs depict behaviors that constitute the strongest evidence of persuasion.

Knowledge Experiment

Hypothesis: If the principal believes that she and the speaker have common interests, then an increase in the principal's assessment of the probability that the speaker is knowledgeable leads to an increase in the incidence of persuasion.

Control: The principals did not observe the coin toss. The speaker had common interests with the principals but did not observe the coin toss. There were no external forces. All of this was common knowledge.

Treatment: The speaker observed the coin toss.

Control. In the control condition, a principal and the speaker earned equal amounts when the principal made a correct prediction (e.g., both earned $1.00).[12] Both earned nothing from a principal's incorrect prediction.

Because the principals and speaker had common interests, the principals had an undominated strategy to follow the speaker's advice in both the control and treatment conditions. That is, principals could not make themselves worse off, in expectation, by following the speaker's advice every time. To isolate the effect of speaker knowledge on persuasion, we therefore paid all principals in the knowledge experiment a small sum

---

[11]This probability comes from a binomial distribution. We are thus assuming that each prediction is independent and identically distributed.

[12]As explained previously, to reduce the extent to which our findings depend on the particular parameter values in a single experiment, we ran all of our experiments several times under slightly different conditions. For example, we paid the principals $1.00 for a correct prediction in one experiment, but only 50 cents in another experiment. We found that these variations had no impact on the results. For more information, consult: http:\\polisciexplab.ucsd.edu.

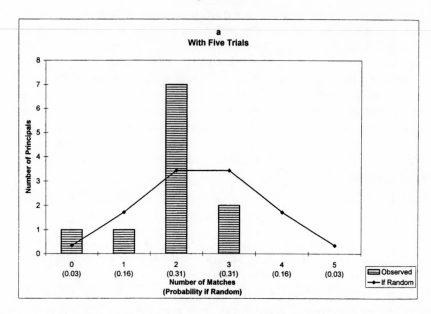

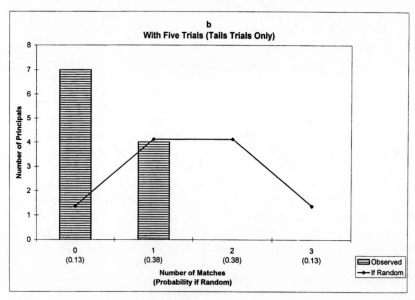

Figure 7.1. Knowledge experiment: control condition.

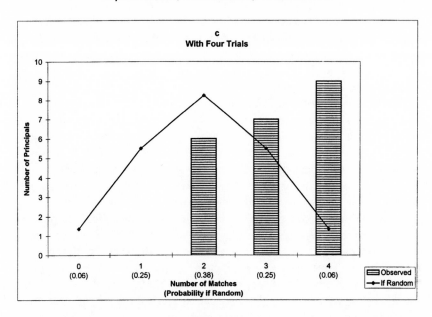

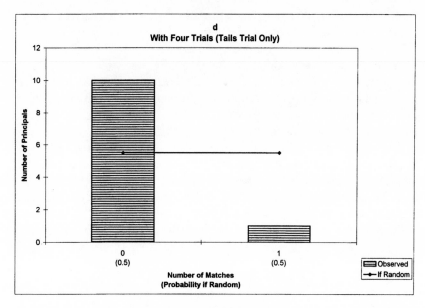

Figure 7.1. (*cont.*)

117

(e.g., 10 cents) for predicting heads, regardless of whether this prediction was correct or incorrect. We expected that principals would choose heads in the control condition, regardless of the speaker's signal, and would follow the speaker's advice in the treatment condition, regardless of whether they heard "heads" or "tails."

Figure 7.1 displays the principals' behaviors in a *control* condition that consisted of five trials. In Figure 7.1a we can see that the principals' predictions did not consistently match the speaker's advice. Specifically, the predictions of seven principals matched the speaker's advice two out of five times, two principals matched the speaker's advice three out of five times, one principal matched the speaker one time, and one principal never made a prediction that matched the speaker's advice. Figure 7.1b presents the same result more starkly. It shows the principals' responses only for the trials in which the speaker reported "tails." In these cases, the speaker's advice (tails) was always at odds with the choice that would maximize the principal's expected payoff (i.e., heads). In these cases, we expected that the principals would ignore the speaker.[13] Figure 7.1b confirms that most principals chose heads regardless of the speaker's advice to choose tails (indeed, seven of ten principals always picked heads). The probability that *one* string of *randomly* chosen predictions would match the speaker's statement zero out of three times is .13. Thus, the fact that the predictions of seven out of eleven principals never matched the speaker's statement (when the speaker stated "tails") is strong evidence that the principals were enticed by the 10 cents for predicting heads. Figures 7.1c and 7.1d present results for the cases where the control condition consisted of four trials. In these figures, we observe similar patterns of behavior.[14]

Overall, in the control conditions, the principals' predictions matched the speaker's advice 63 percent (90/143) of the time. In addition, the speaker sent a veracious report approximately 46 percent (6/13) of the time and the principals made reasoned choices approximately 50 percent (71/143) of the time.

For just the trials where the speaker signaled tails, the principals' predictions matched the speaker's advice only 11 percent (5/44) of the

[13]The principal's expected value from following the ill-informed speaker's advice to choose tails was $(.5)*(1 \text{ dollar}) + (.5)*(0 \text{ cents}) = 50$ cents. This is less than the principal's expected value from ignoring the speaker's advice and, instead, opting for heads $- (.5)*(1 \text{ dollar}) + (.5)*(0 \text{ cents}) + (10 \text{ cents}) = 60$ cents.

[14]The large percentage of the principals whose predictions matched the speaker's advice in the treatment reported in Figure 7.1c is deceiving, as the speaker signaled heads in three of the four trials. Figure 7.1d shows that when the speaker signaled tails, most principals opted for heads.

time, the speaker sent a veracious report 50 percent (2/4) of the time, and the principals made reasoned choices approximately 57 percent (25/44) of the time. These results suggest that principals ignored speakers who lacked knowledge despite the fact that they knew of the speakers' common interests.[15]

Treatment. Our treatment introduced a speaker who had *knowledge*, as well as *common interests*. Introducing this stimulus changed behaviors considerably. Figure 7.2 contains results from a ten-trial treatment condition. Figure 7.2a displays the results from all trials, while Figure 7.2b again shows the results only from those trials in which the speaker reported tails. Figures 7.2c, 7.2d, and 7.2e contain results from four trial treatment conditions.[16]

In all cases, and in contrast with the control condition, the predictions of the principals in the treatment condition *consistently matched* the speaker's advice – even when the speaker reported tails. For example, Figure 7.2b shows that seven out of eleven principals predicted tails *every time* the speaker advised it, despite the guaranteed payoff from choosing heads. The probability that one string of randomly chosen predictions would match the speaker's statement six out of six times is less than 2 percent. The probability that *seven out of eleven* strings would feature six of six matches, if principals acted randomly, is nearly zero. Therefore, our findings constitute strong evidence of persuasion. The other parts of Figure 7.2 indicate analogous behavior.

Overall, in the treatment condition, the principals' predictions matched the speaker's advice 92 percent (174/190) of the time. In addition, the speaker sent a veracious report approximately 94 percent (17/18) of the time, and the principals made reasoned choices approximately 86 percent (164/190) of the time. This last statistic mimics behaviors in the complete information benchmark trials.

In our knowledge experiment, only principals in the treatment condition consistently used the speaker's signal as an effective substitute for the information they lacked. Therefore, we have strong support for the hypothesis that when the speaker and principal have common interests,

[15]In the treatment with five trials, we covertly offered the speaker $5.00 to state tails 60 percent of the time. We did this to assure that the speaker would sometimes signal tails, which would supply us with observations where the speaker's statement (tails) differed from the principal's dominant strategy (choose heads). We announced the use of this procedure at the end of the experiment.
[16]Figure 7.2c differs from Figure 7.2a only in the number of trials that we administered. Figures 7.2d and 7.2e have a similar relationship to Figure 7.2b. Figures 7.2d and 7.2e differ only in the number of times that the speakers signaled tails across experiments.

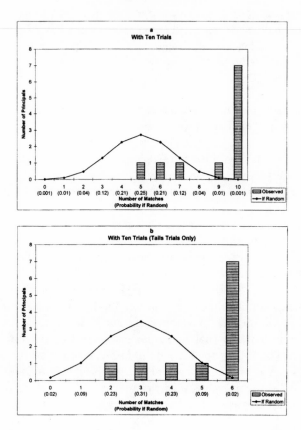

Figure 7.2. Knowledge experiment: treatment condition.

increasing the speaker's knowledge induces persuasion and allows people who lack information to make reasoned choices.

Variations on the Treatment. We ran two variations of the knowledge treatment. The point of the first variation was to show how *perceived* speaker knowledge would affect persuasion. We expect that perceived speaker knowledge, and not actual speaker knowledge, is a necessary condition for persuasion.

To test this hypothesis, we used a ten-sided die to determine speaker knowledge. We rolled the die once per trial. If the die landed on 1 though 7, then we showed the coin-toss outcome to the speaker; otherwise, we did not. The speaker, of course, knew whether or not he was knowledge-

120

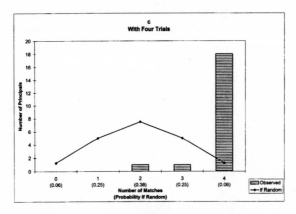

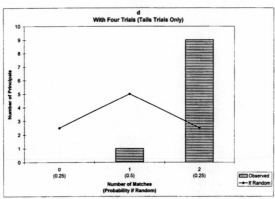

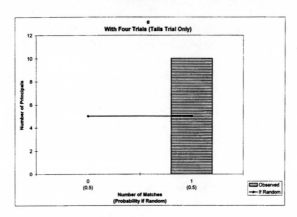

Figure 7.2. (*cont.*)

able when making his statements. By contrast, the principals knew only that there was a 70 percent chance that the speaker was knowledgeable.

Figure 7.3 contains the principals' behavior strings from this treatment. Given the parameters in our experiment, we expected that the principals would follow the speaker's advice if they believed that the probability that the speaker was knowledgeable was greater than 50 percent. Therefore, we expected persuasion in this variation of the treatment. Figure 7.3a shows that most of the principals' predictions matched the speaker's advice in this treatment. While the probability that one string of randomly chosen predictions would match the speaker's statement every time is .001, the predictions of seven out of eleven principals in this treatment matched the speaker's statement every time. As Figure 7.3b shows, the principals' predictions matched the statements even when the speaker signaled "tails." Overall, in this variation of the knowledge treatment, the principals' predictions matched the speaker's advice 90 percent (99/110) of the time.

We expected persuasion in all trials of this treatment because the conditions for persuasion were satisfied. We did not, however, expect reasoned choices in all of these trials. The reason for this latter expectation was that the speaker had knowledge in only 70 percent of the trials. While we expected reasoned choice in these trials, we did not expect reasoned choice as often in the other 30 percent of the trials.

In the fourteen trials where the speaker actually had knowledge, the conditions for enlightenment as well as the conditions for persuasion were satisfied. In these trials, the speaker sent a veracious report 100 percent (7/7) of the time and the principals made reasoned choices approximately 87 percent (67/77) of the time. By contrast, in the three trials where the speaker did not have knowledge, the conditions for persuasion were satisfied, while the conditions for enlightenment were not. In these trials, the speaker *unknowingly* sent a veracious report in two of three trials. The principals' predictions matched this advice 97 percent (32/33) of the time and made reasoned choices approximately 70 percent (23/33) of the time (a figure that, given observed principal behaviors, would have been lower had the speaker unknowingly sent more false reports). In sum, persuasion and reasoned choice occurred when the speaker was actually knowledgeable, whereas reasoned choice occurred with a lower frequency when the speaker actually lacked knowledge. Together, the results from the original knowledge treatment and this variation provide strong support for the expectation that perceived speaker knowledge, when accompanied by common interests, induces persuasion and facilitates reasoned choice.

In our second variation of the knowledge treatment, we examined the case where the speaker lacked knowledge and had conflicting interests.

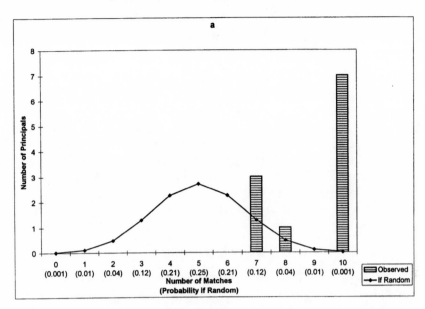

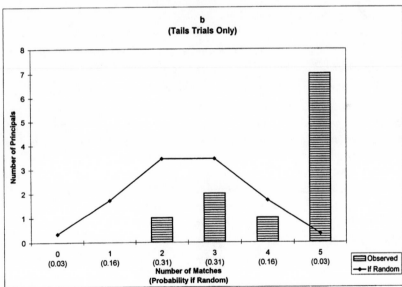

Figure 7.3. Knowledge experiment: treatment condition with 70 percent knowledge.

Experiments

We ran this treatment to establish that a speaker who lacked both knowledge and common interests would be no more (or less) persuasive than a speaker who lacked either characteristic.

Specifically, we did not show the speaker the coin-toss outcome and paid him 50 cents for each *incorrect* principal prediction. We expected that the principals would not follow the speaker's advice in this treatment. Figure 7.4 confirms that, indeed, the principals' predictions did not consistently match the speaker's advice; specifically, the principals' predictions matched the speaker's advice only 33 percent (18/55) of the time. In addition, the speaker made a truthful report 60 percent (3/5) of the time, and the principals made reasoned choices 58 percent (32/55) of the time.[17] These results resemble the behaviors we observed in the incomplete information benchmark trials and the control condition, both as we expected.

Interest Experiment

Hypothesis: If the principal believes that the speaker is knowledgeable, then an increase in the principal's assessment of the probability that the speaker has common interests leads to an increase in the incidence of persuasion.

Control: The principals did not observe the coin toss. The speaker had conflicting interests and observed the coin toss. There were no external forces. All of this was common knowledge.

Treatment: The speaker and principals had common interests.

Control. In the control condition of the interest experiment, we showed the speaker the coin-toss outcome and paid the speaker for each *incorrect* principal prediction. We expected that principals in the control condition would not follow the speaker's advice and would make reasoned choices at the same rate as in the incomplete information benchmark trials.[18] Figure 7.5 displays the results for the control condition.

Every bar graph in Figure 7.5 depicts a distribution of principal-behavior strings that resembles random behavior. Indeed, the figures show that the modal principal behavior in most of the experiments was to follow the speaker's advice about half of the time.[19] In short, the princi-

---

[17]We again covertly offered the speaker $5.00 to report tails 60 percent of the time.

[18]In this experiment, and all subsequent experiments, there was nothing to be gained by paying the principal a small fee (e.g., 10 cents) for choosing heads (as we did in the speaker knowledge experiment). Therefore, we made no such payment.

[19]Figures 7.5c, 7.5d, and 7.5e present results from variations where the speaker could choose not to send a signal. When this occurred, the principals made correct predictions four out of nine times (44 percent).

124

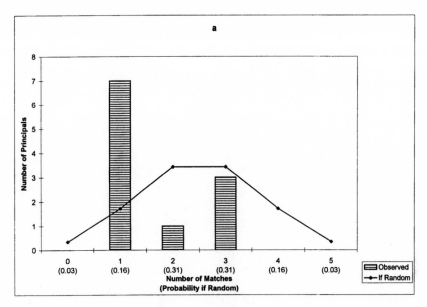

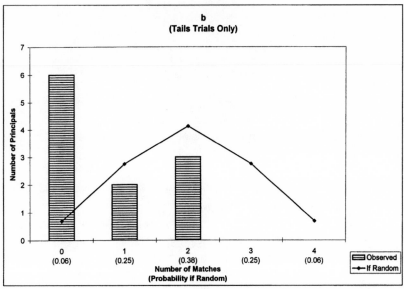

Figure 7.4. Knowledge experiment: conflicting interests and no knowledge.

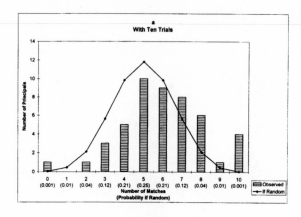

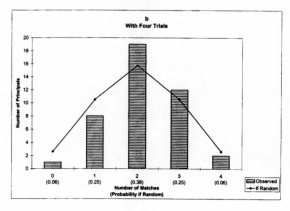

Figure 7.5. Interest experiment: control condition.

pals' behaviors in the control condition mimicked the behaviors observed in the incomplete information benchmark trials.

Overall, in the control condition, the principals' predictions matched the speaker's advice 59 percent (452/771) of the time and the speaker sent a veracious report approximately 58 percent (46/79) of the time. In addition, the principals made reasoned choices approximately 54 percent (413/771) of the time. These results suggest that principals ignored knowledgeable speakers who lacked common interests.

Treatment. As Figure 7.6 shows, the introduction of a knowledgeable speaker who had common interests vastly increased the incidence of persuasion. In every graph, the distribution of the principals' behavior

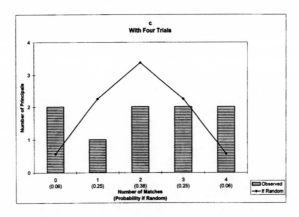

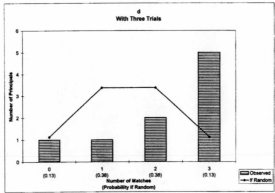

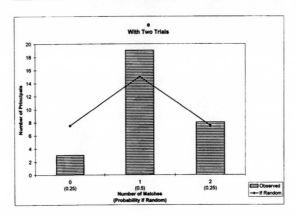

Figure 7.5. (*cont.*)

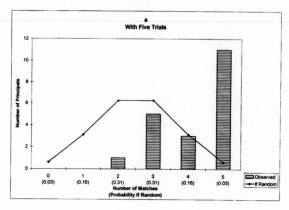

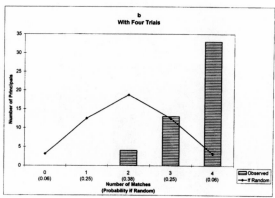

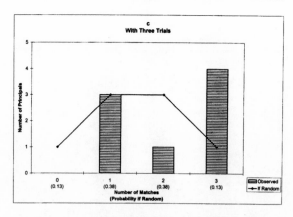

Figure 7.6. Interest experiment: treatment condition.

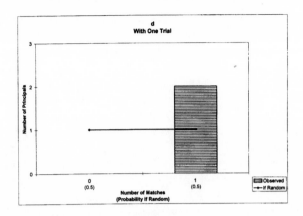

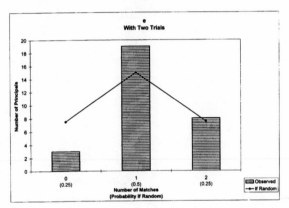

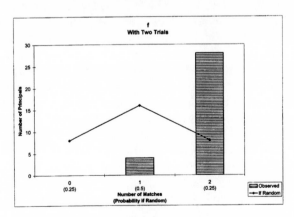

Figure 7.6. (*cont.*)

strings is heavily skewed to the right, suggesting high incidences of persuasion. In Figure 7.6a, for example, the predictions of over half of the principals matched the speaker's advice *every time*. Given the .03 probability that one string of randomly chosen predictions would match the speaker's statement every time, these strings constitute strong evidence of persuasion. The other parts of Figure 7.6 provide similar results; the principals' predictions consistently matched the speaker's advice.[20]

Overall, in the treatment condition, the principals' predictions matched the speaker's advice 88 percent (372/422) of the time and the speaker sent a veracious report approximately 98 percent (48/49) of the time. In addition, the principals made reasoned choices approximately 87 percent (366/422) of the time. These statistics mimic behaviors in the complete information benchmark trials. They suggest that principals regularly used the speaker's signal as an effective substitute for the information they lacked. Comparing behaviors in the control and treatment conditions provides very strong support for our hypothesis; when the speaker was knowledgeable, increasing the commonality of speaker and principal interests induced persuasion and allowed people who lacked information to make reasoned choices.

Variations on the Treatment. We ran two further variations of the interest treatment. The point of the first variation was to show how *perceived* speaker interests affect persuasion. We expect that perceived common interests, and not actual common interests, are a necessary condition for persuasion.

To test this expectation, we used a ten-sided die to determine whether or not the speaker had common or conflicting interests. We rolled the die once per trial. We told all subjects that if the die landed on 1 though 7, then we would pay the speaker for each correct prediction that a principal made; otherwise, we would pay the speaker for each incorrect prediction. Thus, the speaker knew whether or not he had common or conflicting interests, but the principals knew only that there was a 70 percent chance of common interests and a 30 percent chance of conflicting interests.

Figure 7.7a displays the results from this treatment. Given the parameters of the experiment, we expected that principals would follow the speaker's advice (i.e., the principals would follow because the probability of common interests was greater than 50 percent). We found that the

---

[20]Figures 7.6e and 7.6f present results from variations where the speaker could choose not to send a signal. When the speaker did not send a signal, the principals made correct predictions eleven out of eighteen times (61 percent).

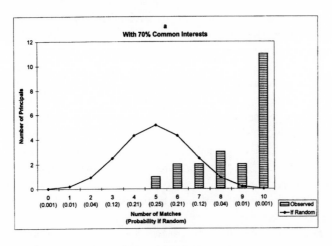

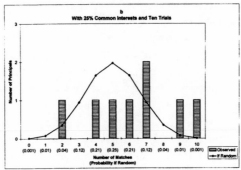

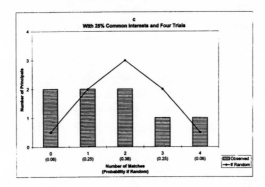

Figure 7.7. Interest experiment: variations on the treatment condition.

131

predictions of a majority of principals matched the speaker's advice *every time*. This too provides strong support for our hypothesis, as it is extremely unlikely that even one string of randomly chosen predictions would match the speaker's statement every time. Overall, in this variation of the interests treatment, the principals' predictions matched the speaker's advice 87 percent (183/210) of the time.

We expected persuasion in all trials of this treatment because the conditions for persuasion were satisfied. We did not, however, expect reasoned choices in all of these trials. The reason for this latter expectation was that the speaker had common interests and, therefore, had an incentive to send a truthful signal in only 70 percent of the trials. While we expected reasoned choices in these trials, we did not expect reasoned choice in the remaining trials.

In the fourteen trials where the speaker actually had common interests, the conditions for persuasion as well as the conditions for enlightenment were satisfied. In these trials, the speaker sent a veracious report approximately 79 percent (11/14) of the time and the principals made reasoned choices approximately 69 percent (102/147) of the time. By contrast, in the six trials where the speaker actually had conflicting interests, the conditions for persuasion were satisfied, while the conditions for enlightenment were not. In these trials, the speaker sent a veracious report approximately 33 percent (2/6) of the time and the principals made reasoned choices approximately 49 percent (31/63) of the time. These results provide support for our expectations, as we can reject the null hypothesis of random behavior.

In our second variation of the interest treatment, we used an eight-sided die to determine whether or not the speaker had common or conflicting interests. We rolled the die once for every trial in this treatment. We told subjects that if the die landed on 1 or 2, then we would pay the speaker for each correct prediction that a principal made; otherwise, we would pay them for each incorrect prediction. Thus, the speaker knew whether or not he had common or conflicting interests, but the principals knew only that there was a 25 percent chance of common interests and a 75 percent chance of conflicting interests. We expected that this level of common interests (being below 50 percent) would *not* be sufficient to induce persuasion, regardless of whether the speaker actually had common or conflicting interests.

Figures 7.7b and 7.7c display the results from this treatment. They show that the distribution of principals' predictions does not significantly differ from the distribution that random behavior would have generated. In this treatment, the principals' predictions matched the speaker's advice

56 percent (63/112) of the time. In addition, the speaker made a truthful report 50 percent (7/14) of the time, and the principals made reasoned choices 46 percent (51/112) of the time.[21] The principals' behaviors in this variation mimicked the behaviors in incomplete information benchmark trials.

Penalty-for-Lying Experiments

Hypothesis: If the principal believes that the speaker is knowledgeable, then an increase in the penalty for lying leads to an increase in the incidence of persuasion.

Control: The principals did not observe the coin toss. The speaker had conflicting interests and observed the coin toss. There were no external forces. All of this was common knowledge.

Treatment: We introduced a penalty for lying.

Control. The control for these experiments was the same as the control in the speaker interest experiment. Recall that, in this condition, the principals' predictions matched the speaker's advice 59 percent (452/771) of the time and made reasoned choices approximately 54 percent (413/771) of the time. Principal behavior in this condition mimicked behavior in the incomplete information benchmark trials.

Treatments. In our penalty-for-lying treatments, as in the control condition, the principal and speaker had conflicting interests. Specifically, the speaker earned $1.00 for each incorrect prediction that a principal made, and principals earned $1.00 for each of their own correct predictions. What distinguished the treatment and control conditions was a penalty for lying – if the speaker made a false statement, then he paid us for doing so, regardless of the principals' subsequent predictions.

In our first penalty-for-lying treatment, we set the penalty for lying at 10 cents. Thus, if the speaker made a *false* statement and the principal made a *correct* prediction, then the speaker reaped net earnings of *minus 10 cents* (i.e., the speaker earned nothing for the correct prediction minus the 10 cent penalty). If the speaker made a *false* statement and the principal made an *incorrect* prediction, then the speaker earned 90 cents (i.e., the speaker earned $1.00 for the incorrect prediction minus the 10 cent penalty). If the speaker makes a true statement, then the speaker's earnings

---

[21]In these trials, the speaker had the choice of reporting heads, reporting tails, or making no statement. In the one trial where the speaker chose not to make a statement, the principals made correct predictions three out of eight times (37.5 percent).

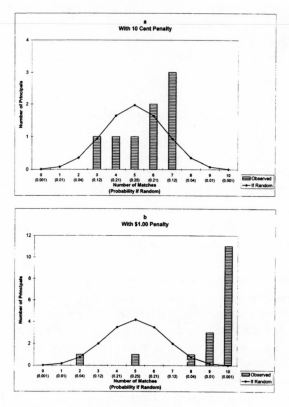

Figure 7.8. Penalty-for-lying experiment: treatment condition.

depend only on the principal's prediction (i.e., the speaker earned $1.00 for an incorrect prediction and nothing for a correct prediction).

We instituted a small penalty for lying in our first treatment to demonstrate that the penalty's effectiveness depends on its ability to make principals believe that the speaker would be induced to tell the truth. We expected that this penalty would be *too low to induce persuasion*. Figure 7.8a shows this to be the case. The distribution of principal behavior strings in this figure mimics random behavior, suggesting an absence of persuasion.

Overall, the speaker sent a truthful signal approximately 70 percent (7/10) of the time. Compared with the control setting, the 10 cent penalty induced truth telling. However, the principals apparently chose not to believe many of these statements, as their predictions matched the speak-

134

er's advice only 56 percent (45/80) of the time. In addition, the principals made reasoned choices approximately 41 percent (33/80) of the time.

Our second penalty-for-lying treatment increased the penalty to $1.00. We expected that this penalty would induce persuasion, and Figure 7.8b suggests that it did. In the presence of a $1.00 penalty for lying, principals consistently chose to believe speakers whom they knew to have conflicting interests. Specifically, the predictions of eleven out of seventeen principals matched the speaker's statement every time.

Overall, in this variation of the penalties-for-lying treatment, the speaker sent a truthful signal approximately 80 percent (16/20) of the time; the principals' predictions matched the speaker's advice 89 percent (152/170) of the time; and the principals made reasoned choices approximately 74 percent (126/170) of the time. These results demonstrate that penalties for lying can induce principals who lack information to believe speakers who have conflicting interests and, therefore, facilitate reasoned choice.[22]

Verification Experiments

Hypothesis: If the principal believes that the speaker is knowledgeable, then an increase in the probability of verification leads to an increase in the incidence of persuasion.

Control: The principals did not observe the coin toss. The speaker did. The speaker knew whether he and the principals had common or conflicting interests. The principals did not know this. The principals did, however, know that there was a 25 percent chance of common interests and a 75 percent chance of conflicting interests. There were no external forces. All of this was common knowledge.

Treatment: We introduced the threat of verification.

In our verification experiment, the principals had incomplete information about the speaker's preferences. Specifically, we rolled an eight-sided die once for every trial in this experiment. We told all subjects that if the die landed on 1 or 2, then we would pay the speaker for each correct prediction that a principal made; otherwise, we would pay the speaker for each incorrect prediction. The speaker knew whether or not he had common or conflicting interests, but the principals knew only that there

---

[22]We also ran experiments with a 90 or 91 cent penalty for lying. Our expectations for these cases were unclear as they depended heavily on unobservable factors like the subjects' degree of risk aversion. We found that behaviors in these cases were a mixture of the behaviors in the 10 cent penalty and $1.00 penalty treatments. Specifically, the speaker sent a veracious report 74 percent of the time (28/38); the principals' predictions matched the speaker's advice 81 percent of the time (263/324); and the principals made reasoned choices two-thirds of the time (218/324).

was a 25 percent chance of common interests and a 75 percent chance of conflicting interests.

We ran the verification experiment under these conditions because we suspected that these conditions would produce nontrivial interactions. By contrast, we suspected that the experiment would have been trivial had the principals *known* the speaker to be knowledgeable and to have common interests (as verification should have been irrelevant, in this case). Similarly, if the principals *knew* the speaker to have conflicting interests, then we expected that the principals would have an incentive to ignore the speaker. As a result, any observed reactions to our verification treatment would have had nothing to do with the principals' assessments of speaker incentives.

Control. In the control condition there was no verification. Figures 7.7b and 7.7c (described previously) display the results from our control condition. In this condition, the principals' predictions matched the speaker's advice 56 percent (63/112) of the time, the speaker made a truthful report 50 percent (7/14) of the time, and the principals made reasoned choices 46 percent (51/112) of the time.

Treatments. Verification has two related effects. First, it reduces the value of lying. That is, knowledgeable speakers who have conflicting interests and face the threat of verification generally gain less from their interaction with a principal than is the case under no such threat. Second, verification gives principals a stronger reason to believe the speaker.

To test both of these hypotheses, we introduced a slight change to our experimental design. Unlike previous experiments, we offered the speaker a choice: Pay us, the experimenters, to make a statement or remain silent. If the speaker chose to make a statement, then we charged him $2.00 and allowed his earnings to be determined by the principals' choices. If the speaker chose not to make a statement, then we charged the speaker nothing, did not allow him to make a statement, and paid the speaker nothing. As a result, when the speaker chose not to make a statement, principals made choices without receiving any advice (unless there was verification). We offered speakers this choice to gauge how verification affected the value of communication to speakers.

We instituted the threat of verification by rolling a ten-sided die. If the die landed on 1 through 7, then we verified; otherwise, we did not. To put it another way, for every trial in the verification treatment there was a 70 percent chance that we would report the true coin-toss outcome, regardless of the speaker's action.

Two aspects of this experimental design were particularly important. First, the speaker did not know, before making his statement, whether or not verification would occur. Second, the principals had no way of

Information, Persuasion, and Choice

knowing whether the message they heard came directly from the speaker or was our verification – the principals merely heard "heads" or "tails." The speaker and principals knew that there was a 70 percent chance of verification in each trial.

We expected that when the principals and the speaker had common interests, the speaker would send truthful signals. By contrast, when the principals and the speaker had conflicting interests, we expected that the speaker would not send a signal. Furthermore, we expected that the principals would follow the advice of any statement that they heard.[23]

Figure 7.9 presents the results for our verification treatment. The predictions of eleven of nineteen principals matched the announced statement *every time*. Overall, in this treatment, the principals' predictions matched the announcement 88 percent (260/294) of the time.

In the trials where verification occurred, the conditions for both persuasion and enlightenment were satisfied (regardless of the speaker's interests). Therefore, in these trials we expected a high incidence of persuasion and reasoned choice. In fact, the principals' predictions matched the announcement and the principals made reasoned choices approximately 86 percent (187/217) of the time.

In trials where there was no verification but the speaker actually had common interests, the conditions for persuasion and the conditions for enlightenment were also satisfied. In these trials, speakers sent truthful signals in six of six trials; principals' predictions matched the signals approximately 97 percent (55/57) of the time; and principals made reasoned choices approximately 97 percent (55/57) of the time.

We also expected that *the speaker would make a statement only if he and the principal had common interests*. In fact, when the speaker and principal had common interests, speakers made a statement 100 percent (9/9) of the time.

In trials where there was no verification and the speaker had conflicting interests, the conditions for enlightenment were not satisfied. In these trials, we did not expect the speaker to make a statement, and we expected the incidence of reasoned choice to be about 50 percent – the same as

[23]We expected that speakers in this treatment would make a statement only if they had common interests with the principals. This follows because the 70 percent threat of verification made statements unprofitable, in expectation, for speakers with conflicting interests. To see this, consider that in equilibrium, the principals had a dominant strategy to follow the announced statement. So, if there were ten principals, for example, the $2.00 fee for making a statement is equivalent to a 20 cent fee per principal. Given this information, the speaker's expected payoff when the speaker earned 50 cents for each incorrect prediction was: $(.7)^*(-20 \text{ cents}) + (.3)^*(50 \text{ cents} - 20 \text{ cents}) = -\$.05$. This amount is less than the expected payoff of $0.00 for not making a statement. Therefore, when the speaker had conflicting interests, it was better for the speaker not to make a statement.

137

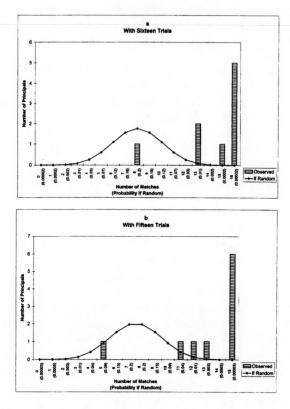

Figure 7.9. Verification experiment: treatment condition.

in the incomplete information benchmark trials. In the trials where the speaker made no statement, the principals made reasoned choices two-thirds (24/36) of the time. On two occasions the speaker who had conflicting interests did make a statement – contrary to our expectation. In these trials, one of the two signals was truthful. The principals' predictions matched these signals 90 percent (18/20) of the time, and principals made reasoned choices 40 percent (8/20) of the time.[24] While speaker behavior

[24]We also administered a verification treatment where the speaker and principal always had conflicting interests, and we verified 70 percent of the time. In these trials, the speaker never made a statement that was not verified. The principals' predictions matched the announcement and the principals made reasoned choices 98 percent (62/63) of the time. The speaker chose not to make a statement and there was no verification two times (i.e., there was no announcement). In these cases, fifteen out of twenty-one principals made reasoned choices (71 percent).

in these trials was not as we expected, the principals' responses were. In general, the verification experiments provide strong support for the hypothesis that verification makes principals who lack information more likely to make reasoned choices.

Costly Effort Experiments

Hypothesis: If the principal believes that the speaker is knowledgeable, then an increase in the speaker's observable costly effort leads to an increase in the incidence of persuasion.

Control: The principals did not know which alternative was better for them. The speaker observed the coin toss that determined which alternative was better. The speaker knew whether he and the principals had common or conflicting interests. There were no external forces. All of this was common knowledge.

Treatment: We introduced an opportunity for the speaker to exert observable costly effort.

In our theory, we examine the situation where a knowledgeable speaker has an opportunity to send a costly signal to the principal. When a knowledgeable speaker undertakes costly effort to advocate a change in the status quo, the principal can draw a more accurate inference about the size of the proposed change. Specifically, the principal can infer that the change must be worth enough to the speaker to warrant the costs incurred.[25] Thus, the larger the cost paid by the speaker to attempt to change the status quo, the greater must be the proposed change in the status quo. Knowing this can allow the principal to narrow the possible set of alternatives and, by so doing, make reasoned choices.

The design of our costly effort experiment mirrors the structure of our theory. In our experiment, the speaker no longer signaled "better" or "worse." Instead, we offered the speaker the chance to pay a fixed amount to propose a fixed alternative to a preexisting, commonly known status quo. If the speaker chose not to pay, then the trial ended with the principals' making no decisions and the status quo's determining all subjects' payoffs. If the speaker chose to pay, then the principals chose between accepting the speaker's proposal or retaining the status quo, and their choices determined their own and the speaker's earnings.

As in all previous experiments, the consequences of the principals' actions depended on the result of a coin toss. In our costly effort experiment, the principals knew the value of the status quo (i.e., their payoff

---

[25]In Chapter 5, we described how the principal can also learn from an agent's observable costly effort; thus, the experiments discussed here apply to learning from either an agent or a speaker.

139

from the status quo), but they did not know the value of the speaker's proposal. Rather, they knew that the proposal could take on one of two values and that its actual value depended on the outcome of a coin flip. For example, each principal knew that by opting for the status quo, she would earn 40 cents, whereas choosing the proposal would result in a 10 cent payoff if the coin landed on heads or a 60 cent payoff if the coin landed on tails. Thus, when faced with a choice, the principals did not know which alternative provided a higher payoff. As a consequence of this design, all subjects knew that if the coin-toss outcome for a particular trial was, for example, tails, then the principals earned more by choosing the proposal than the status quo, and vice versa if the coin landed on heads. The principals were also uncertain about the speaker's payoff from the proposal; that is, the speaker's payoff from the proposal also took on one of two values, determined by the coin-toss outcome. The speaker, however, unlike the principals, knew the outcome of the coin toss.

The speaker's earnings, as in the previous experiments, were determined by the principals' decisions. If the speaker paid the fixed cost, then he earned a fixed amount (i.e., 60 cents), determined by the coin-toss outcome, for every principal who chose her proposal; the speaker earned nothing for every principal who opted for the status quo. So, if the speaker paid to make a proposal that no principals chose, then the speaker earned nothing and lost the amount he paid to make the proposal. If, on the other hand, the speaker did not pay to make a proposal, then he earned nothing (i.e., the speaker's payoff from the status quo was $0) and lost nothing.

We expected that the speaker would make a proposal only if two conditions held: first, if his payoff from doing so exceeded the cost of making a proposal; and second, if the speaker expected the principals to accept the proposal. If the speaker's earnings from the proposal did not exceed the cost of making the proposal, or if the speaker expected the principals to opt for the status quo, then we expected that the speaker would not make a proposal.

Benchmark. We began this experiment by running new benchmark trials. The purpose of these trials was to determine what speakers and principals would do when the principals knew the consequences of their actions. Such trials provide the basis for asserting that certain choices are "reasoned."

In these trials, principals knew the coin-toss outcomes before they had to make a choice. Therefore, they knew whether choosing the status quo or the proposal would give them a higher payoff. As costly effort would be redundant in these trials, we did not force the speaker to pay to make proposals. We expected that the principals in these trials would choose

140

the higher-paying options (i.e., make reasoned choices). In fact, principals chose the highest-paying alternatives more than 85 percent (152/178) of the time.

Control. Our control condition differed from our costly effort benchmark trials in only one way. In our control condition, the principals did not know the coin-toss outcomes. Therefore, the principals were uncertain about which alternative was better for them. As in most of our previous experiments, the speaker observed the coin toss.

We expected principals to make relatively few reasoned choices in the control condition. In fact, only 135 of 371 (36 percent) of the choices made were reasoned. However, we expected, and observed, that principal behavior in these trials was not random, as it was in the control treatments in the previous experiments. In previous experiments, the expected value of picking heads or tails was equal, all else constant. In our costly effort experiments, the expected value of the proposal and the value of the status quo were typically *not* equal. We found that, in the control condition, 72 percent (266/371) of the principals made choices consistent with maximizing expected value – that is, choosing the proposal only if the expected value of the proposal were greater than the known value of the status quo. For example, if choosing the proposal when the coin lands heads paid the principal 80 cents, and choosing the proposal when the coin lands tails paid 40 cents, then the expected return from choosing the proposal was 60 cents. So if the payoff for choosing the status quo was 50 cents, then choosing the proposal would be consistent with maximizing expected value.

Treatments. In our treatment, we introduced the opportunity for observable, costly effort. In one version of the treatment, we implemented the costly effort effect by charging the speaker 20 cents per principal to make a proposal. *We set the speaker's payoffs in such a way that paying a 20 cent per principal cost to make a proposal would be profitable for the speaker under one coin-toss outcome (e.g., heads) but not the other.*

For example, if the speaker's payoff from the proposal were 60 cents per principal if the coin landed on heads and 10 cents per principal if the coin landed on tails, then we expected the speaker to pay to make a proposal only if the coin landed on heads. This is true because the speaker could make up the 20 cent per principal cost of making a proposal only if the coin landed on heads. Otherwise, the speaker was better off not paying to make a proposal and sticking with the $0 payoff from the status quo. Thus, if the speaker made a proposal, the principals could deduce that the coin landed on heads. In a second version of the treatment, we charged the speaker 40 cents per principal and set payoffs in an analogous manner.

Table 7.3. *Speaker behavior in the benchmark trials.*

Actual speaker behavior	Expected speaker behavior	
	Proposal	Indifferent
Proposal	8	9
No proposal	0	3

In the 20 cent treatment, 142 out of 165 (86 percent) principals made reasoned choices.[26] In the 40 cent treatment, 198 out of 220 (90 percent) principals made reasoned choices.[27] Comparing these behaviors with those of the benchmark trials and control condition strongly suggests that costly effort provided many principals who lacked information about the coin toss with the knowledge that reasoned choice required.

Speaker Behavior. As was the case with our previous hypotheses, we derived our expectation about costly effort from a game theoretic model. This implies that our conclusions depend on the premise that player strategies are part of an equilibrium, which implies that we have particular expectations of speaker behaviors as well. We expected the speaker to make a proposal only if two necessary conditions were met: the speaker's payoff from having principals choose the proposal was higher than his cost of making a proposal and the speaker expected the principals to accept the proposal. If either of these conditions was not met, then we

---

[26]These results include only those trials where we expected the speaker to make a proposal (i.e., when the speaker's payoff from the proposal exceeded the cost of making a proposal and the principals were expected to opt for the proposal, after observing the costly effort). If the speaker made a proposal when his dominant strategy was not to make a proposal, then it was unclear how the principal should respond (as this behavior was off the equilibrium path). Nonetheless, we found that when the speaker made a proposal when he should not have, the principals chose the alternative consistent with an expected value calculation 108 out of 121 times (89 percent) and made reasoned choices 40 out of 121 times (33 percent).

[27]As in the 20 cent condition, these results include only those cases where the speaker was expected to make a proposal (and actually did make a proposal). When the speaker unexpectedly offered a proposal, the principals opted for choice consistent with an expected value calculation fifty-nine out of sixty-six times (89 percent) and made reasoned choices thirty-four out of sixty-six times (51.5 percent).

Table 7.4. *Speaker behavior in the control condition.*

Actual speaker behavior	Expected speaker behavior	
	Proposal	Indifferent
Proposal	11	26
No proposal	1	2

Table 7.5. *Speaker behavior in the treatment conditions.*

20 cent treatment	Expected Speaker Behavior	
Actual speaker behavior	Proposal	No proposal
Proposal	15	11
No proposal	5	9

40 cent treatment	Expected Speaker Behavior	
Actual speaker behavior	Proposal	No proposal
Proposal	20	6
No proposal	0	14

expected the speaker to be indifferent between making a proposal or not, at best.

Table 7.3 depicts the relationship between observed and anticipated speaker behaviors in the benchmark trials. Here, the speakers behaved as expected.

In the control condition, we expected the same speaker behavior. Table 7.4 is consistent with our expectations.

Table 7.5 shows that speaker behavior did not quite match our expectations in the costly effort treatments. Speakers made proposals in thirty-five of the forty trials that we expected they would. However, in the forty trials where we expected no proposals, speakers made seventeen. Our post-experimental questionnaires revealed that some speakers had trouble with the mathematics and others were not motivated to maximize their earnings.

CONCLUSION

In this chapter, we have described a set of experiments designed to test our hypotheses about the political consequences of limited information. We began with a set of benchmark trials. The first benchmark trials allowed us to identify which experimental behaviors constituted reasoned choices. The second set of benchmark trials established what types of decisions subjects would make if they lacked information about the consequences of their actions and had no opportunity to learn. Then we ran a series of experiments on persuasion. We first introduced control conditions where our conditions for persuasion were not satisfied. In these conditions, we found little evidence of persuasion and no higher incidence of reasoned choice than would have occurred by chance. We then introduced treatment conditions. In most of these treatments, our conditions for persuasion were satisfied, and we found strong evidence of persuasion and reasoned choice.

To summarize our findings and conclude this chapter, we introduce Table 7.6. This table shows the frequency of veracious reporting, persuasion, enlightenment, deception, and reasoned choice in all of the experimental treatments where these terms are relevant (i.e., because the format of the costly effort experiments was different, we do not include these trials in the table).

Table 7.6 has five sections. The first summarizes behaviors in the complete information benchmark trials, across all experiments. In these trials, 97 percent of the principals made reasoned choices.

The second section of Table 7.6 summarizes behaviors in all of the trials in which the conditions for persuasion and enlightenment were satisfied. We expected a *high incidence of persuasion, enlightenment, and reasoned choice* in these trials. We were not disappointed. In these trials, subjects who did not see the coin-toss outcomes nonetheless made correct predictions more than 83 percent of the time. Indeed, under certain conditions, principals were able to make the correct prediction at much higher levels, such as in the verification experiments (in the trials where the speaker had common interests but there was no verification) where they made reasoned choices 97 percent of the time. In many cases, they accomplished this feat despite the fact that the speakers were rewarded when principals made incorrect predictions.

The third section of Table 7.6 summarizes behaviors in the incomplete information benchmark trials. In these trials, 48 percent of the principals made reasoned choices.

144

Table 7.6. A summary of speaker and principal behavior.

Section 1. Benchmark Trials: Complete Information

	Veracious report	Persuasion	Enlightenment	Deception	Reasoned choice
Complete information benchmark trials	N/A	N/A	N/A	N/A	97% 376/389

Section 2. Behaviors When the Conditions for Persuasion and the Conditions for Enlightenment Were Satisfied

	Veracious report	Persuasion	Enlightenment	Deception	Reasoned choice
Knowledge and common interests[a]	94 17/18	92 174/190	94 164/174	6 10/174	86 164/190
Knowledge and common interests (tails only)	100 9/9	89 85/96	100 85/85	0 0/85	89 85/96
70% knowledge and common interests (when the speaker had knowledge)	100 7/7	87 67/77	100 67/67	0 0/67	87 67/77
70% knowledge and common interests (when the speaker had knowledge) (tails only)	100 5/5	86 47/55	100 47/47	0 0/47	86 47/55
Common interests and knowledge[b]	98 48/49	88 372/422	98 364/372	2 8/372	87 366/422
70% common interests and knowledge (when common interests)	79 11/14	88 129/147	77 99/129	23 30/129	69 102/147
Conflicting interests and $1.00 penalty	80 16/20	89 152/170	80 121/152	20 31/152	74 126/170

Table 7.6. (cont.)

	Veracious report	Persuasion	Enlightenment	Deception	Reasoned choice
25% common interests and 70% verification (when verified)[c]	N/A	86 187/217	100 187/187	0 0/187	86 187/217
25% common interests and 70% verification (when common interests and not verified)	100 6/6	97 55/57	100 55/55	0 0/55	97 55/57
TOTALS	92 105/114	89 1,136/1,280	93 1,057/1,136	7 79/1,136	83 1,067/1,280

Section 3. Benchmark Trials: Incomplete Information

	Veracious report	Persuasion	Enlightenment	Deception	Reasoned choice
Incomplete information benchmark trials	N/A	N/A	N/A	N/A	48 377/780

Section 4. Behaviors When the Conditions for Persuasion Were Satisfied and the Conditions for Enlightenment Were Not

	Veracious report	Persuasion	Enlightenment	Deception	Reasoned choice
70% knowledge and common interests (when the speaker did not have knowledge)[d]	67 2/3	97 32/33	69 22/32	31 10/32	70 23/33
70% common interests and knowledge (when conflicting interests)	33 2/6	86 54/63	41 22/54	59 32/54	49 31/63
25% common interests and 70% verification (when conflicting interests and not verified)[e]	50 1/2	90 18/20	44 8/18	56 10/18	40 8/20
TOTALS	45 5/11	90 104/116	50 52/104	50 52/104	53 62/116

Section 5. Behaviors When the Conditions for Persuasion Were Not Satisfied

	Veracious report	Persuasion	Enlightenment	Deception	Reasoned choice
No knowledge and common interests	46 6/13	63 90/143	47 42/90	53 48/90	50 71/143
No knowledge and common interests (tails only)	50 2/4	11 5/44	80 4/5	20 1/5	57 25/44
No knowledge and conflicting interests	60 3/5	33 18/55	78 14/18	22 4/18	58 32/55
No knowledge and conflicting interests (tails only)	50 2/4	18 8/44	50 4/8	50 4/8	50 22/44
Conflicting interests and knowledge[f]	58 46/79	59 452/771	60 271/452	40 181/452	54 413/771
25% common interests and knowledge[g]	50 7/14	56 63/112	46 29/63	54 34/63	46 51/112
Conflicting interests and 10 cent penalty	70 7/10	56 45/80	60 27/45	40 18/45	41 33/80
TOTALS	57 69/121	58 668/1,161	57 383/668	43 285/668	52 600/1,161

[a] These results are from the treatment in the knowledge experiment. Recall that we paid principals in this experiment a small amount for predicting heads.

[b] These results are from the treatment in the interest experiment. In some of these trials, the speaker had the option of not making a statement. In two of these trials, the speaker chose not to make a statement, and 11 out of 18 principals made reasoned choices.

[c] The persuasion, enlightenment, and deception statistics are based on the verified announcement.

[d] In these cases, the speaker always reported heads.

[e] The speaker chose not to make a statement four times. In these cases, twenty-four out of thirty-six principals made reasoned choices.

[f] In some of these trials, the speaker had the option of not making a statement. In one of these trials, the speaker chose not to make a statement, and four of nine principals made reasoned choices.

[g] In some of these trials, the speaker had the option of not making a statement. In one of these trials, the speaker chose not to make a statement, and three of eight principals made reasoned choices.

The fourth section of Table 7.6 summarizes all of the trials where the conditions for persuasion were satisfied but the conditions for enlightenment were not. In these trials, we expected a *high incidence of persuasion and deception and a relatively low incidence of reasoned choice.* Again, our observations met our expectations. This is most notable with respect to deception. In our experiments, we say that a principal was deceived when her prediction matched the speaker's statement and the prediction was incorrect. In the trials where we expected persuasion and deception, we saw persuasion approximately 90 percent of the time (104/116). Of the persuasive communications, 50 percent (52/104) served to deceive the principals. Compare this with the incidence of deception in the second section of Table 7.6, where we expected little or no deception. There, only 7 percent (79/1136) of the persuasive communications deceived.

The fifth section of Table 7.6 summarizes the trials where we expected no persuasion and thus a lower percentage of reasoned choice as well. Our expectations were again confirmed. Persuasion and reasoned choice both dropped to near 50 percent, what we would expect to observe if the principals were choosing randomly.

Table 7.6 clearly demonstrates how important the conditions for persuasion and enlightenment are in determining who can and cannot make reasoned choices. Over and over again, the table shows how subjects who lacked a crucial piece of information could substitute a statement made by another, when the conditions for persuasion and enlightenment were in force, as the basis for reasoned choice.

Our experimental results provide impressive support for our theory of persuasion. They show that people who were faced with a complex choice chose systematic adaptations as a way to achieve their objectives. In these experiments, reasoned choice required neither principals with complete information about the consequences of their actions nor statements from speakers whom they knew well.

The political consequences of limited information can be quite damaging. However, our experiments clarify when such damage will be done. If people who lack information cannot interact with speakers when the conditions for enlightenment are satisfied, then limited information prevents reasoned choice. Otherwise, limited information may imply nothing about reasoned choice. In these cases, the political consequences of limited information are far less dangerous.

8

Laboratory Experiments
on Delegation

Democracy requires successful delegation. But delegation is fraught with difficulty. If we do not exercise the utmost care, delegation can easily become abdication, where an agent takes actions without regard to his principal's welfare (Kiewiet and McCubbins 1991, Miller 1992).

Delegation becomes abdication when two unfortunate circumstances maintain. The first circumstance is that a principal and an agent have conflicting interests concerning the outcome of delegation. When this circumstance occurs, an agent has an incentive to make proposals that decrease the principal's welfare. The second circumstance is that a principal lacks the information necessary to determine whether her welfare is enhanced or decreased by the agent's proposals.

The central lesson of our theory of delegation is that these unfortunate circumstances can be overcome when the *knowledge* and *incentive conditions* are satisfied (see Theorem 5.1). The knowledge condition is fulfilled if and only if the principal can correctly infer whether the agent's proposal makes her better or worse off than the status quo. The incentive condition is fulfilled only if the agent is motivated to make a proposal that is better than the status quo for the principal.

We also show that enlightenment can lead to the satisfaction of the incentive condition as well as the knowledge condition (Theorem 5.3). To see this, suppose that a principal can distinguish agent proposals that increase her welfare from ones that do not. In this case, the agent knows that making proposals that are worse than the status quo for the principal leads the principal to reject the agent's proposal. It follows that when the principal is enlightened, the agent has an incentive to make only proposals that are better than the status quo for the principal. Thus, a principal's enlightenment can induce an otherwise defiant agent to act in her interests.

In this chapter, we test our theory of delegation. In what follows, we describe a series of experiments that involved subjects' playing the roles

149

of principal, agent, and speaker. As in our experiments on persuasion, an ill-informed principal was asked to choose between two alternatives. A speaker again offered advice to the principal regarding her choice. The novel feature of our delegation experiments was the addition of an agent whose choices affected the payoffs of the other players. In some settings, the conditions for enlightenment were satisfied; in others they were not.

The point of our experiments was to show how satisfaction of the conditions for enlightenment affects the agent's incentives. We expected that if the conditions for enlightenment were satisfied, then agents would make proposals that benefited principals. Indeed, this is what we observed. As a result, our experiments support the conclusion that if the conditions for enlightenment are satisfied, then *delegation can succeed even when the principal lacks information and the principal and the agent have conflicting interests.*

In what follows we first describe our experiments' design. We then review four experiments on the relationship between interests, information, the conditions for enlightenment, and delegation.

EXPERIMENTAL DESIGN

We ran our experiments on delegation during the first six months of 1996. Our subject pool and method for recruiting subjects were identical to those described in the previous chapter.

We designed each experimental trial to emulate our theory of delegation. Thus, each trial began with an agent's deciding whether or not to make a proposal to a principal. If the agent did not make a proposal, then the trial ended and the agent and the principal each received a status quo payoff. If the agent made a proposal, then the principal effectively accepted or rejected the agent's proposal by predicting the outcome of a hidden coin toss. Before the principal made her prediction, however, the speaker made a statement to the principal, advising the principal to predict heads or tails. When the agent made a proposal, each player's payoff depended on the accuracy of the principal's prediction.

This experimental design provides a valid test of our expectations only if the experimental analogies are faithful to our theory. We list our most important experimental analogies in Table 8.1.[1]

At the top of Table 8.1, we list premise–analogy pairs that were *constant* within our experiments. We call these analogies constant because

---

[1]To enhance this chapter's readability, we omit some details of our experimental design. More information is available at: http:\\polisciexplab.ucsd.edu. As in the experiments described in Chapter 7, we sometimes varied payoff schemes across experimental sessions. We found no evidence that these variations affected the results.

Table 8.1. *Theoretical premises and experimental analogies.*

Theoretical premise	Experimental analogy
Constants	
1. "Our model of delegation requires three people . . . the *principal,* the *speaker,* and the *agent.*"	Each subject was a principal, a speaker, or an agent.
2. "The agent can propose [a single alternative] to the status quo policy. . . . Proposing is costly. . . . If the agent does not pay, then the game ends and each player's earnings are determined by the . . . [status quo]. If the agent pays, then the game continues. . . . The speaker makes his statement [and then] the principal chooses [the proposal or the status quo]."	The agent chose whether or not to make a proposal. If the agent chose not to make a proposal, then the game ended with the agent and the principal each earning a fixed positive amount. If the agent chose to make a proposal, then the principal predicted the outcome of a coin toss. Before the principal made a coin-toss prediction, however, the speaker advised the principal to predict either "heads" or "tails." The accuracy of the principal's coin-toss prediction determined whether the agent and/or the principal earned *more* than the fixed amount or *nothing.*
3. "We assume that the principal has beliefs about, but may not know, [which alternative is better]."	The principal did not observe the coin-toss outcome before making a prediction.
4. "The principal . . . is goal oriented."	If the agent did not make a proposal, then the principal earned a small fixed amount that was independent of the coin toss. If the agent made a proposal, then the principal earned more than the fixed amount if he or she made a *correct* prediction and earned nothing if he or she made an *incorrect* prediction.
5. "The speaker sends a signal of "better" or "worse" to the principal . . . and need not tell the truth."	The speaker signaled "heads" or "tails" to the principal. The speaker need not tell the truth.
Agent interest variable	
1. "Nature chooses whether the agent and principal have *common* or *conflicting* interests."	The experimenters chose whether the agent and the principal had common or conflicting interests.
1a. The agent and principal have *common* interests.	If the agent made a proposal and the principal predicted *correctly,* then the agent earned more than the fixed amount. If the agent made a proposal and the principal predicted *incorrectly,* then the agent earned nothing.
1b. The agent and principal have *conflicting* interests.	If the agent made a proposal and the principal predicted *correctly,* then

151

Table 8.1. (*cont.*)

Theoretical premise	Experimental analogy
	the agent earned nothing. If the agent made a proposal and the principal predicted *incorrectly,* then the agent earned more than the fixed amount.
Speaker characteristic variables	
2. "Nature chooses whether the speaker and principal have *common* or *conflicting* interests."	The experimenters chose whether the speaker and the principal had common or conflicting interests.
2a. The speaker and principal have *common* interests.	If the principal made a *correct* prediction, then the speaker earned a positive amount. If the principal made an *incorrect* prediction, then the speaker earned nothing.
2b. The speaker and principal have *conflicting* interests.	If the principal made a *correct* prediction, then the speaker earned nothing. If the principal made an *incorrect* prediction, then the speaker earned a positive amount.
3. Nature chooses "speaker knows whether x is better or worse than y" with probability $k \in [0, 1]$ and "speaker does not know whether x is better or worse than y" with probability $1\text{-}k$.	The experimenters chose whether or not the speaker observed the coin toss.
3a. The speaker has complete information.	The speaker observed the coin toss.
3b. The speaker has incomplete information.	The speaker did not observe the coin toss.
External force variables	
4. "We represent [penalties for lying] as a cost *pen* ≥ 0, that the speaker must pay when he sends a false signal."	
4a. No penalties for lying.	No penalties for lying.
4b. Penalties for lying.	The speaker paid a penalty if he or she made a false statement.
5. Verification: "After the speaker speaks, but before the principal chooses, nature reveals to the principal whether x is better or worse for her."	
5a. No verification.	No verification.
5b. Verification.	The experimenters revealed the true coin-toss outcome to the principal with probability v.

we used them in all of our experimental conditions. At the bottom of Table 8.1, we list premise–analogy pairs that *varied* within our experiments. We tested our expectations by varying these analogies. We next describe these analogies in greater detail.

The Constant Analogies

The first constant analogy concerned the participants. In our theory, we model communication as an interaction between an *agent,* a *speaker,* and a *principal.* In our experiment, we selected subjects to play each of these roles.

The second constant analogy concerned the sequence of events. In our theory, the *agent* chooses whether or not to propose an alternative to a common knowledge status quo. Making a proposal is costly for the agent and can confer benefits to him only if the principal accepts the proposal. By contrast, choosing not to make a proposal is costless for the agent. If the agent does not pay the cost of making a proposal, then the game ends and all players' utilities are determined by the spatial distance between their ideal points and the status quo. If the agent pays, then the player's utilities are determined by whether or not the principal accepts the proposal. That is, the principal either accepts the agent's proposal or rejects it in favor of a common knowledge status quo.

In our experiments, the agent faced an analogous dilemma. The agent chose whether or not to make a proposal. If the agent chose not to make a proposal, then the agent and the principal earned a status quo payoff, a fixed positive amount. If the agent chose to make a proposal, then the speaker made a statement and the principal made a prediction about a coin-toss outcome. When the agent proposed, each player's earnings depended on the accuracy of the principal's prediction. Thus, the cost imposed on the agent for making a proposal was the forgone guaranteed payoff from the status quo.

The third constant analogy concerned the principal's choice. In our theory of delegation, the principal is uncertain as to whether the agent's proposal is better or worse for her than the status quo. In our experiments, the principal did not observe the coin-toss outcome before making a prediction and was thus uncertain about which alternative – heads or tails – would yield the greatest payoff.[2]

---

[2]In essence, the principal was deciding whether to accept or reject the agent's proposal; however, a coin toss determined whether accepting or rejecting the agent's proposal generated higher earnings for the principal than the status quo fixed amount. Thus, the important decision for the principal, and the one we focused on, was the coin-toss prediction.

Experiments

In our persuasion experiments, the principal's personal knowledge of coin-toss outcomes was an experimental variable – in some treatments the principal observed the coin tosses, in other treatments the principal did not. In our delegation experiments, *the principal never observed the coin-toss outcomes.*

The fourth constant analogy concerned the consequences of the principal's choices. In both our theory and experiments, if the agent did not make a proposal, then the principal earned a fixed amount from the status quo (e.g., 70 cents). By contrast, if the agent made a proposal, then the principal earned more than the fixed amount when she made a *correct prediction* (e.g., $1.00) and earned nothing when she made an incorrect prediction.

The fifth constant analogy concerned the speaker's choices. In our theory of delegation, the speaker signals "better" or "worse" and does not have to tell the truth. In our experiments, the speaker signaled "heads" or "tails" and did not have to tell the truth.[3]

The Variable Analogies

We used the variable analogies to test our hypotheses. Our experiments on delegation included three types of variable analogies: *agent interest* variables, *speaker characteristic* variables, and *external force* variables.

The agent interest variable concerned the relationship between the principal's and agent's interests. In some of our experimental trials, the principal and agent had *common interests*. In these trials, if the agent made a proposal and the principal made a correct prediction, then the agent earned more than the (status quo) fixed amount; by contrast, if the principal made an incorrect prediction, then the agent earned nothing.[4] In other trials, the principal and agent had *conflicting interests*. In these trials, if the agent made a proposal and the principal made an incorrect prediction, then the agent earned more than the (status quo) fixed amount; if the principal made a correct prediction, however, the agent earned nothing.[5] We always showed the agent, and never showed the principal, the coin-toss outcomes.

---

[3]Because the principal's choice of heads or tails was actually analogous to accepting or rejecting the agent's proposal, the speaker's signal of heads or tails was also analogous to signaling "better" or "worse."

[4]Recall that if the agent did not make a proposal, then he earned a fixed amount.

[5]In most of the trials where the agent and principal had common interests, we paid the agent $1.40 if he made no proposal, $2.00 if he made a proposal and the principal made a correct prediction, and nothing if he made a proposal and the principal made an incorrect prediction. In trials where the principal and agent had conflicting interests, we switched the latter two components of the agent's payoff structure.

Delegation

The speaker characteristic variables – whether the speaker and the principal had common or conflicting interests, and whether the speaker observed the coin toss – are the same as they were in Chapter 7. Similarly, the external forces variables – penalties for lying and verification – are identical to those used in our persuasion experiments.[6]

In some trials, where the speaker possessed knowledge and either had common interests with the principal or faced sufficient external forces, we expected the speaker to enlighten the principal. We call these trials the *treatment condition*. When these conditions were not met, we refer to the trials as the *control condition*.

In the treatment condition, the principal was expected to learn the coin-toss outcome from the speaker, and, thus, the agent was expected to make a proposal only if he had common interests with the principal. This follows because the agent's expected payoff from making a proposal exceeded the (status quo) fixed amount only when the agent and the principal had common interests.[7]

In the control condition, we expected the principal's predictions to be correct about half of the time. The agent's payoff structure was such that if the agent expected the principal's predictions to be correct only half of the time, then the agent's expected return from proposing was less than the expected return from making no proposal.[8] *So, we expected that when the agent and the principal had common interests, the presence of an enlightened principal would induce the agent to make a proposal. Otherwise, we expected the agent not to make a proposal.*

The ten analogies in Table 8.1 constitute the basic design of our delegation experiments. As was true with our persuasion experiments, the design of our delegation experiments presented subjects with simple and familiar situations; we were extremely careful not to suggest particu-

[6]We did not run an experiment on costly effort in this chapter as it would have been redundant. To see why, recall from our discussion in Chapter 5 that costly effort has the same effect on the principal's beliefs regardless of whether the speaker or the agent pays the cost. Therefore, we could learn nothing new by running costly entry experiments where the agent, rather than the speaker, paid the cost. We also ran no experiments where the principal was uncertain about the speaker's interests as the purpose of those experiments was to point out the difference between actual and observed speaker characteristics on persuasion. We would derive little substantive benefit from repeating that exercise here.

[7]Given the payoffs discussed in footnote 5, when the agent had common interests with an enlightened principal, the agent expected to earn \$2.00 from making a proposal, which is greater than the \$1.40 fixed-amount payoff. When the agent had conflicting interests with an enlightened principal, he expected to earn nothing from making a proposal and thus was expected to opt for the \$1.40 fixed payoff.

[8]Given the payoffs discussed in a previous footnote, the agent's expected payoff from a making a proposal in the control condition was $.5 * (\$2.00) + .5 * (\$0) = \$1.00$ and the agent's payoff from the fixed amount was \$1.40.

lar behaviors to subjects; we gave subjects quizzes on the instructions; and most subjects achieved perfect scores on these quizzes. As a result, we are confident about our ability to use the data from our experiments to draw meaningful inferences about our hypotheses on delegation.

Other Design Elements

To make the experiments even more like our theory, we took two precautions to limit what subjects could learn about one another. First, we used partitions to prevent visual contact. Subjects in our experiments could not see one another. Second, we prevented subjects from talking to one another. With one exception, these precautions were identical to the precautions we described in Chapter 7. The exception was that we extended these precautions to cover the agent. Therefore, no subject could identify the agent by sight or sound, nor could the agent identify any other subject by sight or sound.

Two additional elements of our experimental design allowed us to conduct our experiments in a cost-effective way. First, we allowed the agent, principal, and speaker to interact multiple times. In our theory, there is a single interaction. Ideally, we would have liked to have the agent, principal, and speaker in our experiments to interact just once. However, setting up our experiments required significant labor, time, and expense. It was impractical to invite subjects to come to our laboratory for the purpose of making just one decision. Therefore, we had the agent, speaker, and principal interact many times.

As in our persuasion experiments, we again took precautions to mitigate any consequences of repeated play. Specifically, in all of our experiments, we did not provide subjects with any information about the past choices of any other subject. So, subjects *first* learned how much they earned *after the experiment was completed*. Moreover, subjects learned only the sum total of their earnings; we did not give them detailed information about particular choices. Therefore, the subjects never learned which predictions were correct and which were incorrect. They also never learned when the speaker told the truth and when the speaker lied. During the experiment, our subjects had absolutely no information about what other subjects did in the past. As a result, they had an incentive to treat every interaction with the speaker (or the principal) as though it were the only interaction.

In our delegation experiments, reducing repeated play effects required one additional step. In each trial, the agent had the choice either to make a proposal or not. Had we provided the principal with information about these decisions (e.g., if we announced "in this round the agent chose not to make a proposal"), then we would have provided the principal with information that could have affected her beliefs about agent behavior in later trials. To preserve the single-play analogy, we did not give the principal this information. Instead, the principal made a prediction (heads or tails) in every trial, regardless of whether or not the agent made a proposal. To make our experiments analogous to our theory, however, we based the principal's earnings on the accuracy of her prediction only if the agent made a proposal (and so informed the subjects). That is, if the agent chose not to make a proposal, the principal earned the status quo fixed amount, regardless of her prediction.

The second additional design element is that we ran experiments with one speaker, one principal, and eight to ten agents.[9] In our theory, by contrast, we study the interaction between one speaker, one principal, and one agent. Our decision to use multiple agents was motivated by our desire to generate experimental data on *how the conditions for enlightenment affected agent behavior*. Our design allowed us to gather the data we desired at a much lower price than running with one agent per principal.

Again, we took precautions to ensure that subjects had the same incentives they would have had if there had been only one agent. First, we prevented agents from affecting one another's earnings by paying them only for their own decisions. Second, and as we described previously, we prevented the agents from affecting one another's earnings indirectly by either seeing one another, hearing one another, or receiving information about the previous choices of other players. Therefore, the agents' earnings were affected neither directly nor indirectly by the choices of the other agents. We also presented all agents with exactly the same set of incentives. Because the principal and the speaker knew that the agents all faced the same incentives and because they could not receive feedback about previous outcomes, the principal and speaker had no basis upon which to discriminate among agents. Therefore, from the principal's and speaker's perspectives, it was as if they were interacting with just one agent.[10]

[9]At the outset of each new experimental condition, we selected one subject to be the principal and one subject to be the speaker. All of the other subjects acted as agents. To make the experiment less abstract, we referred to the principal as "predictor," the speaker as "reporter," and the agents as "stage one players" during the experiment.
[10]For example, in some treatments we paid the principal $1.00 every time she made a correct prediction and an agent made a proposal. So, if ten agents made proposals and the principal made a correct prediction, then the principal earned $10.00. If we had just one agent and paid the principal $10.00 for every correct prediction when the agent made a proposal, then our expectations about the principal's incentives (and expected earnings) would be identical.

157

Experiments

Each of our experimental sessions involved two experimenters, two to four assistants, and eight to twelve subjects. To familiarize our subjects with the basic structure of the experiment, we began each session with the trials described in Chapter 7.[11] We then introduced two to four experimental conditions. At the conclusion of the last trial, we asked all subjects to fill out a post-experimental questionnaire; we then paid them and ended the session.

We ran four delegation experiments in which we varied one of four variable analogies in Table 8.1. We varied the speaker's interests, the speaker's knowledge, the likelihood of verification, and the imposition on the speaker of a penalty for lying. The point of each experiment was to show how these variations affected the agent's behavior.

Speaker Knowledge Experiment

Hypothesis: If the principal and speaker have common interests, then making the speaker knowledgeable will induce an agent to make proposals that are favorable to the principal.

Control: The principal and speaker did not observe the coin toss. The principal and speaker had common interests. There were no external forces. All of this was common knowledge.

Treatment: The speaker observed the coin toss.

Our first experiment examined the effect of a variance in the speaker's knowledge on the agent's behavior. In our theory, the conditions for enlightenment are satisfied only if a speaker who has common interests with a principal is also knowledgeable.

Each agent earned 65 cents if he chose not to make a proposal. In trials where the agents and the principal had common interests, each agent earned $1.00 if he made a proposal and the principal made a correct prediction and earned nothing for making a proposal when the principal made an incorrect prediction. In trials where the agents and the principal had conflicting interests, each agent earned nothing if he made a proposal and the principal made a correct prediction and earned $1.00 for making a proposal when the principal made an incorrect prediction.

To isolate the relationship between the speaker's knowledge and the agent's behavior in this experiment, we gave the speaker and principal

---

[11]The results from these trials were included in the data reported in Chapter 7.

common interests.[12] However, as we discussed in the knowledge experiment of Chapter 7, when the principal and speaker had common interests, the principal had a weakly dominant strategy to follow the speaker's advice regardless of the speaker's knowledge. To isolate the effect of the speaker's knowledge, we again paid the principal a small amount (e.g., 10 cents) for choosing heads.

Given this payoff structure for the agent and principal, we expected the set of agent behaviors described in Table 8.2.

We expected that the agents would make proposals under the conditions in cells 5 and 6 where they had common interests with the principal and the speaker saw the coin-toss outcome (i.e., the conditions for enlightenment were satisfied). We also hypothesized that the agents would make proposals under the conditions in cells 1 and 4 as well. This follows because the principal's equilibrium behavior, when in the midst of a speaker who lacked knowledge, was to predict heads (because of the guaranteed payment for doing so). So, when the agents observed that the coin landed on heads and they had common interests with the principal, the agents had reason to believe that the principal would choose heads, and, therefore, they had an incentive to make a proposal (cell 1).[13] Likewise, the agents had an incentive to make a proposal when the coin landed on tails and the agents had conflicting interests with the principal (cell 4).

Figure 8.1a depicts the agents' behavior in the experimental conditions that correspond to cell 1 in Table 8.2. The horizontal axis shows the number of proposals made, while the vertical axis displays the number of agents who made the given number of proposals. Thus, Figure 8.1a shows that fourteen of eighteen agents made proposals in every trial. The likelihood of seeing this distribution of proposal strings if the agents proposed randomly (as we define random behavior in Chapter 7) is very close to zero. Thus, the observed behaviors strongly support our expectation.

In Figure 8.1b, we report agent behavior strings for the experimental conditions that correspond to cell 2 in Table 8.2. In this case, we expected no proposals to be made. In these trials, sixteen of eighteen agents chose never to make a proposal. The difference between the agents' behavior in cells 1 and 2 could not be more stark.

---

[12]In these experiments, the principal earned (a status quo payoff of) 65 cents when an agent made no proposal. The principal earned $1.00 if an agent made a proposal and she made a correct prediction. If an agent made a proposal and the principal made an incorrect prediction, the principal earned nothing. To establish common interests between principal and speaker, we paid the speaker $1.00 for each correct prediction the principal made.

[13]The agents always observed the coin-toss outcome.

Table 8.2. Expectations about agent behavior in the knowledge experiment.

	The speaker does not see the coin-toss outcome		The speaker sees the coin-toss outcome	
	Agent–principal common interests	Agent–principal conflicting interests	Agent–principal common interests	Agent–principal conflicting interests
Coin lands on heads	Agent proposes (1)	Agent does not propose (3)	Agent proposes (5)	Agent does not propose (7)
Coin lands on tails	Agent does not propose (2)	Agent proposes (4)	Agent proposes (6)	Agent does not propose (8)

Delegation

Figures 8.1c and 8.1d depict the agents' behavior for the experimental conditions that correspond to cells 3 and 4 of Table 8.2, respectively. We expected no proposals when the coin landed on heads (cell 3) and many proposals when the coin landed on tails (cell 4). As expected, sixteen of eighteen agents in Figure 8.1c made no proposals, while fifteen of eighteen agents in Figure 8.1d always made proposals. These results strongly support our hypotheses about agent behavior.

Figures 8.1e through 8.1h depict the agents' behavior in the four treatments where the speaker was knowledgeable (i.e., the treatment conditions). Because the speaker and principal also had common interests, the conditions for enlightenment were satisfied in each case. Therefore, the agents in the experiment should have expected the principal to make correct predictions. As a result, *the agents should have made a proposal if and only if they and the principal had common interests.* Figures 8.1e (for heads) and 8.1f (for tails) depict the agents' behavior strings for this case and show that twenty-three of twenty-four agents always chose to propose, as we hypothesized. Figures 8.1g (for heads) and 8.1h (for tails) depict the agents' behaviors when the agents and the principal had conflicting interests. We expected that the agents would not make any proposals in these instances. Again, we see a stark contrast with the agents' behavior in the previous two figures, as the figures show that eighteen of twenty-four agents made no proposals. Each of these distributions provides strong support for our hypotheses about the agents' behavior.

To see more clearly how the variation in speaker knowledge affected the agents' behavior, compare Figure 8.1f with Figure 8.1b. In both situations the coin landed on tails and in both situations the principal earned a small fixed amount (i.e., 10 cents) for choosing heads. The only difference between the two conditions is that in Figure 8.1f, the speaker was knowledgeable whereas in the conditions reflected by the results in Figure 8.1b, the speaker lacked knowledge. In Figure 8.1b, sixteen of eighteen agents chose *never* to make a proposal. In Figure 8.1f, *every agent* (twelve out of twelve) *made a proposal every time.* Thus, the presence of an enlightened principal led the agents to make proposals that they would not have otherwise made to an unenlightened principal. This confirms our theoretical expectations.

A comparison of Figure 8.1d with Figure 8.1h shows another effect of speaker knowledge on the agents' behavior. Again, the only difference between the experimental conditions that generated these figures was that the speaker was knowledgeable in the latter case. In Figure 8.1d, fifteen of eighteen agents always made proposals. In Figure 8.1h, eight of twelve agents never made a proposal. Thus, it appears that the presence of a knowledgeable speaker again induced the agents to change their behavior.

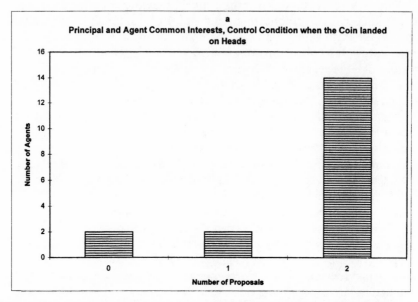

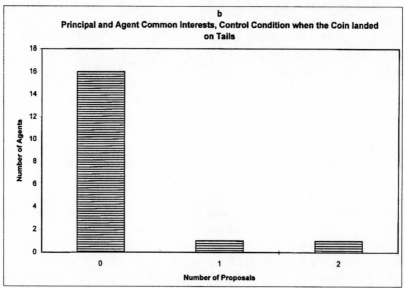

Figure 8.1. Knowledge experiment.

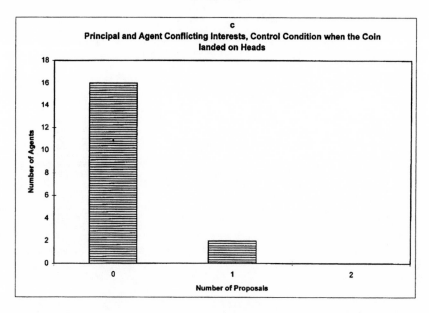

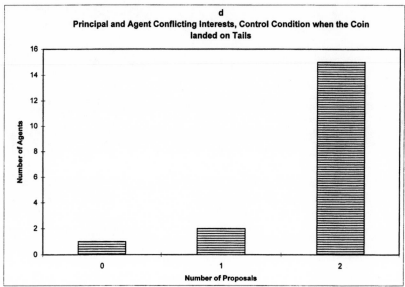

Figure 8.1. (*cont.*)

Experiments

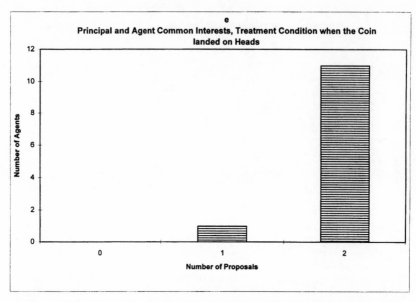

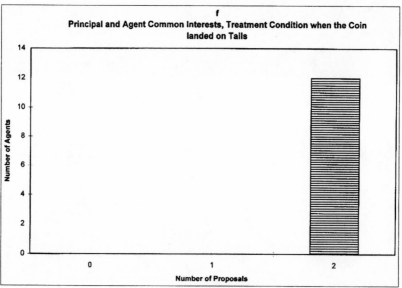

Figure 8.1. (*cont.*)

164

Delegation

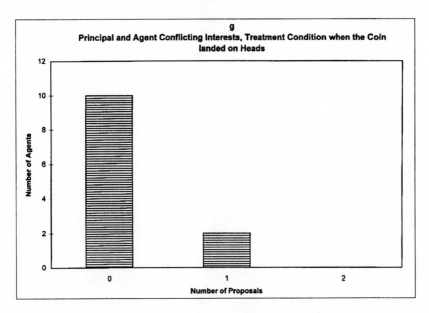

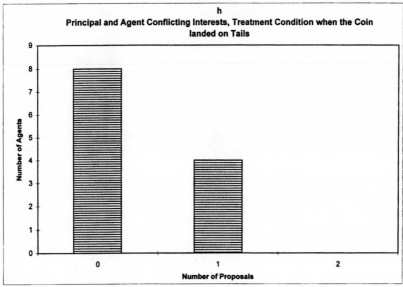

Figure 8.1. (*cont.*)

Experiments

In Table 8.3, we summarize the agents' behaviors in the knowledge experiment. Each cell entry gives the agents' mean percentage of proposals (along with the number of agents in each condition). In the four cells (1, 4, 5, and 6) where we expected proposals, we usually saw them (varying from 83 percent in cell 1 to a high of 100 percent in cell 6). When we expected no proposals, the agents rarely made them (varying from a low of 6 percent to a high of 17 percent). In sum, variations in speaker knowledge corresponded to dramatic and predictable changes in the agents' behavior.

Speaker Interest Experiment

Hypothesis: If the speaker is knowledgeable and there are no external forces, then giving the speaker and principal common interests will induce an agent who has common interests with the principal to make proposals that are favorable to the principal.

Control: The principal did not observe the coin toss. The speaker did. The speaker and principal had conflicting interests. There were no external forces. All of this was common knowledge.

Treatment: The speaker and principal had common interests.

Our second experiment isolated the effect of variations in the speaker's interests on the agents' behavior. We concluded earlier that if a knowledgeable speaker has common interests with the principal, then the conditions for enlightenment are satisfied. By contrast, if a knowledgeable speaker's interests conflict with the principal's, then the conditions for enlightenment are not satisfied. When the conditions for enlightenment are satisfied, the agents' actions will be beneficial to the principal, all else constant. To isolate the relationship between speaker interests and agents' behavior in this experiment, we held speaker knowledge constant.

In the control condition, the speaker and principal had conflicting interests. For example, we paid the speaker 50 cents every time the principal made an incorrect prediction. In the treatment condition, they had common interests – we paid the speaker 50 cents every time the principal made a correct prediction. We expected that the agents would make proposals only in the trials where the speaker, the principal, and the agents had common interests. In all other cases, we expected that the agents would not make proposals. Table 8.4 summarizes these expectations.

Figures 8.2a and 8.2b depict distributions of agent behavior strings from control condition trials (i.e., the speaker and the principal had conflicting interests) where the agents and the principal had conflicting interests. We expected no proposals in these trials, and the figures strongly

Table 8.3. *Agent behavior in the speaker knowledge experiment. Mean percentage of proposals.*

	The speaker does not see the coin-toss outcome		The speaker sees the coin-toss outcome	
	Agent–principal common interests	Agent–principal conflicting interests	Agent–principal common interests	Agent–principal conflicting interests
Coin lands on heads (# of agents)	83% (18)	6 (18)	96 (12)	8 (12)
Coin lands on tails (# of agents)	8 (18)	89 (18)	100 (12)	17 (12)

Table 8.4. *Expectations about agent behavior in the speaker interest, penalty-for-lying, and verification experiments.*

	Agent–principal common interests	Agent–principal conflicting interests
Treatment[a]	Agent proposes	Agent does not propose
Control[b]	Agent does not propose	Agent does not propose

[a]The speaker was expected to enlighten the principal.
[b]The speaker was not expected to enlighten the principal.

support this expectation. Approximately 65 percent of the agents never made a proposal. The remaining agents offered proposals in only a few trials.

We next review agent behavior strings from trials under the control condition (i.e., the speaker and the principal had conflicting interests) where the agents and principal had common interests. In these trials, each agent earned $1.20 for making no proposal, earned $2.00 for making a proposal when the principal predicted correctly, and earned nothing for making a proposal when the principal predicted incorrectly.[14] Given these parameters, we expected the agents to make proposals only if the probability that the principal would correctly predict the coin toss was at least 60 percent. Because the conditions for enlightenment were not satisfied, we expected that the principal would make random predictions (as this term is defined in Chapter 7) and that the agents would not make proposals in these trials.

Figures 8.2c and 8.2d display the agent behavior strings for these trials. In these trials, the bulk of the agents never made any proposals. In both figures, the median agent made no proposals. This again provides strong support for our expectations.

Figures 8.2e and 8.2f depict agent behavior strings from treatment condition trials (i.e., the principal and the speaker had common interests) where the agents and the principal had conflicting interests. In this case, the satisfaction of the conditions for enlightenment should have induced the agents not to make proposals. As expected, a majority of agents never made a proposal; indeed, the median agent never made a proposal.

Figures 8.2g and 8.2h depict agent behavior strings from treatment condition trials (i.e., the principal and the speaker had common interests)

[14]This payoff scheme varied slightly across experiments, but these variations had no substantive impact.

where the agents and principal had common interests. Because the conditions for enlightenment were satisfied (and thus, the probability of a correct prediction was at or near 100 percent), we expected that the agents would offer proposals in these trials.

While the results reported in Figure 8.2g confirm our expectation, the results reported in Figure 8.2h are more ambiguous. The principal's ability to acquire knowledge led agents to make more proposals. The modal agent reported in Figure 8.2g always made a proposal. We expected the same pattern in Figure 8.2h, but, by and large, the agents in this treatment chose not to make proposals, contrary to our hypothesis. The modal agent in this treatment made a proposal just 25 percent of the time. Nonetheless, when compared with the agents' proposal depicted in Figures 8.2a through 8.2f, we see a significant increase in proposals by the agents. Overall, then, the evidence provides support for our expectations.

Of course, there is a ready explanation for the agents' reluctance to make proposals in the trials of treatment condition where the agents and the principal had common interests. That explanation is risk aversion.

In our theory, agents are risk neutral. The presence of risk-averse subjects in our experiments weakened the faithfulness of our experimental analogies. However, simple comparative statics on our theory reveal that if agents were risk averse, then we should have expected to observe a lower incidence of proposals in the treatment condition (when the agents and principals had common interests). To see why, recall that each agent faced a choice between a guaranteed payoff of $1.20 or a payoff of $2.00 that depended on the principal's ability to make a correct prediction. Risk-averse subjects would have found the fixed payoff more satisfying than risk-neutral ones. To put it another way, even when the conditions for enlightenment were satisfied, it would not have required a great degree of risk aversion to lead agents not to propose.[15]

Table 8.5 summarizes our observations of the agents' behaviors in this experiment. Each cell reports the agents' mean percentage of proposals,

[15]Our post-experimental questionnaires suggested that the agents' risk aversion was facilitated by our experiments' complexity. Our theory of delegation involves some nontrivial calculations, especially for the agent. Because the agent moves first, he must anticipate the speaker's and principal's behavior in order to determine whether he is better off proposing or not proposing. In this experiment, we expected that an agent would make a proposal only if he had common interests with the principal and believed that the principal would make a correct coin-toss prediction with a probability of 60 percent or greater. In our experiment, we expected this requirement to be satisfied only if the conditions for enlightenment were satisfied. In reality, forming such an expectation was not a trivial task for our subjects.

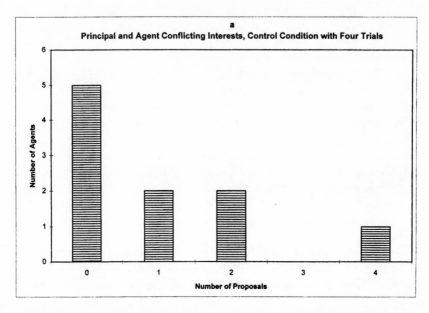

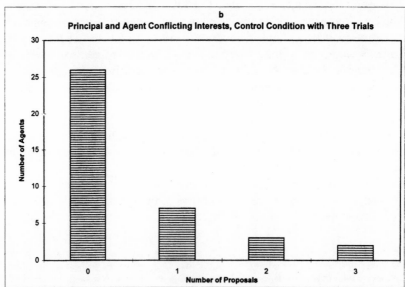

Figure 8.2. Interest experiment.

170

Delegation

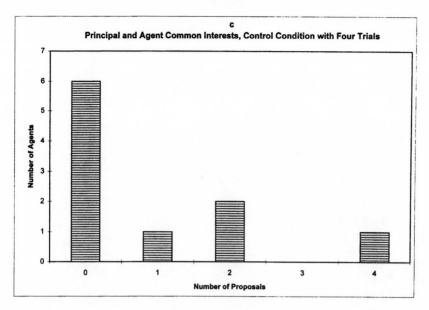

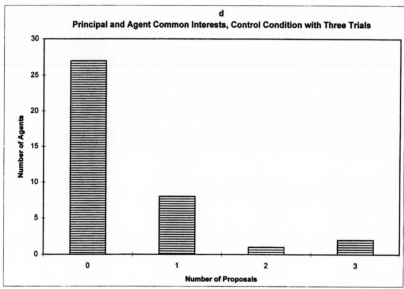

Figure 8.2. (*cont.*)

Experiments

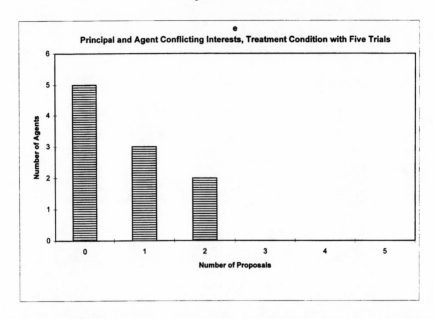

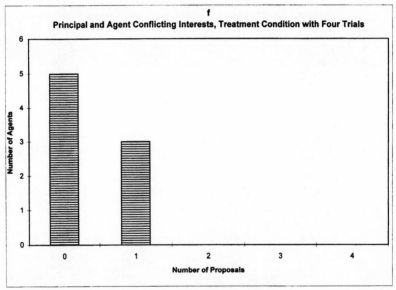

Figure 8.2. (*cont.*)

172

Delegation

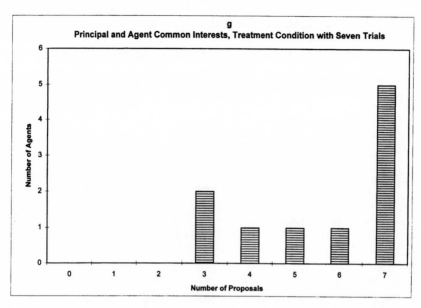

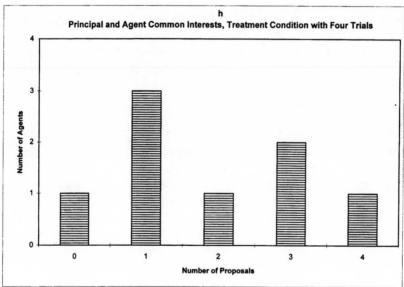

Figure 8.2. (*cont.*)

Experiments

Table 8.5. *Agent behavior in the speaker interest experiment.*

	Agent–principal common interests		Agent–principal conflicting interests	
Treatment	65[a]	18[c]	12	18
	(.33)[b]		(.15)	
Control	16	48	18	48
	(.28)		(.30)	

[a]Agents' mean percentage of proposals.
[b]Standard deviation.
[c]Total number of agents (observations).

the standard deviation, and the number of agents for the given condition.[16] In the cell where we expected proposals (i.e., the treatment condition where the principal and agent had common interests), the agents' mean percentage of proposals was 65 percent. In each of the other cells, where we expected no proposals, the agents were significantly less likely to make proposals (varying from a low of 12 percent to a high of 18 percent). Clearly, the principal's ability to become enlightened induced the agents to take actions that they otherwise would not have taken.

Penalties-for-Lying Experiment

Hypothesis: If the speaker is knowledgeable and has interests that conflict with those of the principal, then introducing a sufficient penalty for lying on the speaker will induce an agent who has common interests with the principal to make proposals that are favorable to the principal.

Control: The principal did not observe the coin toss. The speaker did. The speaker and principal had conflicting interests. There were no external forces. All of this was common knowledge.

Treatment: We introduced a penalty for lying on the speaker.

[16]We use percentages in order to standardize the number of proposals; that is, the number of possible proposals differed across experiments, and to account for this we convert the number of proposals each agent made into a percentage. For example, if an agent made one out of three proposals, then we convert this to 33 percent. Also, we use the agents' mean percentage of proposals instead of the total percentage of proposals because we are interested in individual agent behavior.

Delegation

In this experiment, we paid the speaker $5.00 every time the principal made an incorrect prediction and nothing every time the principal made a correct prediction, thereby setting up the conditions for conflicting interests between the speaker and the principal. In the treatment condition, we penalized the speaker $10.00 for making a false statement.

We expected that the principal would ignore the speaker in the control condition (with no penalty for lying) and would follow the speaker's advice in the treatment condition. We also expected that the speaker would send truthful signals in the treatment condition. Because the introduction of the penalty was sufficient to satisfy the conditions for enlightenment, we hypothesized that the agents would make proposals only in those trials of the treatment conditions where the principal and agents had common interests.[17] In all other cases, we expected that the agents would not make proposals (see Table 8.4).

The control condition for this experiment was identical to the control condition for the interest experiment just discussed. That is, the control condition included trials where the speaker and the principal had conflicting interests. Figures 8.2a and 8.2b display the results from the control condition where the agents and the principal had conflicting interests; Figures 8.2c and 8.2d display results from the control condition where the agents and the principal had common interests. In these trials, as discussed previously, the agents made very few proposals.

In Figures 8.3a and 8.3b, we depict agent proposal strings for treatment trials (i.e., the speaker faced a penalty for lying) where the agents and the principal had conflicting interests. The figure shows, as expected, that almost no proposals were made under these circumstances. In Figures 8.3c and 8.3d, we depict agent behavior strings for the treatment trials (i.e., the speaker faced a penalty for lying) where the agents and the principal shared common interests. Figure 8.3c show that only two of the eight agents made a proposal *every* time; however, five of the eight agents made a proposal more than half the time and only one agent never made a proposal. In Figure 8.3d, the agents made proposals 88 percent of the time and the median agent made a proposal two out of three times.

In Table 8.6, we compare the agents' behaviors in the treatment and control conditions for the penalty-for-lying experiments. The cell entries mimic those from Table 8.5, and our expectations are the same as those described in Table 8.4. Again, the incidence of observed proposals matched our expectations very well. The mean percentage of proposals

---

[17]In these experiments, the principal earned nothing if the agent chose the fixed amount and earned $1.00 if the agent made a proposal and she made a correct prediction. The agent earned $1.40 for choosing the fixed amount, earned $2.00 for making a proposal when the principal made a correct prediction, and earned nothing for making a proposal when the principal made an incorrect prediction.

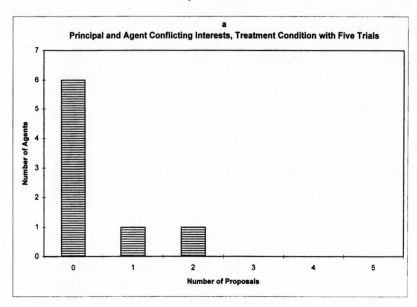

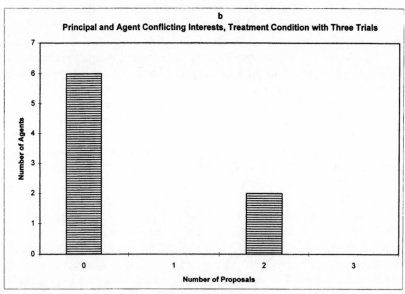

Figure 8.3. Penalty-for-lying experiment.

176

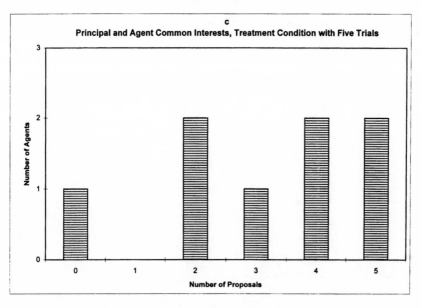

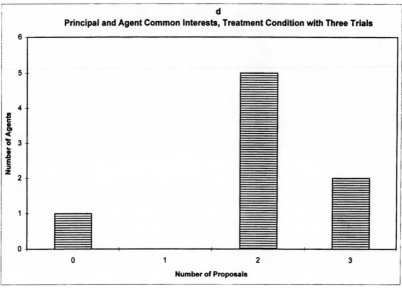

Figure 8.3. (*cont.*)

Table 8.6. *Agent behavior in the penalty-for-lying experiment.*

	Agent–principal common interests		Agent–principal conflicting interests	
Treatment	65	16	12	16
	(.32)		(.24)	
Control	16	48	18	48
	(.28)		(.30)	

in the treatment condition where the agents and the principal had common interests was substantially greater than the mean percentage of proposals in each of the other three cells.

Verification Experiment

Hypothesis: If the speaker is knowledgeable and has interests that conflict with those of the principal, then introducing a sufficient threat of verification will induce an agent who has common interests with the principal to make proposals that are favorable to the principal.

Control: The principal did not observe the coin toss. The speaker did. The speaker and principal had conflicting interests. There were no external forces. All of this was common knowledge.

Treatment: We introduced verification.

The purpose of our final experiment was to isolate the relationship between verification and the agents' behavior. We introduced verification into the experiment in much the same way as described in Chapter 7. After the agents made their decisions, the speaker chose whether or not to pay $2.00 for the privilege of sending a signal. If the speaker paid, then he could signal "heads" or "tails." The speaker earned $5.00 if the principal made an incorrect prediction and earned nothing if the principal made a correct prediction. If the speaker did not pay, then he earned nothing. After the speaker made his decision, we rolled a ten-sided die. If the die landed on 1 though 7, then we replaced the speaker's statement with the true coin-toss outcome, regardless of the speaker's signal. If the die landed on 8, 9, or 10, then we reported the speaker's statement, if any. As before, the principal had no way of knowing whether the signal she received was the speaker's statement or the true coin-toss outcome as replaced by us. The principal knew only that there was a 70 percent chance that the signal she received was the true coin-toss outcome.

As before, we expected the agents to make proposals only in the trials of the treatment condition (i.e., verification could occur) where the agent and principal had common interests (see Table 8.4).[18] The control condition for this experiment was the same as the control condition for the interest experiment and the penalty-for-lying experiment. As discussed previously, in these trials, the agents rarely made proposals.

Figures 8.4a and 8.4b depict the agents' behavior in the trials of the treatment condition (i.e., verification can occur) where the agents and the principal had conflicting interests. As expected, there were very few proposals here as well. Indeed, the median agent never made a proposal.

Figures 8.4c and 8.4d display results from the trials of the treatment condition (i.e., verification could occur) where the agents and the principal had common interests. In Figure 8.4c, more than half of the agents made proposals fewer than three out of six times. Furthermore, the modal agent made a proposal only one out of six times. In Figure 8.4d, the agents' behavior was closer to our expectations, as half of the agents made a proposal at least four out of five times. Nonetheless, these results do not support our expectations. While we can only speculate as to why these agents were reticent to make proposals, the complexity of the experiment and agent risk aversion are again plausible factors.

We summarize the agents' choices in the verification experiments in Table 8.7. The cell entries again mimic those from Table 8.5, and our expectations again are the same as those described in Table 8.4. While this experiment provides our weakest results, the pattern of proposals was still as expected, with substantial differences between the mean percentage of proposals in the treatment condition where the agents and the principal had common interests and the other conditions. These results provide some affirmation for our theory and are impressive given the complexity of this particular experiment.

[18]As in previous experiments, we paid each agent $1.40 if he chose not to make a proposal. If he made a proposal and the principal's prediction was correct (incorrect), then we paid the agent $2.00 (nothing) when the agent and the principal had common interests and nothing ($2.00) when agent and principal interests conflicted. When the agents and the principal had common interests, the agents' expected earnings from making a proposal were $(.7)*(\$2) + (.3)*[(.5)*(\$2)+(.5)*(\$0)]$, which equals $1.70. This is greater than the $1.40 that the agent received from not making a proposal. When the agent's and principal's interests conflicted, the agent's expected value from making a proposal was $(.7)*(\$0) + (.3)*[(.5)*(\$0)+(.5)*(\$2)]$, which equals 30 cents. This is less than the $1.40 that the agent received from not making a proposal.

Experiments

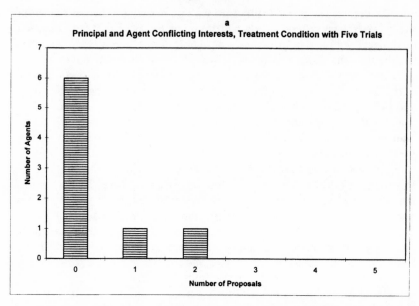

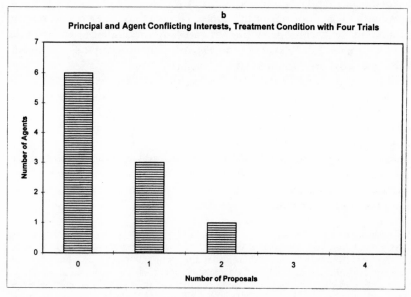

Figure 8.4. Verification experiment.

180

Delegation

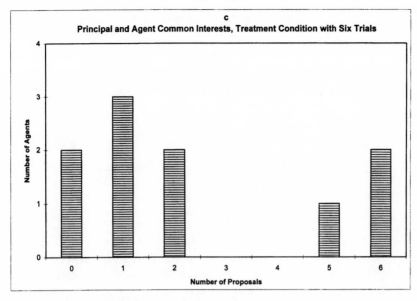

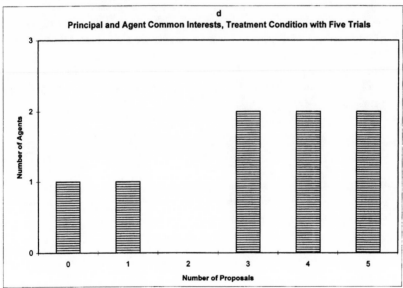

Figure 8.4. (*cont.*)

181

Table 8.7. *Agent behavior in the verification experiment.*

	Agent–principal common interests		Agent–principal conflicting interests	
Treatment	50	18	10	18
	(.39)		(.16)	
Control	16	48	18	48
	(.28)		(.30)	

CONCLUSION

In our delegation experiments, we expected to observe proposals only if the conditions for enlightenment were satisfied and the agents and the principal had common interests. In general, our observations were consistent with our expectations. When we expected proposals, we observed them 50 to 100 percent of the time. When we expected no proposals, we observed them only 6 to 18 percent of the time. The conditions for enlightenment induced agents to make proposals that were favorable to the principal and dissuaded agents from making proposals that were unfavorable to the principal. These experiments suggest that using institutional design to facilitate learning can be an effective way of making delegation successful.

POSTSCRIPT

Our delegation experiments offered opportunities for persuasion. In the following table, we use the data from our delegation experiments to replicate Table 7.6. The new table reveals behaviors analogous to those in our persuasion experiments.

Delegation

Table 8.8 *Persuasion and reasoned choice in the delegation experiments.*

Section 1. Behaviors When the Conditions for Persuasion and the Conditions for Enlightenment Were Satisfied

	Veracious report	Persuasion	Enlightenment	Deception	Reasoned choice
Knowledge and common interests[a]	100% 16/16	94 15/16	100 15/15	0 0/15	94 15/16
Knowledge and common interests (tails only)	100 8/8	88 7/8	100 7/7	0 0/7	88 7/8
Common interests and knowledge[b]	95 19/20	100 20/20	95 19/20	5 1/20	95 19/20
Conflicting interests and penalty for lying	100 16/16	88 14/16	100 14/14	0 0/14	88 14/16
Conflicting interests and verification (when verified)[c]	N/A	64 9/14	100 9/9	0 0/9	64 9/14
TOTALS	98 51/52	88 58/66	98 57/58	2 1/58	86 57/66

Section 2: Behaviors When the Conditions for Persuasion Were Satisfied and the Conditions for Enlightenment Were Not

	Veracious report	Persuasion	Enlightenment	Deception	Reasoned choice
Conflicting interests and verification (when not verified)[d]	0 0/4	100 4/4	0 0/4	100 4/4	0 0/4

Section 3. Behaviors When the Conditions for Persuasion Were Not Satisfied

	Veracious report	Persuasion	Enlightenment	Deception	Reasoned choice
No knowledge and common interests	63 10/16	81 13/16	62 8/13	38 5/13	56 9/16
No knowledge and common interests (tails only)	50 2/4	25 1/4	100 1/1	0 0/1	50 2/4
Conflicting interests and knowledge	72 23/32	59 19/32	79 15/19	21 4/19	63 20/32
TOTALS	69 33/48	67 32/48	72 23/32	28 9/32	60 29/48

[a]These results are from the treatment in the knowledge experiment. Recall that we paid principals in this experiment a small amount of predicting heads.
[b]These results are from the treatment in the interest experiment.
[c]The persuasion, enlightenment, and deception statistics are based on the verified announcement.
[d]The speaker chose not to make a statement 2 times. In these cases, 0 out of 2 principals made reasoned choices.

9

A Survey Experiment
on the Conditions for Persuasion

In this chapter, we use a survey experiment in which more than 1,000 randomly chosen individuals participated to show that that people are selective about whom they choose to believe. From their responses, we find that the best predictors of how a respondent reacts to a speaker's statements are the conditions for persuasion that we derived in Chapter 3. Specifically, *we find that a person's willingness to follow a speaker's advice depends strongly and regularly on that person's perceptions of the speaker's knowledge and trustworthiness.*

We base our findings on a novel survey experiment that confronted more than 1,400 respondents from across the country with a dilemma analogous to that faced by the principal in Chapter 3.[1] That is, *each respondent made a binary choice.* Like the principal in Chapter 3, our respondents' choices were so complex that they *were unlikely to know which of two alternatives was better for them.* Also like the principal, we provided most of our respondents *with an opportunity to learn from others.* And, as in our model, our respondents may have known little about the speaker's knowledge or trustworthiness.

[1]There are many advantages to survey experiments (see Sniderman, Brody, and Tetlock 1991 for a review). However, telephone interviews allow experimenters relatively little control over the physical environment in which the experiment takes place. For example, subjects could have answered our questions while washing the dishes, watching television, or engaging in a wide range of other activities. Because telephone interviews offer such a lack of control, it is reasonable to ask why we would engage in such an exercise. The answer to this question is that we ran this survey experiment *in conjunction with* a series of more controlled laboratory experiments (such experiments were the focus of Chapters 7 and 8). The fact that we ultimately reject this chapter's null hypothesis (and show a strong positive relationship between perceived knowledge, perceived trustworthiness, and persuasion) in two radically different experimental environments demonstrates that the predictive strength of our theory is robust to a broad range of background conditions. Certainly, such success grants a far stronger claim to broad predictive success than would be true if we limited our analysis to only one type of experimental environment.

Conditions for Persuasion

The experiment began with the interviewer's asking the respondent either to support or oppose a specific, complex policy proposal. It was with this question that we created our experimental treatment. The treatment involved giving some, but not all, respondents additional information before we elicited their opinions. Some respondents heard that a speaker, such as Rush Limbaugh, supported the policy proposal. Other respondents heard that the speaker opposed the proposal. The remaining heard neither statement. For the respondents who heard a speaker's statement, we continued the survey experiment with a series of questions about particular speaker attributes. We drew some of these attributes from our theoretical work in Chapter 3, while other attributes came from conventional explanations of persuasion.

We used the survey experiment to evaluate the predictive power of our "conditions for persuasion." Recall that persuasion is *a successful attempt to change the beliefs of another* and that persuasion is a necessary, but not a sufficient, condition for enlightenment. We summarize our conditions for persuasion in compact versions of Chapter 3's theorems.

> *Theorem 3.1: Absent external forces, having perceived common interests is a necessary condition for persuasion.*
>
> *Theorem 3.2: Absent external forces, perceived speaker knowledge is a necessary condition for persuasion.*
>
> *Theorem 3.3: With respect to persuasion, external forces can be substitutes for common interests (and for each other).*

Together, these theorems generate a critical null hypothesis. This null hypothesis is the negation of our prediction about the relationship between perceived speaker knowledge, perceived speaker trustworthiness, and persuasion.[2]

> *Null Hypothesis: The speaker's ability to persuade a respondent is not affected by the respondent's perception of the speaker's trustworthiness or knowledge.*

Recall that all of our claims about enlightenment and delegation depend on Chapter 3's theorems about persuasion as a necessary or sufficient condition for their own validity. This implies that if our survey experiment shows that our theory of persuasion makes bad predictions, then our subsequent conclusions about enlightenment and delegation may also be flawed. However, the survey experiment shows no such thing. To the

---

[2]Unlike in our laboratory experiments on persuasion, we do not report reasoned choice statistics here. The reason, of course, is that it is impossible to know what reasoned choice for our subjects would be.

contrary, our survey experiment allows us to reject this chapter's null hypothesis and provides strong evidence for our predictions. The main implication of our findings is that people are quite selective in choosing whom to believe.

The remainder of the chapter proceeds as follows: First, we describe the experiment. Next, we show that systematic patterns in the responses of our 1,464 subjects allow us to reject this chapter's null hypothesis. Then we show that the conditions for persuasion not only provide good predictions about which statements our respondents chose to believe but also provide better predictions of respondent behavior than other well-known explanations of persuasion.

DESCRIPTION OF THE EXPERIMENT

My main conclusion is that the key premises in any theory that purports to explain the real phenomena of politics are the empirical assumptions about goals, and even more important, about the ways in which people characterize the choice situations that face them. . . . What will happen next is not independent of where the system is right now. And a description of where it is right now must include a description of the subjective view of the situation that informs the choices of the actors.

– Simon 1985: 301

We designed our survey experiment to evaluate how respondents chose whom to believe. The design of the experiment closely followed Simon's advice, as the measures of the independent variables, such as perceived speaker knowledge and trustworthiness, were based on "the subjective view of the situation that informs the choices of the actors."

The Survey

In 1992, a group of seventeen scholars from thirteen universities designed a survey instrument in order to explore the dynamics of political reasoning. *The Multi-Investigator Study on Political Persuasion and Attitude Change* was the fruit of their efforts and contained twelve separate and independently conceived experimental components. The experiment we describe here was one of the twelve components.

The study was conducted at the University of California, Berkeley's Survey Research Center and used computer-assisted telephone interviewing (or CATI) technology. From June 15 to November 4, 1994, the instrument was administered to a national sample of 1,464 respondents who were randomly selected from the population of all English-speaking adults eighteen years of age or older, residing in households with telephones, within the forty-eight contiguous states.[3]

Design

Our experiment began with one of two versions of a question that we designed to measure respondent opinions on a confusing issue.[4]

> *Question 1 with endorsement: Now I am going to ask you a couple of questions about a new issue in American politics – spending money to build prisons. It's been reported that talk show host [SPEAKER] [POSITION] spending money to build more prisons. What do you think? Is spending money to build prisons a good idea or a bad idea?*

> *Question 1 without endorsement: Now I am going to ask you a couple of questions about a new issue in American politics – spending money to build prisons. What do you think? Is spending money to build prisons a good idea or a bad idea?*

Question 1 contains our experimental variation. This variation had two components. First, a random-number generator determined whether Question 1 is read *with* or *without* an endorsement. If Question 1 was read with an endorsement, then the same generator determined whether the speaker was talk show host Rush Limbaugh or talk show host Phil Donahue. Second, a different random-number generator similarly deter-

[3]The sample of telephone numbers for the survey was generated using a procedure called list-assisted random-digit sampling. This recently developed methodology preserves the characteristics of a random sample but takes advantage of the availability of large computer databases of telephone directory information to make the sample more efficient. This method allows a reduction in the number of unproductive calls to nonworking telephone numbers and an increase in the number of households in our sample over the number that would have been achieved by sample random-digit dialing. More information on this sampling method is available in Casady and Lepkowski (1993). Of the 2,234 English-speaking households contacted as a result of this procedure, 686 refused to participate, 68 were never at home, and 16 were unable to participate. The remaining 1,464 households constitute the sample.

[4]Our experiment employs a "post-test only" design. Inferences about persuasion can be drawn in such an experiment when the random assignment of respondents across experimental conditions is likely to ensure that each group would have roughly comparable initial attitudes. Our 1,464 respondents were randomly assigned to only 5 experimental conditions, making the likelihood of initial comparability quite high. Note that in the version of Question 1 on the survey, respondents also had the option of responding "a very good idea" or "a very bad idea." To simplify the presentation, we collapsed such responses into the categories "a good idea" and "a bad idea" respectively. For the eleven respondents who replied "don't know" to Question 1, we supplied a similarly worded follow-up question. Only three respondents replied "don't know" to the follow-up. We dropped these three observations from the data.

mined whether the endorsement, if there was one, was "supports" or "opposes."

The two generators produced, on average, a 10 percent chance that the respondent would hear Question 1 without an endorsement. It was also set so that the statements "Rush Limbaugh supports," "Rush Limbaugh opposes," "Phil Donahue supports," "Phil Donahue opposes" were equally likely (i.e., on average, there was a 22.5 percent chance that a given respondent would hear Question 1 with a particular endorsement).

The survey continued with two questions that were relevant to our attempt to assess the predictive power of our theory. We designed the first of these two questions to elicit a measure of the respondent's perception of the speaker's trustworthiness. The second of these two questions elicited a measure of the respondent's perception of the speaker's knowledge. The order in which we asked these two questions was randomly determined, with each equally likely to be asked first.

> *Question 2: Now I am going to ask you a couple of questions about [SPEAKER]. On most political issues would you say that you and [SPEAKER] agree all of the time, most of the time, only some of the time, or never?*

> *Question 3: How much would you say that [SPEAKER] knows about what will happen if this country spends money to build more prisons – a lot, some, a little, or nothing?*

We followed these questions with a series of standard demographic questions about the respondent's partisanship, ideology, socioeconomic characteristics, and feelings about the speaker.

Why We Chose These Questions

We chose prison spending as an issue focus for three reasons. First, we expected it to be salient for many respondents. We based our expectation on the many public opinion polls in the mid-1990s that showed crime to be a primary concern of many Americans.

Second, we expected the links between ideology and the responses to be unclear. While building more prisons was a conservative, "law and order" issue, spending money to solve problems was more of a liberal, "interventionist" position. In other words, we chose the issue so that our speakers could plausibly support or oppose either proposal.

Third, we expected many respondents to be uncertain about the consequences of accepting either proposal. By contrast, had we chosen an issue whose consequences were transparent, we would expect, and our theory would predict, no relationship between speaker statements and the survey responses – as it is difficult to persuade someone of something they think they know.

Our reasons for choosing Rush Limbaugh and Phil Donahue as speakers had similar foundations. First, we wanted speakers with whom most respondents were likely to be familiar. In fact, only 3 of the 1,340 respondents who heard a version of the question that contained an endorsement had no prior knowledge of the speaker. Second, we chose speakers who were unlikely to be universally trusted or reviled. Third, we chose talk show hosts rather than well-known experts or novices in the areas of corrections or law enforcement, because respondents were likely to vary in their assessments of how much these figures knew.[5]

In sum, we chose issues and speakers in an attempt to get variance in both the dependent variable of interest (respondent attitudes about the issue) and the independent variables of interest (perceived speaker incentives and trustworthiness) in a setting where the issue at hand was likely to be both salient and difficult to understand.

The Match Between the Survey Experiment and the Theory

To the extent that this experimental environment captured all of the assumptions made in our theory of persuasion, our ability to reject the null hypothesis is evidence of our theory's predictive power. To the extent that this experimental environment did not capture all of the theoretical assumptions, we have a bad experiment. So, before we assess the implication of the data for the null hypothesis, we briefly review Chapter 3's assumptions and assess the extent to which our survey experiment re-created these assumptions. We assert that our survey experiment offered good, though not perfect, analogies of the premises in Chapter 3.

In our model, communication requires at least two people: the *principal* and the *speaker*. In our experiment, each respondent played the role of the principal, and Rush Limbaugh or Phil Donahue was the speaker.

In our model, we assume that the principal *must make a binary choice*. In our experiment, we asked the respondent to support or oppose spending money for prisons. This was a binary choice.

In our model, we assume that the *principal is goal oriented*. In our experiment, we knew very little about the goals of our respondents. Some

---

[5]We used more than one speaker to evaluate the robustness of the competing explanations of persuasion. It turns out that none of the predictions we evaluate depend on whether Limbaugh or Donahue was the speaker. We had only two speakers because of time constraints on the survey (i.e., to facilitate all of the experiments, we used all of the time we were allotted with the questions we asked) and because randomizing over more than two speakers would reduce to unacceptably low levels the number of respondents receiving each treatment.

respondents may have had the goal of giving thoughtful responses, while others might have had the goal of ending the phone call as quickly as possible. A considerable challenge for our study was accounting for these myriad goals. Specifically, the more respondents whose goals were not consistent with giving thoughtful responses, the more we stacked the deck against our experiment's being a good analogy of our theory.[6] Because the variety of goals that our respondents could have had only seem to stack the deck against rejecting our hypothesis, our ability to reject the null hypothesis in this environment only strengthens our claim about our theory's predictive power. For this reason, we welcomed the challenge posed by variance in respondent goals.

In our model, we assume that the *speaker is goal oriented and that the principal may not know the speaker's goals.* However, we find that the conditions for persuasion do not depend on what the speaker's goals actually are. *Instead, the conditions for persuasion depend only on the principal's beliefs about these goals.* Thus, what mattered for the purpose of our experiment was our respondents' beliefs about speaker goals. Question 2 was a simple attempt to obtain a very coarse measure of these beliefs.

Similarly, in the model we assume that *the speaker need not have useful private information, and that the principal may be uncertain about how much the speaker knows.* In our survey experiment, Question 3 was a simple attempt to obtain a very coarse measure of the respondents' perceptions of speaker knowledge.

In our model, *the principal may not know which alternative is better for her.* In our experiment, we asked respondents about prison spending, presumably an issue that engendered uncertainty in many people.

In the model, we assume *that the speaker and principal have a limited common language.* In the experiment, speakers said one of two things: "supports" or "opposes." These statements are equivalent to the "better"/ "worse" language we use in the model.

In the model, we assume a particular *sequence of events.* First, each player's beliefs about both the other player and the consequences of his or her own actions are established prior to the play of the game. Second, the speaker says either "better" or "worse." Third, the principal chooses one of the two alternatives. Fourth, the game ends. The interaction between speaker and respondent in the experiment had an equivalent structure to the interaction in the model.

---

[6]The same can be said for the assertion that our responses came from respondents who told us what they thought we wanted to hear. It should be noted, however, that respondents who had no way of knowing the purpose of the experiment were extremely unlikely to know what we wanted to hear.

Conditions for Persuasion

Table 9.1. *Percent reporting that spending money to build more prisons is a good idea.*

Category	% Good	N
All respondents	59.7	1,247
All respondents who:		
Heard supports – either source	59.8	639
Heard opposes – either source	59.3	666
No endorsement	61.4	122
Heard Rush Limbaugh – either position	59.0	622
Heard Phil Donahue – either position	60.0	683
Heard Rush Limbaugh supports	60.7	300
Heard Rush Limbaugh opposes	57.4	322
Heard Phil Donahue supports	59.0	339
Heard Phil Donahue opposes	61.0	344
Democrat	56.1	635
Republican	64.7	588
Independent	53.1	128
Conservative	67.0	544
Liberal	49.0	353

ANALYSIS

In Table 9.1, we present a set of descriptive statistics.[7] These statistics reveal the percentage of subjects who responded that greater prison spending is a "good idea." These statistics show that, while respondents' partisanship and ideology had some effect on their opinions, they were far from deterministic. Table 9.1 also suggests that speaker statements had little effect on our respondents' opinions. For example, respondents who heard "Limbaugh supports" were only a little more likely (3.3 percentage points) to support the issue than was the sample that heard "Limbaugh opposes." Worse yet, the respondents who heard "Donahue supports" were actually *less* likely to support the issue than were the respondents who heard "Donahue opposes." However, a closer look at the data reveals that, instead of ignoring the endorsements we supplied, respondents used these endorsements in systematic and predictable ways.

[7]Lupia (n.d.) conducts a more comprehensive analysis of these data. The results we present here are representative of his findings.

Experiments

Simple Hypothesis Tests

In Table 9.2, we show how the speaker's statements affected the respondent's opinions. We call our measure of perceived speaker trustworthiness *Agrees*. The source of the variable *Agrees* is the responses to Question 2. We call our measure of perceived speaker knowledge *Knows*. The source of the variable *Knows* is the responses to Question 3. For simplicity, we collapse response categories for both variables. We collapse the top two categories of *Agrees* because fewer than ten respondents replied that they "agree all of the time" with either Limbaugh or Donahue. We collapse *Knows* responses into binary categories for expositional clarity.[8]

Theorems 3.1, 3.2, and 3.3 imply that increases in either *Agrees* or *Knows* should increase the likelihood that the response to Question 1 (good idea or bad idea) matched the speaker's endorsement (supports or opposes, respectively). In Table 9.2, the column labeled *Supports–Opposes* measures how often these matches occurred. If all respondent opinions matched speaker statements, then *Supports–Opposes* = −100. If there were no matches, then *Supports–Opposes* = −100. Further, when equal numbers of respondents agreed and disagreed with the speaker, then *Supports–Opposes* = 0.

Table 9.2 reveals that when respondents perceived speakers to be knowledgeable or trustworthy, then matches were more frequent. For example, respondents who reported that they agree with Rush Limbaugh "all or most of the time" and heard "Rush Limbaugh supports" were 22 percentage points more likely to support prison spending than were respondents who reported that they agree with Rush Limbaugh "all or most of the time" and heard "Rush Limbaugh opposes." For respondents who agreed with Limbaugh "some of the time," *Supports–Opposes* = 6, while for respondents who "never" agreed with Limbaugh, *Supports–Opposes* = −22. The effect of Phil Donahue's statements were of the same direction and magnitude.

The fact that the variable *Supports–Opposes* actually takes on negative values implies that people did not necessarily ignore advice from speakers whose trustworthiness or knowledge was suspect. These negative values are stark counterexamples to the claims of game theoretic signaling models (Crawford and Sobel 1982, Gilligan and Krehbiel 1987, 1989). Recall that one claim of these models is that the absence of common interests between speaker and principal necessarily leads to uninformative "cheap talk." If all talk between people with conflicting interests were indeed

---

[8]With respect to the power of our hypothesis tests, note that our measures of perceived speaker knowledge and perceived speaker incentives are quite crude, thus stacking the deck against the hypothesis rejections that would (and ultimately do) bolster the predictive credentials of our theory.

Table 9.2. *Percent who report that spending money to build more prisons is a "good" idea, separated by perceived speaker knowledge or trust.*

Either source said:	Supports % good	Opposes % good	Supports–Opposes	N supports	N opposes
Agrees: all or most	76	51	25	84	75
Agrees: some	62	59	3	341	366
Agrees: never	41	65	–24	98	110
Knows: a lot or some	70	56	14	327	317
Knows: a little or nothing	44	64	–20	217	249

Limbaugh said:	Supports % good	Opposes % good	Supports–Opposes	N Supports	N Opposes
Agrees: all or most	76	54	22	51	54
Agrees: some	66	60	6	150	156
Agrees: never	33	55	–22	60	63
Knows: a lot or some	75	60	15	156	156
Knows: a little or nothing	39	55	–16	107	116

Donahue said:	Supports % good	Opposes % good	Supports–Opposes	N Supports	N Opposes
Agrees: all or most	76	43	33	33	21
Agrees: some	59	59	0	191	210
Agrees: never	53	77	–24	38	47
Knows: a lot or some	66	52	14	171	161
Knows: a little or nothing	49	71	–22	110	131

Experiments

"cheap," then we should never see a negative *Supports–Opposes*. But we do.

However, and as we described in Chapter 3, respondents who believe that both a speaker and his audience have interests that conflict with their own ought to listen to the speaker's advice and do the opposite.[9] In Table 9.2, the manifestation of these beliefs is the negative values of *Supports–Opposes*. Thus, our respondents' reactions to the statements (i.e. the negative *Supports–Opposes* figures) of speakers they distrusted or regarded as ignorant suggest that they were using these statements in the manner that we predicted.

In Table 9.3, we show how the effect of the speaker statements on respondent opinions varied in accordance with particular combinations of *Agrees* and *Knows*. This table further reinforces the predictive success of our theory. That is, for every level of *Agrees*, *Supports–Opposes* increases as *Knows* increases. Table 9.3 reveals that the effect of perceived speaker knowledge and trustworthiness on respondent opinions was more than mere echoes of each other – each had distinct, although complementary effects.

Variations in *Supports–Opposes* in Tables 9.2 and 9.3 are precisely as the propositions of Chapter 3 predict – as either *Agrees* or *Knows* increases, so does *Supports–Opposes*. Moreover, the magnitude of these effects is so large that they allow us to reject the null hypothesis. That is, we treat each entry in Table 9.2 as a stochastically independent random variable from a binomial distribution $b(N, \%\text{Good})$. For every pair of entries, we evaluate the null hypothesis that the means of these distributions are equal. We find that as we move from a low category of *Agrees* or *Knows* to a higher category, we can reject – using 90 percent or 95 percent confidence intervals – the null hypothesis that the relationship between whether the speaker said "supports" or "opposes" and the respondents' propensity to respond "good idea" was unaffected.

Moreover, neither Rush Limbaugh's nor Phil Donahue's *actual* knowledge, interests, incentives, personality, or reputation varied within the experiment – they were exogenous constants. As a result, the variance in the data was not due to any of these conventional explanations of persuasion.

A Comparison with Alternative Explanations

Of course, there are alternative explanations for the patterns revealed in the data. It could be the case that our theory's explanation is a mere restatement of other well-known explanations of persuasion. In order to

[9]See the section on multiple principals in Chapter 3.

Table 9.3. *Percent who report that spending money to build more prisons is a "good" idea, separated by perceived speaker knowledge and trust.*

Agrees	Knows	Supports % good	Opposes % good	Supports–Opposes	N supports	N opposes
all or most	a lot or some	80	49	31	80	70
all or most	a little or nothing	0	80	−80	4	5
some	a lot or some	69	57	12	212	220
some	a little or nothing	51	62	−11	126	138
never	a lot or never	56	69	−13	25	16
never	a little or nothing	36	64	−28	73	89

evaluate our theory against these explanations, we now show how the predictive power of *Agrees* and *Knows* compares with the predictive power of other well-known alternative explanations.

First, we compare the relationship between *Agrees, Knows,* and respondent opinions with the relationship between affect, as measured by conventional feeling thermometer questions, and respondent attitudes. Then, we conduct a similar comparison replacing conventional measures of affect with conventional measures of ideology. We find that our measures of perceived speaker knowledge and trustworthiness provide better predictions of respondent attitudes than do the alternative explanations.

The Role of Affect (as Measured by Feeling Thermometers).   One alternative explanation of persuasion, the affective relationship between speaker and principal, has its roots in psychology. A well-known manifestation of the role of affect in political persuasion scholarship is the likability heuristic (e.g., Petty and Cacioppo 1986). Beliefs such as "people should agree with people they like" or "people I like usually have correct opinions" express the likability heuristic. In his review of the social psychology literature, O'Keefe (1990, 107) states, "Where this heuristic is invoked, liked sources should prove more persuasive than disliked sources."

Feeling thermometers are the conventional measure of "liking." If feeling thermometers are a good measure of liking, and if the likability heuristic is a good predictor of persuasion, then an increase in the speaker's thermometer score should have corresponded with an increase in the percentage of respondents who agreed with his position. In Tables 9.4 and 9.5, we evaluate this hypothesis while simultaneously reevaluating the hypothesis that as *Agrees* and/or *Knows* increases, so should the percentage of respondents who agreed with the speaker's position.

Table 9.4 shows the relationship between thermometer scores, *Agrees, Knows,* and respondent support for prison spending for the subsample who heard that either speaker "supports" this spending. We sort the observations into *columns* based on their response to feeling thermometer questions. We sort the same observations into *rows* based on *Agrees* or *Knows.*

The *likability heuristic* predicts that *as we move from left to right* in any row of Table 9.4, support for more prisons should *increase. Our theory* predicts that, regardless of the value of the feeling thermometer, *as we move from Agrees = "all or most" to Agrees = "never" or from Knows = "a lot or some" to Knows = "a little or nothing,"* support for more prisons should *decrease.*

The likability heuristic's prediction *is false in every case* for which there were at least ten respondents in each category. By contrast, our theory's prediction *is true in all of these cases.* Table 9.4 confirms our

Conditions for Persuasion

Table 9.4. *Respondents who heard either "Rush Limbaugh supports" or "Phil Donahue supports." Percent who reported that stated issue is a good idea, separated by knows, agrees, and feeling thermometer score.*

Donahue supports	Thermometer <50	Thermometer 50	Thermometer 50>	Thermometer as predicted
Agrees: all or most	100[a]	67[a]	74	—
Agrees: some	55	65	56	No
Agrees: never	52	75[a]	0[a]	—
Agrees as predicted	Yes	—	Yes	
Knows: a lot or something	61	71	65	No
Knows: a little or nothing	48	57	37	No
Knows as predicted	Yes	Yes	Yes	

Limbaugh supports	Thermometer <50	Thermometer 50	Thermometer 50>	Thermometer as predicted
Agrees: all or most	100[a]	100[a]	73	—
Agrees: some	61	76	65	No
Agrees: never	29	62[a]	33[a]	—
Agrees as predicted	Yes	—	Yes	
Knows: a lot or something	66	81	76	No
Knows: a little or nothing	37	63	20[a]	No
Knows as predicted	Yes	Yes	Yes	

[a] These entries are based on fewer than 10 observations and are not factored into the prediction evaluation.

expectations that it is possible for people to be persuaded by people they do not like.

In Table 9.5, we run the same comparison for the sample who heard that either speaker "opposes" prison spending. The likability heuristic predicts *that as we move from left to right* in any row of Table 9.5, support for more prisons should *decrease*. Our theory predicts that, regardless of the value of the feeling thermometer, *as we move from Agrees = "all or most" to Agrees = "never" or from Knows = "a lot or some" to Knows = "a little or nothing,"* support for more prisons should *increase*.

Again, the likability heuristic's prediction is true in only four of the nine cases for which there were at least ten respondents in each category. Our theory's prediction is true in seven of ten cases. Seen from this perspective, our measures of perceived speaker knowledge and incentives are far better predictors of the variance in respondent attitudes than are feeling thermometers.

197

Table 9.5. *Respondents who heard either "Rush Limbaugh opposes" or "Phil Donahue opposes." Percent who reported that stated issue is a good idea, separated by knows, agrees, and feeling thermometer score.*

Donahue opposes	Thermometer <50	Thermometer 50	50>	Thermometer as predicted
Agrees: all or most	67[a]	100[a]	37	No
Agrees: some	59	61	52	No
Agrees: never	79	50[a]	67[a]	No
Agrees as predicted	Yes	—	Yes	
Knows: a lot or something	60	56	42	Yes
Knows: a little or nothing	72	70	68	Yes
Knows as predicted	Yes	Yes	Yes	

Limbaugh opposes	Thermometer <50	Thermometer 50	50>	Thermometer as predicted
Agrees: all or most	67[a]	37	55	—
Agrees: some	55	68	67	No
Agrees: never	59	41	100[a]	Yes
Agrees as predicted	Yes	—	Yes	
Knows: a lot or something	60	64	58	No
Knows: a little or nothing	55	52	75[a]	Yes
Knows as predicted	No	No	—	

[a] These entries are based on fewer than 10 observations and are not factored into the prediction evaluation.

We do not, however, draw from these results the conclusion that the likability heuristic is wrong. In fact, we see our explanation of how people choose whom to believe as a complement to the basic insight that the likability heuristic offers – people are systematic and selective in choosing whose advice to follow. Indeed, our theory explains that persuasiveness is determined by a principal's "feelings" about the speaker (i.e., the principal's beliefs about the commonality of the speaker's interests with her own) as well as perceptions of speaker knowledge and certain external forces that affect the speaker's incentives. Thus, these two explanations, while different, are not contradictory.

Our explanation for the failure of the "affect" variable to explain variance in our respondents' opinions is that feeling thermometers are a *terrible* measure of what it is about a speaker that induces a principal to follow or ignore his advice. Feeling thermometers do not allow for such factors as a speaker's perceived knowledge or interests, which can mediate the manner in which a respondent's feelings affect his or her attitudes toward others. As a result, feeling thermometers should not be used in attempts to understand persuasion.

The Role of Ideology. Another explanation of persuasion, the claim that people are more likely to believe speakers who share their ideology, has its roots in studies of voting behavior and public opinion. Its insight is analogous to that of the likability heuristic and is expressed by beliefs such as "people should agree with people who have the same ideological beliefs" or "people like me usually have correct opinions."

We asked all of our respondents standard survey questions about their ideology. We first asked if they were conservative or liberal. We then asked follow-up questions to assess the strength of their convictions. While most scholars use responses to the two questions to produce seven-point ideology scales, we focus on the difference between liberals and conservatives. We do this not to bias the presentation; if anything our presentation of ideology overstates its impact.[10]

If our measure of ideology is accurate, then an ideology-based explanation of persuasion leads to the following predictions. Respondents are more likely to agree with the opinions of speakers who share their ideology than they are to agree with speakers who do not share their ideology. In Table 9.6, we evaluate this hypothesis while simultaneously reevaluating the hypothesis that as *Agrees* and/or *Knows* increases, so should the percentage of respondents who agree with the speaker's position.

The top of Table 9.6 shows the relationship between ideology, *Agrees, Knows,* and respondent support for prison spending for the subsample who heard that either speaker "supports" this spending. The bottom of the table shows the same relationship for the subsample who heard that either speaker "opposes" this spending. We sort the observations into *columns* based on their response to ideology questions. We sort the same observations into *rows* based on *Agrees* or *Knows*.

The ideology-based prediction is that conservatives should have been more likely than liberals to support prisons when Rush Limbaugh did and less likely to voice their support when Phil Donahue did. Our theory predicts that *as we move from Agrees = "all or most" to Agrees = "never" or from Knows = "a lot or some" to Knows = "a little or nothing,"* the propensity to support more prisons should *decrease.* The opposite predictions hold for the case where the speaker says "opposes."

---

[10]Specifically, the between-group (i.e., conservative versus liberal) effects are far greater in magnitude than the within-group effects (i.e., strong conservative versus weak conservative).

Table 9.6. *Percent reporting that stated issue is a good idea, separated by knows, agrees, and speaker ideology.*

Supports

Speaker:	Rush Limbaugh			Phil Donahue		
Respondent:	Cons.	Lib.	Ideology as predicted	Cons.	Lib.	Ideology as predicted
Agrees: all or most	78	40ᵃ	—	82	67ᵃ	—
Agrees: some	65	53	Yes	60	60	No
Agrees: never	33ᵃ	34	—	57	25ᵃ	—
Agrees as predicted	Yes	Yes		Yes	—	
Knows: a lot or some	74	59	Yes	66	59	Yes
Knows: a little or nothing	46	32	Yes	55	57	No
Knows as predicted	Yes	Yes		Yes	Yes	

Opposes

Speaker:	Rush Limbaugh			Phil Donahue		
Respondent:	Cons.	Lib.	Ideology as predicted	Cons.	Lib.	Ideology as predicted
Agrees: all or most	56	0ᵃ	—	50ᵃ	50	—
Agrees: some	69	53	No	64	53	No
Agrees: never	60ᵃ	65	—	80	60ᵃ	—
Agrees as predicted	Yes	Yes		Yes	Yes	
Knows: a lot or some	62	54	No	59	46	No
Knows: a little or nothing	72	56	No	78	69	No
Knows as predicted	Yes	Yes		Yes	Yes	

ᵃ These cell entries are based on fewer than ten observations and are not factored into the prediction evaluation.

The ideology-based prediction *is true in only three of the twelve cases* for which there were at least ten respondents in each category. By contrast, our theory's prediction *is true in all fifteen cases.* Table 9.6 confirms our expectations that it is possible for people to be persuaded by others with ideological leanings different from their own.

Of course, this table does not show that ideology is irrelevant in the context of the formation of opinions. In fact, it is quite clear that all else constant, conservative respondents were more likely to support prison spending. What this table does suggest, however, is that claims such as "*Agrees* and *Knows* are mere restatements of the effect of ideology" are plainly false. Even within the subset of conservative respondents and the subset of liberal respondents, perceived speaker knowledge and trust-worthiness were major determinants of how people chose whom to believe.[11]

CONCLUSION

To summarize, we find that in a survey experiment where *Agrees* and *Knows* were, at best, crude measures of perceived speaker knowledge and trustworthiness, respectively, they were also strong and consistent predictors of the extent to which respondent attitudes matched speaker statements. We interpret these findings to provide compelling support for our claim that people are selective about whom they choose to believe. As did the principal in our theory of persuasion, our respondents showed a tendency to follow the advice of speakers whom they perceived to be both knowledgeable and trustworthy and to ignore the advice of speakers who lacked these characteristics.

[11]We have run an equivalent analysis for the effect of partisanship. We do not include it here because the partisanship explanation fares nowhere near as well as ideology when it is compared with *Agrees* and *Knows*.

PART III

Implications for Institutional Design

10

The Institutions of Knowledge

Democracy is rule by the people. In all modern democracies the people elect or appoint legislative assemblies, executives, commissions, judges, and juries to make decisions on their behalf. These elections and appointments constitute a delegation of the people's sovereign authority to rule.

Institutions define and shape these delegations. Constitutions, statutes, administrative rules and procedure, court decisions, norms, practices, and customs define these delegations and shape the incentives of democratic principals and agents alike.[1]

But it is not enough, for the success of democratic delegations, that institutions alter the incentives of democratic agents. Rather, it is also necessary that the incentive-altering effects of institutions make agents and speakers trustworthy *and* that democratic principals perceive institutions to have this effect. That is, the incentive effects of democratic institutions must be salutary (i.e., offer agents and speakers an incentive to be trustworthy) and must be believed widely to have this effect. Democratic institutions can, in this way, establish the conditions for persuasion, enlightenment, and reasoned choice. Consequently, political institutions can help to resolve the democratic dilemma.

In this chapter, we examine some of the central institutions of modern democracy and investigate the incentives they create. Our purpose is to demonstrate that electoral, legislative, bureaucratic, and judicial institutions can also be the insitutions of knowledge. To do this, we examine

[1]The study of institutions and their incentive-altering effects has a long and storied tradition, dating to Montesquieu (1748), Madison (1788), and Smith (1776). Modern scholars have further argued that institutions serve to solve various collective dilemmas, such as policy instability, coordination, and the Prisoners' Dilemma (see, for example, Miller 1992, North 1990, Ostrom 1990, Shepsle 1979, Shepsle and Weingast 1981, Weingast and Marshall 1988). Others have argued that institutions mitigate certain management problems (see, for example, Alchian and Demsetz 1972, Baron 1992, Demski and Sappington 1989, Myerson 1989, Tirole 1988).

the incentive effects of democratic institutions to ascertain when they promote the conditions for enlightenment and reasoned choice.

ELECTORAL INSTITUTIONS

Of democracy's delegations, the one that is most often indicated as a failure is the delegation from the people to their elected representatives. It seems to many that reasoned choice is beyond the capability of the vast majority of the democratic citizenry. While it is indisputable that voters know little of the details of politics and government, this fact alone does not imply that they are incapable of reasoned choices. Instead, we need to ascertain if there are ready substitutes for the knowledge voters lack.

In this section, we address the question "Do electoral institutions help voters to acquire useful substitutes for the knowledge they lack?" To do this, we identify institutions that help voters use the substitutes that are available to them. Specifically, we describe institutions that clarify the interests of political speakers, that induce observable and costly effort by political speakers, and that create the threat of verification.

Clarifying Interests

For many of the issues they face, voters have access to simple cues that help guide their decisions. During election campaigns, numerous speakers – from political parties and candidates to interest groups, media organizations, friends, and family – offer advice to voters about how they should cast their ballots. A problem arises, however, in the fact that no person can attend to all available cues. Voters *must choose* to treat different cues differently. As a consequence, they follow some cues and reject or ignore the rest.

How voters make these choices is inherent in the varying value and usage of party cues. Party identification is a well-known and widely used voter cue (see, for example, Downs 1957; Campbell et al. 1960; Nie, Verba, and Petrocik 1976; Fiorina 1981; Enelow and Hinich 1984; Popkin 1991; Sniderman, Brody, and Tetlock 1991). It is, however, not an equally valuable cue for all voters or in all situations. Party identification is a useful cue only if it conveys information about knowledge and trust. If voters are to be influenced by partisan appeals, then they must perceive speakers who share their party identification to be knowledgeable. They must also have some basis for trusting these speakers. This basis for trust can be forged from the perception of either common interests with speakers from their own party or from the presence of some external force that makes these speakers trustworthy.

The Institutions of Knowledge

It follows that electoral institutions which affect voters' perceptions can also affect the value of the party cue and thus the propensity with which voters will use party cues as substitutes for the detailed information they lack. As an example, some electoral systems, such as those that use single-member plurality districts, affect voters' perceptions by inducing candidates for office to act in predicable ways. Single-member plurality districts favor large parties by rewarding them with a disproportionately large share of legislative seats (Rae 1971, Lijphart 1994). As a result, these systems tend to support only two large parties (Cox 1997, Duverger 1954), and thus candidates have an incentive to coordinate their policy positions with those of other members of these two parties. By so doing, they can establish a reliable party brand name that provides a useful cue to voters about candidates' policy positions. This, in turn, can affect voter perceptions by clarifying a candidate's interests.[2]

Closed-list proportional representation systems offer similar incentives to politicians. In these systems, voters cast ballots for parties and not for individual candidates. Additionally, in many countries, only parties whose vote totals surpass some legal threshold (e.g., 5 percent) are eligible to earn seats. Recognizing this reward structure, parties work to make their "brand names" effective by linking policy positions and outcomes to the party (Cox 1997). Not surprisingly, party is the only widely used voting cue in closed-list proportional representation systems.

What is true for political parties is often true for interest groups as well, especially broadly based "peak associations." If these groups want to be influential, then they have an incentive to take coherent and reliable policy positions on issues important to their members. These groups also have an incentive to create reliable brand names that voters can use as a cue in determining who is knowledgeable and trustworthy (see Lupia 1994, Page and Shapiro 1992).

Of course, merely forming a political party or an interest group does not assure persuasive power. People have an incentive to attend to or use these judgmental shortcuts only if they believe that doing so will help them avoid costly mistakes. Obscure groups, or groups for whom institutions do not provide sufficient incentives for the creation of a perception of reliability, will be ignored. Moreover, if electoral institutions change in ways that make existing parties or groups take inconsistent or incoherent positions, then such changes can weaken the value of the cues that these groups provide. Under these circumstances, political candi-

---

[2]Clarifying interests is perhaps the most important effect here, but if voters understand that candidates are supervised by their party's leadership or co-partisans, then they understand that statements made by a candidate may be subject to verification or a penalty for lying. This too can forge the basis for trust between voters and candidates.

dates will find it increasingly difficult to persuade voters that the policies they advocate are the better course for society, and that they deserve election.

The general lesson to be drawn here is that *there are regular, cognitively driven, institutionally influenced reasons that any cue, including those based on party, ideology, gender, or race, is effective.* These cues are effective only when voters perceive them to be better indicators of a candidate's or speaker's knowledge and trust than other available cues.[3] It follows that, to understand why people cast the votes they do, we must understand how they choose among the cues available to them and how institutions affect these choices.[4]

Verification

Competition between candidates for election, between news organizations, between interest groups, and among citizens eager to affect the policy process *can* generate the conditions for enlightenment by establishing the context for verification. Electoral institutions promote competition in a variety of ways.[5] Some governments, for example, provide equal television time to all political parties, and others limit the amount candidates or parties can advertise (see, for example, Dalton, 1989: 249). There is also important variance in the extent to which electoral institutions erect barriers to entry for people, groups, and parties who want to compete for office. For example, qualification for the ballot in many countries requires only a nominal filing fee or the collection of a minimal number of signatures. Other governments go further and even reimburse campaign expenses.[6]

This competition is enhanced by the establishment of a free press. The existence of a free press increases the likelihood that campaign statements will be verified. While competition can create multiple potential verifiers, freedom of the press provides these verifiers with an avenue whereby they

---

[3]If this were not true, then a cue's effectiveness would not vary across issues or across voters. But if there are two things that all of us know, they are that we use different cues to make different decisions and that we have the freedom to choose which cues to use.

[4]For example, we need to determine why voters use some cues such as media endorsements in some elections and use different cues such as interest group endorsements in different elections.

[5]Denzau, Riker, and Shepsle (1985) argue that because of electoral considerations, presidents are induced to reveal truthfully their preferences when making proposals to Congress.

[6]In Germany, for example, the "parties receive a subsidy for campaign expenses according to the number of votes they receive" (Dalton 1989: 280). Also see Katz and Mair (1995) for a general discussion.

can provide public verification of political statements. This creates the opportunity for a competition of ideas and further increases the likelihood of verification. By facilitating competition, these institutional features can increase the threat of verification and can thus increase the likelihood that voters will be capable of reasoned choice.

Costly Effort

Many of the costs of communicating campaign messages to voters can be observed or surmised. Campaign finance disclosure laws, for example, require that campaign committees and lobbyists publicly identify all significant contributors and the amount contributed by each.[7] This enables voters to identify what groups or individuals support a given candidate or initiative and how much a change in the status quo policy is worth to them. Thus, if people are reasonably happy with the status quo and would therefore like to see only a small change in policy, and if they observe the sponsor of a ballot initiative spending several million dollars to affect the election, then, without any further information, they can infer that the initiative proposes a very large change in the status quo and that they should vote against it.[8]

Spending by candidates can have the same effect. In a primary election, for example, where party cannot serve as a cue, voters can observe how much each candidate spends in order to gauge the differences between them. If a challenger, in this case, mounts a very expensive campaign against an incumbent, voters can infer, again without any other information, that many knowledgeable contributors believed that there are substantial personal and policy differences between the challenger and the incumbent.[9] The idea here is that if a voter observes a knowledgeable person giving up something of value for the purpose of obtaining a particular outcome, then the voter can use this observation to draw an inference about how he or she should vote.

When voters use a candidate's costly effort to gauge the potential differences between the candidate and his or her opponent, however, they must be sure that the costs are not subsidized or limited. That is, if the

[7]Examples of financial disclosure laws include the Federal Elections Campaign Act of 1974 and the California Political Reform Act of 1974. While *Buckley v. Valeo* struck down many of the provisions of the California Political Reform Act, including those concerning expenditure limits and source restrictions, the extensive public disclosure rules were left untouched.

[8]A potential problem with financial disclosure laws concerns the difficulty in identifying contributors who attempt to hide their identity by using vague pseudonyms or acronyms.

[9]Because the incumbent has access to a variety of free resources, gauging the incumbent's costly effort is much more difficult (see Jacobson 1990).

state pays all campaign expenses, then it may be misleading to distinguish candidates based on the costs of their efforts. Furthermore, if there are strict spending limits, the level of costs may not reflect the extent of the differences between two candidates or issues. U.S. presidential elections offer public subsidization and limited spending, and therefore, costly effort is not as useful a cue as it would be otherwise.

LEGISLATIVE INSTITUTIONS

In voting on legislative proposals, legislators have access to myriad information sources. They can call on their colleagues, on officials in the executive branch, and on their staff for expert testimony. In addition, legislative committees often can subpoena experts from industry, universities, and social groups. While testimony given at legislative hearings is subject to penalties for lying (i.e., perjury), the basic problem for legislators will be to sort trustworthy from nontrustworthy advisors. We turn now to a discussion of the mechanisms by which legislators sort advice.[10]

Common Interests

Legislators spend a substantial amount of time and energy identifying the people and groups they can trust (Fenno 1973, 1978; Kingdon 1977). For example, when a new party or coalition takes control of government, one of its most important tasks is to appoint cabinet ministers (see Laver and Shepsle 1994). Similarly, at the beginning of each Congress, the election of leaders and the appointment of members to committees are two of the most important business items. Members of Congress place great importance on screening those who control the House's agenda (Fenno 1973; Krehbiel 1991; Polsby 1968; Polsby, Gallaher, and Rundquist 1969; Rohde and Shepsle 1973; Shepsle 1978; Smith and Deering 1990) and seek to align the interests of committees and leaders to the broader interests of the majority party (Cox and McCubbins 1993, Kiewiet and McCubbins 1991).

Further, on many issues for which they lack expertise legislators turn to like-minded colleagues or their party whips for advice. For example, on various issues for which they lack expertise, members of Congress identify knowledgeable and like-minded members whose endorsements

---

[10]For general discussions of legislative rules and their effect on legislative behavior and decisions, see, for example, Cox and McCubbins (1993), Huber (1992), Kiewiet and McCubbins (1991), Krehbiel (1991), Rohde (1991), Shepsle and Weingast (1987), Stewart (1989), Tsebelis (1990), Weingast (1979), and Weingast and Marshall (1988).

and actions they can follow (Kingdon 1973; Jackson 1974; Matthews and Stimson 1970, 1975; McConachie 1898).

Of course, in some instances, the interests of the membership of a committee are sufficiently different from the interests of the rest of the majority party (e.g., the members of the U.S. House Agriculture Committee are often seen to be more sympathetic to farm and rural interests than are other members; see Cox and McCubbins 1993). Absent external forces, we would not expect endorsements from these committees to be persuasive (as Krehbiel 1991 has argued). Similarly, differences between party leaders and backbenchers may render leadership stands unpersuasive (as happened on the issue of banking regulation and taxes within Japan's ruling Liberal Democratic Party; see Rosenbluth 1989). In cases where common interests are absent, persuasion and trust require external forces. In what follows, we describe examples of such forces.

Penalties for Lying

Legislators use penalties for lying to create a basis for trust in contexts where trust would otherwise be absent. For instance, trustworthiness and, implicitly, penalties for breaking a trust are the basis of many behavioral norms in the U.S. Congress (Fenno 1973). Often, penalties for breaking a trust are enforced not by the chamber or the membership but by party leaders (Cox and McCubbins 1994, Schickler and Rich 1997). In parliamentary democracies, where parties tend to have more control over their members' electoral prospects than is true in the United States, penalties for lying can be quite severe, including loss of office and expulsion from the party. The threat of sanction is also thought to hold lobbyists in line (Evans 1991a, 1991b; Hall and Wayman 1990; Herzberg and Unruh 1970; Wright 1990).[11]

Of course, if a penalty for lying or the likelihood of its enforcement is small, then the penalty will dissuade few liars. As a consequence, the penalty may be insufficient to generate trust. For example, scientists' opinions, expert testimony, and remarks made during open floor time by representatives while the House is in recess are not greatly affected by penalties for lying. This may be one reason why legislators frequently ignore this type of testimony.

Verification

Political philosophers and institutional designers alike have recognized the benefits of competition among information providers (e.g., Machiavelli,

[11]There are, of course, legal sanctions for perjury in giving testimony before legislative hearings.

Montesquieu, Madison in *The Federalists*).[12] The constitutional structure of government determines the number and quality of competing information sources available to legislators. In legislatures that are open to the opposition, to the media, and to interest groups, for example, verification becomes much more likely than when it is closed. Consequently, there is more competition in some countries than others, and there is therefore a higher likelihood that statements made by legislative proponents and opponents will be verified.

The design of legislative structure and process is the key to creating competition between information providers. As we have argued elsewhere, legislative procedure is an example (Lupia and McCubbins 1994c). Take, for example, the legislative process in the U.S. House of Representatives wherein a bill must survive many steps before it can be sent to the Senate and the president and be implemented as a new policy.[13] These steps are sketched in Figure 10.1.

Figure 10.1 depicts two important facts about the legislative process. First, the process by which bills are passed sets up a dual system of agenda control wherein control over the agenda is shared by both committees and party leaders.[14] Furthermore, there are numerous points in the legislative process where backbenchers can check the actions of the majority party leadership. Prominent among these is the control over the agenda exercised by congressional committees. These many steps establish a system of checks and balances whereby the ambitions of the majority party leadership are pitted against the ambitions of the party's backbenchers. The House legislative process, thus, makes it likely that statements made by both the House leadership and House committees will be verified. Figure 10.1 highlights the positions in the legislative process that are controlled by the majority party leadership, such as the speakership or the Steering and Policy Committee (Cox and McCubbins 1993, Kiewiet and McCubbins 1991), as contrasted to the positions that are responsive to the party's backbenchers, such as committees and subcommittees.

Figure 10.1 also depicts a second way in which the legislative process pits ambition against ambition. As the figure shows, a bill must be introduced, referred to a committee, and then to a subcommittee. From there, important measures also go through the Rules Committee before being debated and voted on the House floor. Once enacted, new legislation is then subject to the budget and reconciliation process, and the appropriations process, each with its own sets of committees, and each with its

---

[12]Also see Cameron and Jung (1992) and Milgrom and Roberts (1986).

[13]Tsebelis (1995) describes similar procedure for parliamentary systems.

[14]Recognition of a dual system of agenda control brings together Weingast and Marshall's (1988) theory of the industrial organization of Congress with Cox and McCubbins's (1993) theory of party government.

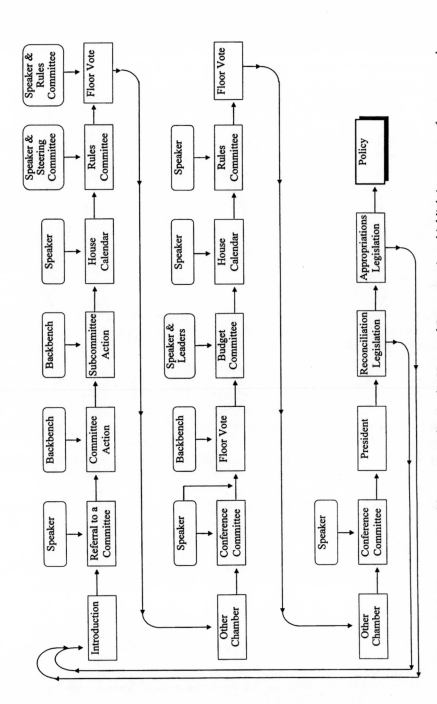

Figure 10.1. How a proposal becomes a policy in the House of Representatives, highlighting aspects of party control.

own rules and procedure, before the policy enacted by the legislation can be implemented. Through this process, substantive policymaking committees (such as the aforementioned Agriculture Committee) are checked by the Appropriations Committee, the Rules Committee, and the Budget Committee (which are "control" committees, designed and appointed for this purpose; see Cox and McCubbins 1993). In this way, members of various committees, each with expertise on the important legislation before the House, can verify the statements and claims made by others in the legislative process. To the extent that the ambitions of these various actors are adversarial, or to the extent that other institutional features make one or more of these actors trustworthy, the system of checks and balances described in Figure 10.1 will generate the context for verification.

A similar system of checks and balances, in this case between backbenchers and frontbenchers, existed for most of the postwar period in Japan. During the period it controlled government, the Liberal Democratic Party (LDP) established its own system of committees, the Policy Affairs Research Council (*Seimu Chosakai* or PARC; see Ramseyer and Rosenbluth 1993). These committees reviewed government policy proposals before they were submitted to the Diet and thus provided backbenchers with information to parry the official reports of the cabinet and the corresponding Diet committees. "Coordinating Councils" (*shingikai*) also put interest group representatives at the policymaking table with bureaucrats and scholars. Any of these groups was thereby privy to information that might otherwise be hidden from backbenchers. In each instance, the members of these committees and councils could act to verify the statements of others in the policymaking process.[15]

While the legislative procedure in the British Parliament is similar, its system of checks and balances is not as robust as in the United States and Japan. The Parliament, for example, has no intraparty equivalents to the PARC committees or coordinating councils. Even the legislative committees of Parliament are impermanent structures, subject to the whims of the majority party leadership. Thus, in terms of numbers of potential verifiers, it seems that U.S. legislators are best off among our three examples, while British backbenchers are worst off.

Costly Effort

Legislative rules, procedures, and practices often impose costs on the actions of legislators, thereby establishing the conditions for enlighten-

---

[15]The advent of coalition government in Japan in 1993 implies competition within the cabinet, as the parties in the coalition seek advantage, and therefore might lead to increased prospects for verification.

ment and reasoned choice. For instance, drafting legislative proposals, holding hearings and investigations, writing reports, striking deals, and whipping up support for legislation all require the expenditure of valuable resources (e.g., time, effort, and money).

Furthermore, in many countries, obtaining funding for a new program requires more work than does the acquisition of additional funding for existing programs (e.g., separate authorizing legislation makes new programs eligible for consideration in the budget process; see McCubbins and Noble 1995a,b). In the United States, for example, large changes in the spending appropriated for a program require either a written explanation for the change or new legislation that changes the program's authority (Kiewiet and McCubbins 1991). Thus, the creation of new budget authority or substantial changes in budget authority require the expenditure of costly effort on the part of the proponents of these budget shifts. Again, without any other information, legislators can infer that the proposals represent a large change in policy. By observing the effort involved in making these proposals, legislators can infer something about the magnitude of the change being proposed. This inference alone may be sufficient to enable legislators to make reasoned choices about accepting or rejecting the proposals.

BUREAUCRATIC INSTITUTIONS

Legislators often delegate the job of policy development to bureaucrats, presidents, and government ministers. The potential advantage of this type of delegation is that bureaucrats may have expertise that legislators lack. As a result, legislators may be able to rely on the bureaucracy to formulate policies that they themselves would have formulated if they had spent the time and resources necessary to acquire the bureaucracy's level of expertise. The potential drawback of delegation is that a bureaucrat who possesses both expertise and policymaking authority can also take actions that make legislators worse off than if they had never delegated (Niskanen 1971, Wildavsky 1974). In this case, the act of delegation is equivalent to abdication, wherein the will of the people, as expressed by their choice of elected representatives, neither constrains nor motivates the formulation of public policy (Lowi 1979, Sundquist 1981). The legislator's dilemma concerns how to realize the potential benefits of delegation without abdicating control over policy (Calvert, Moran, and Weingast 1987; Calvert, McCubbins, and Weingast 1989; Harris 1964; Kiewiet and McCubbins 1991; McCubbins and Schwartz 1984; Wilmerding 1943). In this section, we describe institutions that facilitate successful delegation by legislators to the bureaucracy.

Implications for Institutional Design

Clarifying Interests

Legislators appoint agents to serve in the bureaucracy. This ability gives legislators considerable latitude in determining (*ex ante*) their agents' interests. All else constant, legislators have an incentive to appoint agents whose interests are common to their own (i.e., doing so leads to satisfaction of the *Incentive Condition* that we defined in Chapter 5). By appointing these agents, legislators stack the deck in favor of successful delegation before delegation begins (McCubbins 1985; McCubbins, Noll, and Weingast 1987, 1989 – see also Cornell, Noll, and Weingast 1976; Ferejohn and Shipan 1990; Noll 1971a, 1987; Noll and Owen 1983; Spiller 1990; Spiller and Ferejohn 1992).

Of course, screening appointments is fraught with difficulty (Spence 1974). To circumvent these difficulties, legislators can use the structure and process of bureaucratic decision making to affect the bureaucracy's incentives. In so doing, legislators can affect the conditions for persuasion, enlightenment, and reasoned choice by structuring the agency so that it has common interests with the legislative coalition that oversees it.

To see this, consider that an agency's incentives are determined by three factors. First are the interests of the personnel apppointed to the agency. Second are the rules by which agency personnel make decisions (e.g., whose vote counts and how votes are aggregated). Third is the political environment in which the agency personnel make decisions. Structure and process can be used to affect the latter two factors.[16]

The U.S. National Environment Policy Act (NEPA) of 1969 provides an example of how a legislature can structure the rules of decision making so as to ensure that an agency's interests align with the politically relevant constituency. In the 1960s, environmental and conservation groups in the United States became substantially better organized and more relevant politically. Through NEPA, Congress imposed new procedures that required all agencies to file environmental impact statements on proposed projects. This change forced agencies to assess the environmental costs of their proposed activities. NEPA gave environmental actors a new, effective avenue of participation in agency decisions and enabled participation at a much earlier junction than had previously been possible. The requirements of the act also provided environmental groups with an increased ability to press suits against federal agencies. These changes stopped, delayed, or altered numerous federal projects, from dams to nuclear power plants to highways.

More generally, in all agency decisions, proof must be offered to support a proposal. The establishment of the burden of proof perhaps

---

[16]Regarding the effects of structure and process on bureaucratic agent selection in other countries, see Spiller and Urbiztondo (1994).

best illustrates how legislatures can structure bureaucratic incentives. The burden of proof affects agency decisions most apparently when there is great uncertainty. In such a circumstance, proving anything – either that a regulation is needed to solve a problem, or that it is unnecessary – can be difficult, if not impossible. Hence, assigning either advocates or opponents of regulation a rigorous burden of proof essentially guarantees that they cannot obtain their preferred policy outcome.

For example, the U.S. Federal Food, Drug and Cosmetics Act of 1938, as amended, requires that before a pharmaceutical company can market a new drug, it must first prove that the drug is both safe and efficacious. By contrast, with the Toxic Substances Control Act (TSCA) of 1976 Congress required that the Environmental Protection Agency (EPA), before regulating a new chemical, prove that the chemical is hazardous to human health or the environment. The reversionary outcome is that new chemicals are allowed to be marketed. The results of the differences in the burden of proof are stark: Few new drugs are marketed in the United States, while the EPA has managed to regulate none of the 50,000 chemicals in commerce under these provisions in the Toxic Substances Control Act.

Changing the rules that govern decision making alters the agency's incentives and the outcomes of policymaking as well. Take, for example, the Civil Aeronautics Act of 1938. The Act originally stacked the deck in favor of economic development for existing airlines by placing the burden of proof on prospective entrants for existing air routes. Specifically, prospective entrants had to prove that their entry into a market would not harm the economic well-being of extant carriers. The Civil Aeronautics Board, created by the Act, was renowned for its favoritism toward existing air carriers. At the end of the 1970s, the Kennedy amendments shifted the burden of proof by requiring the existing carriers to prove that the increased competition would be harmful to social welfare. Thus, the burden of proof was no longer placed upon prospective entrants, making their entry far more tractable. Moreover, the newly established burden of proof under the Kennedy amendments tied the hands of existing airlines who sought to sustain their oligopoly, previously protected under federal regulations.

Ultimately, the point of this type of procedural deck stacking is not to preselect policy but rather to cope with uncertainty about the most desirable policy action by making certain that the winners in the political battle over the underlying legislation will also be the winners in the process of implementing the program. By enfranchising interests that are represented in the legislative majority, a legislature need not closely supervise the agency to ensure that it serves the legislature's interests but can allow an agency to operate on "autopilot" (McCubbins, Noll, and

217

Implications for Institutional Design

Weingast 1987: 271). Agencies themselves will follow the same logic in their internal structure (Ferejohn 1987, Wood 1988). Likewise, in political systems with a separately elected executive, the executive will also attempt to mirror the political and electoral forces that he or she faces in the orders and rules imposed on the bureaucracy (Eskridge and Ferejohn 1992, Macey 1992, Moe 1990).[17] The result is, again, that the purposes of an administrative agency are structured to be common to the legislative coalition that created it.

Legislatures can further limit the potential mischief of agency agenda control by carefully setting the reversionary policy in the enabling statute that established the agency. For example, consider the creation of entitlement spending specified by statute, when an agency has no discretion in how or to whom it allocates funds. Another example is seen in the widespread use of "sunset" provisions, whereby an agency's legal authority expires unless the legislature passes a new law to renew the agency's mandate.

Structure and process can thus be used to structure an agency's incentives so that the entity created has common interests with the legislators who created it. In this way, legislators can come to trust statements made by agency personnel, as they operate under the structure and process that defines the agency's decision rules.

Structure and process also can be used to affect an agency's decision-making environment. One way to do this is to assign agenda control to multiple agencies. In this case, no single agency has the ability to establish its own agenda in a particular policy arena. Moreover, agencies with overlapping jurisdictions will be direct competitors for budgets and statutory authority, which further increases their incentive to please political leaders.

This kind of overlapping jurisdictional authority is common in parliamentary systems. For example, in Japan the authority to set electricity prices is vested in a working group composed of representatives from several ministries (Ramseyer and Rosenbluth 1993: 46–58; on German administrative procedure, see Rose-Ackerman 1994; in general, see Weaver and Rockman 1993). The U.S. Congress has also pursued this

[17]The courts also can play a role in the political control of the bureaucracy. Administrative procedures can affect an agency's policy agenda only if they are enforced, and their enforcement can be delegated by the legislature to the courts, in which case procedure can have an effect with minimal effort required on the part of politicians (McCubbins, Noll, and Weingast 1987; Shapiro 1986). For supervision by the courts to serve this function, judicial remedy must be highly likely when the agency violates its rules. If so, the courts, and the constituents who bring suit, guarantee compliance with procedural constraints, which in turn guarantees that the agency choice will mirror political preferences without any need for political oversight (McCubbins and Schwartz 1984).

strategy. In regulating workplace safety, the National Institute for Occupational Safety and Health (NIOSH) in the Department of Commerce must first identify a health or safety hazard. Only then can the agency charged with regulating workplace safety, the Occupational Safety and Health Administration (OSHA) in the Department of Labor, promulgate a rule regulating the identified problem.

Finally, legislatures also possess numerous other *ex post* mechanisms with which to influence bureaucratic behavior. These mechanisms add up to what Weingast (1984) refers to as "the big club behind the door" (see also Fiorina 1977). In discussing the Congress, Weingast (1984: 155–6) notes, "Ex post sanctions . . . create ex ante incentives for bureaucrats to serve congressmen." That is, Congress's big stick engenders the well-known "law of anticipated reactions." By structuring an agency's incentives in this way, legislators can shape an agency's incentives so that the agency's interests are compatible with the interests of the coalition that created it. Agency statements, then, can be more persuasive, more reliable, and more enlightening.

Verification

Agency statements and actions face the threat of verification from legislative oversight. McCubbins and Schwartz (1984) distinguish two ways that the legislature oversees the bureaucracy. Police patrol oversight is centralized, active, and direct; the legislature examines a sample of executive agency activities, with the aim of detecting and remedying any violations of legislative goals and, by its surveillance, discouraging such violations. In contrast, fire alarm oversight is less centralized and involves less active and direct intervention. Instead of examining a sample of administrative decisions, the legislature establishes a system of rules, procedures, and informal practices that enable individual citizens and organized interest groups to examine administrative decisions, to charge executive agencies with violating legislative goals, and to seek remedies from agencies, courts, and the legislature itself. Fire alarms, in essence, act to verify bureaucratic statements and actions.

Fire alarm oversight has several characteristics that are valuable to political leaders. To begin with, leaders do not have to spend a great deal of time looking for trouble. Waiting for trouble to be brought to their attention assures that if there is trouble, it is of a type that is important to constituents. In addition, responding to the complaints of constituents allows political leaders to advertise, claim credit for fixing the problem, and take popular issue-specific positions (Fiorina 1977). In contrast, trouble discovered by actively patrolling might not concern any constituents at all and thus yields no electoral benefit for members. Thus, political leaders are likely to prefer the low-risk, high-reward strategy of fire alarm oversight to the more risky and potentially costly police patrol system. Moreover, a predominantly fire alarm oversight policy is likely to be more effective in securing compliance with legislative goals, for it brings within it targeted sanctions and rewards.[18]

While fire alarm oversight may be the preferred oversight policy, the use of fire alarm oversight is problematic. On each issue that requires oversight, there is likely to be a plethora of fire alarms. The problem is sorting credible from noncredible fire alarms (Lupia and McCubbins 1994b).

The creation of credible (i.e., knowledgeable and trusted) fire alarms involves establishing appropriate procedures for managing the collection and dissemination of information about an agency's activities (Banks and Weingast 1992; McCubbins, Noll, and Weingast 1987, 1989). These rules ensure that fire alarms are, in fact, knowledgeable with respect to agency proceedings. The U.S. Administrative Procedure Act of 1946 (APA) as amended and as interpreted by the courts, for example, establishes several provisions that open up agency proceedings and allow groups access to an agency's agenda. First, an agency cannot announce a new policy without warning but must instead give "notice" that it will consider an issue and do so without prejudice or bias in favor of any particular action. Second, agencies must solicit "comments" and allow all interested parties to communicate their views. Third, agencies must allow "participation" in the decision-making process, with the extent often mandated by the organic statute creating the agency as well as by the courts (McCubbins and Page 1986). If hearings are held, parties may be allowed to bring forth testimony and evidence and often to cross-examine other witnesses. Fourth, agencies must deal explicitly with the evidence presented to them and provide a rationalizable link between the evidence and their decisions. Fifth, agencies must "make available" a record of the final vote of each member in every proceeding. Numerous countries have adopted measures similar to the U.S. APA in order to achieve political control of the bureaucracy (Spiller 1996).

These requirements facilitate the creation of credible fire alarms in at least three ways. First, they ensure that agencies cannot secretly conspire to make public policy. Rather, the agency must announce its intentions to consider an issue well in advance of any decision. Second, agencies must solicit valuable political information (i.e., they must acquire knowledge useful to their political overseers). The notice and comment provisions assure that the agency learns the identity of the relevant political

---

[18]Recent surveys have, in fact, shown that fire alarm oversight is the modal type of congressional oversight (Aberbach 1990, Ogul and Rockman 1990). Nevertheless, police patrol oversight is more comprehensive and effective than is commonly believed.

interests to the decision and something about the political costs and benefits associated with various actions. That participation is not universal (and may even be stacked) should not entail political costs. Diffuse groups that do not participate, even when their interests are at stake, are much less likely to become an electoral force in comparison with those that do participate. Third, the entire proceeding is public, and rules against *ex parte* contact protect against secret deals. The effect is that numerous groups are able to give and acquire knowledge regarding an agency's actions.

Adversarial competition among fire alarms also serves to establish their credibility (Lupia and McCubbins 1994b). Well-heeled interest groups seem to have substantial "access" in Washington. They contribute heavily to congressional reelection campaigns, and, in turn, members of Congress find time in their hectic schedules to listen to what these groups have to say. But a member's time is finite – committee meetings, floor debates, and trips back home to shake hands and kiss babies clutter their schedules, leaving only narrow windows of opportunity for interest groups. Because there are literally thousands of interest groups lobbying in Congress for every conceivable cause, the competition among interest groups is likely to be fierce. It follows (as Bauer, Pool, and Dexter 1963 found) that the wise interest group is one that guards its access jealously by providing legislators with accurate, succinct information on its favored issues, because once a member of Congress's trust has been broken by an overzealous lobbying effort, there may be little opportunity to win it back. Interest groups, in other words, may well compete to play the role of verifier for legislators. For verification to be effective, only some of these groups, the verifiers, must satisfy the conditions for persuasion and enlightenment.

Legislators also have constructed adversarial fire alarm systems and "verifier" agencies to monitor the actions of other actors. The most famous is the Office of Management and Budget (OMB). This office, created in the 1921 Budget and Accounting Act, helps the president compile and submit an executive budget. The OMB and the president have authorization to propose legislative changes directly to Congress as long as they can justify in detail their proposed changes. The Budget Act also created the General Accounting Office (GAO), a special agent of Congress (not a part of the executive branch). The GAO acts as a sort of trustee for legislators. It is both Congress's auditor and accountant (examining agency's books at the end of the fiscal year) and comptroller (checking the flow of funds to agencies throughout the year against what has been authorized and appropriated by law). In addition, the GAO performs special investigations of agency policy performance under standing authority and by special request of individual members of Congress. Taken together, the structure and process of administrative decision making ensure that knowledgeable and trustworthy groups act to verify bureaucratic statements and actions.

Costly Effort

Consider, next, the issue of cost. All agency actions require the use of scarce resources – that is, the bearing of some cost. Again, legislators may be able to infer much about the substance of agency proposals by observing these costs. Every agency has limited resources in terms of both budget and staffing; hence, bureaucrats must make choices as to how they will spend these resources. It follows that when bureaucrats choose any particular action, they send a signal that they believe that the benefits of taking that action outweight the costs.

Agency actions necessarily fall into one of two categories: (1) general rule making or statement of policy and (2) applications of general rules and policies to specific cases or situations. The U.S. Congress has imposed costs on agencies to taking actions of either sort (see Bonfield and Asimow 1989). The broadest imposition of these legislative-sponsored costs arises from the U.S. Administrative Procedure Act of 1946 (APA). The APA established general criteria that administrative agencies must satisfy when creating new policies or writing rules of general applicability. Agencies must give public notice announcing their intentions to make policy of a specific sort. They then must solicit comments from interested groups and individuals who wish to express their views on the proposed content of a new policy. After drafting a proposed rule, they must expose that draft to public criticism and, before implementing a new rule, must show evidence that they have considered public criticism and have not arbitrarily rejected it or arbitrarily inserted new provisions into the rule without first exposing them to public review. Each of these stages in the rule-making process consumes time and resources (at the very least, bureaucrats must maintain the paper trail). Beyond the provisions of the APA, Congress affects agency rule making with statutes authorizing regulatory activities and through administrative mandates (McCubbins, Noll, and Weingast 1987, 1989, 1994).

Congress also chooses the level of cost to impose on agencies by establishing the number and range of regulatory decisions subject to review by other agencies or courts. TSCA again provides an example of this sort of costly action. The act requires the EPA to regulate substances found toxic to human life; in pursuance of this goal, the EPA has to propose test rules for determining whether or not a substance is in fact toxic, mutagenic, or carcinogenic before it can then promulgate a rule for regulating the substance. Thus, if it wants to regulate a chemical, the EPA must undertake two costly actions: design a test rule and write implementation regulation. The chemical producers, on the other hand, need not prove that their new product is not toxic and therefore face very low costs in introducing a new chemical.

In sharp contrast to this process, the introduction of a new drug requires that the pharmaceutical company bear the cost of proving that a new product satisfies the safety requirements laid out by the Food and Drug Administration. Unlike the introduction of new chemicals, it is quite costly to introduce a new drug. These costs enable legislators and regulators to evaluate the potential change in the status quo that would result from the introduction of a new drug.

The definition of evidentiary standards in courts can often raise or lower the cost of agency action. Evidence law includes determining both the burden of producing evidence and the burden of persuasion (Bonfield and Asimow 1989: 574–575). The burden of proof determines who must present evidence (bear costs) in order to proceed with a regulatory action. The burden of persuasion describes the tests a party must meet in order to carry an issue. For example, some laws require that any new rule must pass a cost–benefit analysis before it can become practice. The Office of Management and Budget, for example, created the Office of Information and Regulatory Affairs (OIRA) under the Paperwork Reduction Act of 1980 to check the growth of federal paperwork demands on small businesses. President Ronald Reagan interpreted the Act as a mandate for cost–benefit analysis of major regulations when he issued Executive Order 12291 directing federal agencies to review their regulations and authorizing OIRA to monitor agency compliance with the order (the controversies raised by this executive order are discussed in Kiewiet and McCubbins 1991: 180–2).

LEGAL INSTITUTIONS

Trial procedure determines when and how litigants can introduce and challenge evidence, as well as when and how lawyers can make and refute arguments. We review some of these procedures, identifying some that can establish the conditions for enlightenment. The best-known example of these rules are the sanctions commonly imposed for perjury, which are the equivalent of penalties for lying. Demonstrating that such procedures exist is sufficient to demonstrate that judicial institutions can help relatively uninformed jurors make reasoned choices.

Knowledge

Prosecutors and defendants often rely on expert testimony for corroborative evidence. Rules of evidence govern what constitutes an "expert."

The California civil law code, for example, contains strict requirements for speakers by allowing testimony only from individuals with first-hand, personal knowledge or with special knowledge or experience.[19] Furthermore, when one side introduces scientific evidence, it must show that the research methods used to obtain the evidence are generally accepted by the relevant scientific community.[20] In addition, an opposing attorney can question any witness's recollection or perceptive ability.[21] In sum, the rules of evidence help to assure that the speakers on whom judges and jurors rely are, in fact, knowledgeable about the topic on which they are giving testimony.

Common Interests

In a criminal trial, jurors also know what outcomes the two competing sides want. The prosecution wants a conviction and the defense wants a dismissal or acquittal. Moreover, everybody knows that lawyers benefit from decisions that favor their clients. Thus, courtroom settings present an unusually clear window to speaker interests.

In a courtroom, some speaker interests are transparent. Police officers are presumed to be enforcing the law, not their own whims (although sometimes this becomes the central debate in a case); experts are often thought to be impartial, though paid experts are often suspect; friends, family, employees, ex-spouses, and victims tend to have obvious axes to grind. The bottom line is that the motives of many, though not all, witnesses can easily be surmised. Indeed, in cases where motives are not obvious, trial attorneys often spend considerable effort to point them out to jurors. With visible motives, jurors can make judgments about a witness's trustworthiness by making standard inferences about the witness's interests. Furthermore, the rules of evidence assure the dismissal of any witness who is shown to have poor character, a reputation for lying, or biases.[22]

Verification

The very heart of trial procedure provides the real threat of verification. Almost every statement that an interested party makes to a jury in a

---

[19]See the California civil law Ev. C § 702 and Ev. C § 801.
[20]See the following, from California civil law: *People v. Kelly* (1976) 17 C3d 24, 30–31, 130 CR 144, 148–49; and *People v. Leahy* (1974) 8 C4th 587, 604, 34 Cr2d 663, 673.
[21]See the California civil law Ev. C § 780.
[22]See the California civil law Ev. C § 780.

courtroom is subject to a challenge.[23] Moreover, if cross-examination reveals that a witness made false statements, then that witness is subject to penalties for perjury. Thus, it is reasonable for every person in the courtroom to base his or her beliefs about the truthfulness of every witness's statement on the fact that every witness faces both the threat of verification and real penalties for lying.

Common rules of evidence are entirely consistent with our model of how people learn. Evidence based on hearsay, for example, or any other type of evidence that is not subject to verification is inadmissible in a court of law.[24] Further, jurors know, or are told, what evidence is easy to verify and what evidence is costly to verify. Jurors often believe evidence that is easy to verify but is not challenged. However, jurors tend to discount evidence that opposing counsel does challenge (especially if counsel refutes it). A jury, further, is less likely to believe evidence that is difficult or impossible for opposing counsel to verify.

UNENLIGHTENING DEMOCRATIC INSTITUTIONS

We have thus far identified a series of institutions that facilitate successful delegation and reasoned choice by generating the conditions for enlightenment. We now turn our attention to institutions that have the opposite effect.

Nonpartisan elections seem to us a classic example of an institutional reform that hinders reasoned choice. In partisan elections, parties have incentives to develop policy brand names. In so doing, partisan elections create incentives for consistent behavior on the part of legislators and cues that can help voters make reasoned choices. In nonpartisan elections, this type of information transmission is disallowed. Without parties, there is less of an incentive for collective responsibility among legislators and no central partisan authority to hold individual legislators accountable (Cox and McCubbins 1993).

Term limits are another reform that seems likely to hinder reasoned choice. Some advocates of term limits claim that by removing long-term incumbents and increasing electoral competition, more responsive policy

---

[23]The California civil law code, for example, states that an opposing attorney may seek to impeach a witness by arguing that the facts (admitted evidence) are contrary to the witness's testimony or inconsistent with his or her prior statements (Ev. C § 780).

[24]Hearsay refers to any out-of-court statement offered as truth or fact. Hearsay is disallowed because of the inability to verify the veracity of such statements (i.e., cross-examination is impossible). A deposition, on the other hand, is admissible because the individual whose testimony the deposition is against must be present at or at least have been given notice of the deposition, thereby allowing for cross-examination (verification).

outcomes (i.e., more successful electoral delegations) will result.[25] In its simplest form, their argument consists of three premises and a conclusion. The first premise is that term limits remove long-term incumbents. The second premise is that removing long-term incumbents empowers potential challengers, thereby increasing electoral competition. The third premise is that increasing electoral competition will lead to more responsive policy outcomes. The argument concludes that term limits lead to more responsive policy outcomes.

If we give proponents of term limits the benefit of the doubt and assume that their first two premises are correct, must we conclude, as they do, that term limits will lead to more responsive policy outcomes? Using insights about the dynamics of persuasion similar to our own, Gerber and Lupia (1996) find that term limits need not spawn responsive legislation or political competition. That is, they show that the introduction of new candidates for office into a race facilitates neither persuasion nor enlightenment. Therefore, Gerber and Lupia show that term limits are neither a necessary nor a sufficient condition for successful electoral delegation. For example, if a potential challenger is not sufficiently persuasive to influence voter behavior, then increasing competition by adding (empowering) this challenger (i.e., term limits) cannot affect the incentives of other candidates and as a result may have no effect on whether any candidate satisfies the incentive condition.

In addition to being neither necessary nor sufficient for more enlightened electoral campaigns and more successful electoral delegations, term limits also remove some of the most informative stimuli available to the modern voter. For example, incumbents have public histories, whereas many challengers for office do not. Voters can use the histories of candidates to estimate the consequences of reelecting the incumbent (Downs 1957, Fiorina 1981, Key 1966). Moreover, people who face reelection and who believe that their electoral principals may hold them accountable for their actions have an incentive to take actions that improve their principals' welfare. People whom term limits prohibit from seeking reelection have no incentive to increase the welfare of their principals. At a minimum, then, it is difficult to reconcile the simultaneous desire for term limits and for electoral outcomes based on enlightened voters' decisions.

Another, and more general, idea for improving modern democracy is to encourage ordinary citizens to deliberate on political matters (Fishkin 1991, Habermas 1984). The idea behind this proposal is that citizens

---

[25]Petracca (1990) uses this type of argument to conclude that term limits will produce legislators who are more responsive to their constituents' preferences. Similarly, Will (1992) uses this type of argument to conclude that term limits will make legislators more responsive to (a paternalistic notion of) the public interest.

who deliberate will enlighten one another and vastly improve political decision making. Were persuasion and enlightenment the same thing, deliberative environments would indeed be the ideal solution to the mischiefs of complexity. Regrettably, they are not the same.

Deliberation differs from enlightenment when the most persuasive people in a group are not knowledgeable or the most persuasive (and/or knowledgeable) people have an incentive to mislead the less knowledgeable members. The mere construction of a deliberative setting does not guarantee that the cream of the collective's knowledge will rise to the top and be spread evenly across the group. This is not to say that deliberation cannot be beneficial, but it is to say that deliberation is far more likely to be beneficial if it takes place in a context that generates the conditions for enlightenment.

CONCLUSION

Voters, legislators, and jurors delegate to others and tend to lack information about the consequences of their actions. In many cases, these actors have opportunities to obtain knowledge from the endorsements or testimony of others. The ability of voters, legislators, and jurors to make reasoned choices and delegate successfully depends on whether their opportunities to gain knowledge actually produce knowledge. Were people able to discern the interests and expertise of others, they could make choices about whom to believe that would generate the knowledge they need. In many cases, however, people lack this ability because they do not know one another well.

In this chapter, we have described institutions that do (and do not) facilitate reasoned choice and successful delegation by helping people choose whom to believe. By clarifying other peoples' interests, imposing penalties for lying, introducing the threat of verification, or requiring costly effort, institutions enable voters, legislators, and jurors to make more accurate predictions about the consequences of their actions. Our examination of modern democratic institutions reveals some of the ways in which existing institutions do (or do not) help democratic principals mitigate the democratic dilemma.

Afterword

Conclusions of academic texts are places for authors to wax nostalgic about their intellectual travails or to embark on a circuitous survey of the possible implications of their book's accomplishments. Both can be meaningful endeavors. Neither occurs here.

Our decision about how to conclude *The Democratic Dilemma* is motivated by a lesson from Chapter 2: When many stimuli compete for attention, the opportunity costs of attending to any particular stimulus is quite high; therefore, people should attend to only those stimuli that are very likely to cause the avoidance of very costly mistakes. This lesson reminds us that our readers, who have other stimuli to attend to, want us to wrap things up quickly. So that is what we shall do.

Our goal is to allow readers to make more accurate judgments about the political consequences of limited information. To this end, we conclude that people who want to make reasoned choices need not know all potentially pertinent details about the consequences of their actions. What they need, instead, is the ability to generate accurate predictions. In the previous chapters, we have identified the conditions under which interactions with speakers whose attributes or institutional contexts make their statements persuasive and enlightening allow people who lack information to make reasoned choices.

In the end, *The Democratic Dilemma* shows how basic elements of human cognition interact with the incentive-altering effects of political institutions to determine each person's capacity for reasoned choice. Its lessons about how people learn and how people choose are important for the study of democracy. These lessons help us better explain critical democratic relationships such as the one between a voter's interests and his or her votes, the one between a legislator's intentions and a bureaucrat's actions, and the one between a juror's knowledge and the verdicts he or she supports. With these explanations in hand, students of democracy can better distinguish competent voters, jurors, and legislators from incompetent ones. This ability, more than any other, is the key to understanding, and where possible resolving, the democratic dilemma.

Appendices

Appendix to Chapter 2

We now present a formal version of our theory. We do this to show how our conclusions follow from our premises. Our goal is to make the theory's logic accessible to a wide audience. At the request of the publisher, we have moved some of the proofs to our web site (http://polisciexplab. ucsd.edu).

We proceed in the following manner. Instead of presenting one all-encompassing model of attention, communication, and delegation, we present a series of smaller, more focused models. We begin by presenting our model of attention. This is followed by models of communication and delegation, respectively. Individually, these models reveal important relationships between complexity, scarcity, and choice. Collectively, they constitute our theory.

There is a hierarchical relationship between our models. Our delegation model is based on our communication models, and both are based on our attention model. This hierarchy allows us to generate relevant conclusions with minimal losses of generality.

Presenting the theory in this way reduces the number of logical steps required to derive any one of our conclusions from a well-defined set of premises. As a result, more readers should be able to follow our logic than would be the case if we presented an all-encompassing model. Readers who are interested in examining related all-encompassing models should consult our previous publications (Lupia and McCubbins 1994a, 1994b; Lupia and McCubbins 1994c).

This appendix is partitioned into three sections that correspond to our theories of attention, communication, and delegation, respectively. We begin each section by stating our assumptions about player objectives, opportunities, and knowledge. We end each section with our conclusions about attention, persuasion, enlightenment, deception, reasoned choice, and delegation. In between, we trace the logical steps that link premises to conclusions. Unless otherwise stated, and there will be important ex-

233

ceptions, we assume that all elements of every model are common knowledge.

1. A MODEL OF ATTENTION

Premises

A *principal* has an ideal point, $p \in [0, 1]$. Her task is to choose one of two exogenously and independently determined alternatives, $x \in [0, 1]$ or $y \in [0, 1]$. Note that the assumption "$x \in [0, 1]$ and $y \in [0, 1]$" is without a loss of generality to the assumption that x and y are points in any finite-dimensional space.

Unlike our models of communication and delegation, there is only one actor in our model of attention. Therefore, we use decision theory and not game theory to derive conclusions about her actions. The principal's choice of x or y depends on her objectives, knowledge, and opportunities. We now describe each in turn.

The principal's objective is to maximize her expected utility. We say that the principal maximizes *ex ante* expected utility when making a decision before she has exhausted pre-payoff opportunities to acquire information, and that the principal maximizes *ex post* expected utility when she must choose after she has exhausted these opportunities (see Holmstrom and Myerson 1983).

From the principal's choice of x or y, she derives utility $-|x - p|$ or $-|y - p|$, respectively. That is, the principal prefers the alternative whose spatial location is closest to p. Note that our conclusions – or trivial variants of them – remain valid if the shape of the principal's utility function is in a large class of quasi-concave utility functions. Our conclusions merely require that decreases in utility are weakly monotonic with respect to increases in the spatial distance between ideal points and outcomes (and with respect to cost increases introduced below).

The principal has incomplete information about the personal consequence of her actions. That is, the principal may not *know* whether x or y is closer to p. She does, however, have *beliefs* about which is closer. Specifically, the principal knows that the true spatial location of x is determined by a single random draw from the distribution X, where X has support on a known subset of $[0, 1]$. To put it another way, the principal has beliefs about the range of possible locations of x and about the likelihood that each possible location is the true one. The principal does not, however, know which location was actually drawn. The principal has similar information about y. That is, she knows that y is the result of a single draw from the distribution Y, where Y has support on a subset of $[0, 1]$.

Appendix to Chapter 2

The principal's opportunities are implicit in the model's sequence of events. First, the principal decides whether to acquire information (described in greater detail below). Next, the principal chooses x or y. Finally, the game ends and the principal receives a payoff.

With respect to the principal's information acquisition decision, she has three options. The principal can:

- Pay nothing and learn nothing.
- Pay $c_{xy} \geq 0$ for the opportunity to learn the location of x and y with probability q_{xy} and learn nothing with probability $1 - q_{xy}$. This is equivalent to the decision to purchase the most detailed information available.
- Pay $c_x \geq 0$ for the opportunity to learn the location of x with probability q_x and learn nothing with probability $1 - q_x$. When the principal chooses this option, she purchases a relatively vague signal even though the option to purchase more detailed information is available.

We think of c_x and c_{xy} as cognitive opportunity costs and q_x and q_{xy} as cognitive transaction costs. That is, the c terms are the scarce energies required to acquire information and the $1 - q$ terms are the frictions associated with processing a stimulus into a helpful form. We treat c_x, c_{xy}, q_x, and q_{xy} as fixed and exogenous.

For simplicity and without a loss of generality, we make the following assumptions about how the principal breaks ties: If x and y provide the principal with the same expected utility, then the principal chooses y; if paying for information and not paying for it provide equal expected utility, then the principal does not pay; if two pieces of information provide equal expected utility at the time of purchase, then the principal pays for the less expensive piece.

Let $CL_p(x)$ be the set of $y \in [0, 1]$ that is *closer to p than x* and let $CL_p(y)$ be the set of $x \in [0, 1]$ that is *closer to p than y*. Then, $\int_{CL_{p(y)}} |y - p| - |x - p| dX$ is the expected return from learning x for a given value of y and $\int \int_{CL_{p(y)}} |y - p| - |x - p| dX dY$ is the expected return from learning x given beliefs Y. Note that the set of x over which the integral is taken is the set of x that is closer to the principal's ideal point than y. To put it another way, paying for information can be beneficial only if it prevents the principal from making a costly mistake (choosing y when x is closer to p).

If $-\int |y - p| dY \geq -\int |x - p| dX$, then the return from paying c_{xy} is $q_{xy} \times (\int \int_{CL_{p(y)}} |y - p| - |x - p| dX dY)$. Otherwise, it is $q_{xy} \times (\int \int_{CL_{p(x)}} |x - p| - |y - p| dY dX)$.

Let $CL_p(Y)$ be the set of x for which $-|x - p| > -\int |y - p| dY$. $CL_p(Y)$ is the set of x that provides higher utility than the expected value of y,

235

given beliefs Y. If the principal knows y, then $CL_p(y) = CL_p(Y)$. Let $\neg$ $CL_p(Y)$ be the set of x for which $-|x - p| \leq - \int |y - p| dY$.

Let $B_x = q_x \times (\int_{CL_{p(y)}} \int_{CL_{p(Y)}} |y - p| - |x - p| dXdY)$, $L_y = q_x \times (\int_{CL_{p(x)}} \int_{CL_{p(Y)}} |y - p| - |x - p| dXdY)$, $B_y = q_x \times (\int_{CL_{p(x)}} \int \neg_{CL_{p(Y)}} |y - p| - |x - p| dXdY)$, and $L_x = q_x = (\int_{CL_{p(y)}} \int \neg_{CL_{p(Y)}} |y - p| - |x - p| dXdY)$. In words, B_x is the expected benefit of observing a value of x which correctly suggests that x is closer to p than y. L_y is the expected loss from observing a value of x which incorrectly suggests that x is closer to p than y. The definitions of B_y and L_x parallel those of B_x and L_y, respectively. The terms L_x and L_y identify the circumstances under which acquiring incomplete information – in this case learning only x – can *cause* the principal to make a costly mistake. The existence of such circumstances is but one reason why the principal may rationally choose not to acquire more information. Note that if $-\int |y - p| dY \geq -\int |x - p| dX$, then the expected benefit to the principal of paying c_x is $B_x - L_y$. Otherwise, it is $B_y - L_x$.

Proposition 2.1: The principal uses the following rule to determine her actions.

If $-\int |y - p| dY \geq -\int |x - p| dX$,

- *and $[q_{xy} \times (\int \int_{CL_{p(y)}} |y - p| - |x - p| dXdY)] - c_{xy} > max (B_x - L_y - c_x, 0)$, then the principal pays c_{xy}.*
- *and $B_x - L_y - c_x \geq [q_{xy} \times (\int \int_{CL_{p(y)}} |y - p| - |x - p| dXdY)] - c_{xy}$ and $B_x - L_y - c_x > 0$, then the principal pays c_x.*

If $-\int |x - p| dX > -\int |y - p| dY$,

- *and $[q_{xy} \times (\int \int_{CL_{p(x)}} |x - p| - |y - p| dYdX)] - c_{xy} > max (B_y - L_x - c_x, 0)$, then the principal pays c_{xy}.*
- *and $B_y - L_x - c_x \geq [q_{xy} \times (\int \int_{CL_{p(x)}} |x - p| - |y - p| dYdX)] - c_{xy}$ and $B_y - L_x - c_x > 0$, then the principal pays c_x.*

Otherwise, the principal does not pay.
If, as a result of paying c_{xy}, the principal observes both x and y, then she chooses y if and only if $-|y - p| > -|x - p|$. If, as a result of paying c_x the principal observes x, then she chooses y if and only if $-\int |y - p| dY \geq - |x - p|$. If the principal observes neither x nor y, then she chooses y if and only if $-\int |y - p| dY \geq -\int |x - p| dX$. Otherwise, the principal chooses x.

As the game is decision theoretic, the proof of the proposition is trivial. To falsify it, one would have to either contradict the assumption of utility maximization, change the definition of p, x, y, X, Y, c_x, c_{xy}, q_x or q_{xy}, or change the sequence of events.

Conclusions from Our Attention Model

We will now prove the validity of the Chapter 2 theorems. To unite the mathematics of the model with the theory as presented in the text, we make the following analogies.

- If $-\int |y - p| dY \geq -\int |x - p| dX$, then the *expected cost of a mistake* is $\int\int_{CLp(y)} |y - p| - |x - p| dXdY$. Otherwise, it is $\int\int_{CLp(x)} |x - p| - |y - p| dYdX$.
- *Attention to a particular stimulus* is either the decision to pay c_{xy} or the decision to pay c_x.
- *The probability that attending to a particular stimulus is sufficient to prevent a mistake* is $[q_{xy} \times \int\int_{CLp(y)} dXdY]$ or $[q_x \times \int_{CLp(y)} \int_{CLp(Y)} dXdY]$

  if $-\int |y - p| dY \geq -\int |x - p| dX$. Otherwise, it is $[q_{xy} \times \int\int_{CLp(x)} dXdY]$ or $[q_x \times \int_{CLp(x)} \int_{\neg CLp(Y)} dXdY]$.

- *The probability that attending to a particular stimulus is sufficient to cause a costly mistake* is $[q_x \times \int_{CLp(x)} \int_{CLp(Y)} dXdY]$ if $-\int |y - p| dY \geq -\int |x - p| dX$. Otherwise, it is $q_x \times \int_{CLp(y)} \int_{\neg CLp(Y)} dXdY$.

- *Induces attention to a particular stimulus* is a change from not paying c_x (or c_{xy}) to paying for it.
- *Reduces attention to a particular stimulus* is a change from paying c_x (or c_{xy}) to not paying for it.

  Proof of Theorem 2.1: (*More information is neither necessary nor sufficient for reasoned choice.*)

By contradiction, suppose that more information is necessary for reasoned choice and that Y has all of its support in $CL_p(x)$. Then, by supposition, the principal cannot make a reasoned choice without learning the precise location of y. However, it is also true, by the supposition, that the principal can infer that y is closer to p than is x, without learning y. Therefore, learning the exact location of y cannot be necessary for reasoned choice.

Now suppose that more information is sufficient for reasoned choice. Because the principal can choose not to learn x and y, then knowing either x or y must be sufficient for a reasoned choice. Suppose that $p = .3$, $x = .8$, the principal learns x, and Y is uniformly distributed. Therefore, the expected utility of y is greater than the expected value of x for the principal. Suppose that $y = .9$. Thus, learning x is not sufficient to make a reasoned choice. QED.

> *Proof of Corollaries 1 and 2 to Theorem 2.1: (An increase in either the expected cost of a mistake or the probability that attending to a particular stimulus is sufficient to prevent a mistake, either induces attention to the stimulus or has no effect.)*

Consider the case $-\int |y - p|dY \geq -\int |x - p|dX$ (the other case follows straightforwardly). Next suppose that there is an increase in the expected

cost of a mistake. Then, by definition there is an increase in $\iint_{\overline{CLp(x)}} |y - p|$

$|-|x - p|dXdY$ and an increase in $[q_{xy} \times \iint_{\overline{CLp(x)}} |y - p|-|x - p|dXdY]$

$- c_{xy}$. From Proposition 2.1, it follows that such an increase could induce the principal only to pay for the opportunity to pay to learn x and y. Similar reasoning shows why an increase in the probability that attending to a stimulus is sufficient to prevent a mistake has the same effect. QED.

> *Proof of Corollary 3 to Theorem 2.1: (If an increase in the probability that attending to a particular stimulus is sufficient to cause a mistake is larger than a consequent increase in the probability that attending to a particular stimulus is sufficient to prevent a mistake, then attention to that stimulus is either reduced or has no effect.)*

Consider the case $-\int |y - p|dY \geq -\int |x - p|dX$ (the other case follows straightforwardly). Next suppose that there is an increase in the probability that attending to a particular stimulus is sufficient to cause a mistake that is larger than a consequent increase in the probability that attending to that stimulus is sufficient to prevent a mistake. Then, by definition there is an increase in $\int_{CLp(x)} \int_{CLp(Y)} dXdY - \int_{CLp(y)} \int_{CLp(Y)} dXdY$. This increase implies a decrease in $B_x - L_y - c_x$. From Proposition 2.1, it follows that such an increase could induce the principal only not to pay c_x. Otherwise, the increase has no effect. QED.

As noted in the text, Theorem 2.2 (*People have an incentive to ignore many stimuli*) requires two additional premises. The first premise is that there are thousands of stimuli to which a person could attend. The second premise is that the opportunity cost of paying attention in the general case is substantially higher than if there are one or two stimuli competing for attention. Within the context of the model, we represent these premises with the assumption that c_x and c_{xy} are high relative to all of the model's other parameters. Theorem 2.2 and its corollary follow straightforwardly.

Appendix to Chapter 3

Here, we first present our basic communication model. Then, we extend it in three ways. Our basic model and each of its extensions allow us to derive the necessary and sufficient conditions for persuasion presented in the text. All mathematical terms are in italics.

THE BASIC MODEL

We model communication as a game between two players, a speaker and a principal. The principal chooses one of two alternatives, called x and y. The speaker sends a signal to the principal about his choice. We depict the extensive form in Figure 3.1.

The sequence of events begins with three probabilistic choices by nature. We denote these choices $n = \{n_b, n_c, n_k\}$. The order of these choices is irrelevant. In Figure 3.1, we order the choices in the way that makes the extensive form (notably the speaker's information sets) easiest to draw. Below, we order nature's choices in the way that makes them easiest to describe.

One of nature's three choices determines the "state of the world." We denote this choice $n_b \in \{better, worse\}$. This choice determines whether x is *better* or *worse* than y for the principal. Nature chooses the state $n_b = better$ with probability $b \in [0, 1]$ and the state $n_b = worse$ with probability $1\text{-}b$. The principal does not know n_b. The principal does, however, have prior beliefs about the "state of the world." These beliefs are represented by the probability b.

If $n_b = better$ and the principal chooses x, then the principal earns utility $U \geq 0$. If $n_b = worse$ and if the principal chooses x, then she earns utility $\underline{U} \leq 0$. We assume, without a loss of generality, that if the principal chooses y, then she earns utility 0. So if $n_b = better$, then it is better for the principal to choose x than it is for her to choose y. If $n_b = worse$, then it is worse for the principal to choose x than it is for her to choose y.

Another of nature's three choices determines what the speaker knows about the "state of the world." We denote this choice $n_k \in \{n_b, \varnothing\}$. Nature allows the speaker to know n_b $(n_k = n_b)$ with probability $k \in [0, 1]$ and makes no such revelation (chooses $n_k = \varnothing$) with probability 1-k. We assume that the speaker knows n_k and that the principal does not. So, when $k \in (0, 1)$, the speaker has private information about his knowledge of "the state of the world." The principal's beliefs about the speaker's knowledge are represented by the probability k.

The third of nature's three choices determines whether the speaker and principal have common or conflicting interests. We denote this choice $n_c \in \{common, conflicting\}$. Nature chooses $n_c = common$ with probability $c \in [0, 1]$ and $n_c = conflicting$ with probability 1-c. We assume that the speaker knows n_c and that the principal does not. So, when $c \in (0, 1)$, the speaker has private information about whether he and the principal have common or conflicting interests. The principal's prior beliefs about the speaker's interests (n_c) are represented by the probability c.

Together, n_b and n_c determine how the principal's choice affects the speaker's utility. If $n_c = common$, then the speaker benefits when the principal makes a utility-maximizing decision; the speaker receives utility $Z \geq 0$ when the principal receives utility $U \geq 0$ and receives utility $\underline{Z} \leq 0$ when the principal receives utility $\underline{U} \leq 0$. If $n_c = conflicting$, then the speaker benefits when the principal *does not* make a utility-maximizing choice; the speaker receives utility $\underline{Z} \leq 0$ when the principal receives utility $U \geq 0$ and receives utility $Z \geq 0$ when the principal receives utility $\underline{U} \leq 0$. As before, we normalize speaker utility by setting it equal to 0 when the principal chooses y.

After nature makes her three choices, the gaming begins. First, the speaker sends a signal to the principal. We denote this signal $s \in \{B, W\}$. $s = B$ is the signal "I assert that x is better than y for the principal." $s = W$ is the signal "I assert that x is worse than y for the principal." The speaker selects which signal to make and need not tell the truth. Next, the principal chooses x or y. Then, the game ends and both players receive a utility payoff.

THE EQUILIBRIUM CONCEPT

To derive precise deductive inferences about player beliefs and strategies from the model, we employ an additional premise: We assume that a refined version of sequential equilibrium is the appropriate solution concept for our model. We use this section to motivate both the sequential equilibrium concept and the refinement we use.

A sequential equilibrium has two components. The first component is a strategy profile that prescribes, for every information set, a probability distribution over available actions. We use the vector π to denote a typical strategy profile and the scalar h to denote a typical information set.

A sequential equilibrium's second component is a system of beliefs. A system of beliefs assigns probabilities to the decision nodes within every information set. We use the vector μ to denote a typical system of beliefs. So, $\mu(h)$ is a player's beliefs about which of several *unobservable* events – the decision nodes within information set h – has lead to his present *observable* situation: the information set h. Formally, μ is a function from $d \in D$, the set of decision nodes, to $[0, 1]$, such that for every information set h, $\Sigma_{d \in h} \mu(d) = 1$. We make the usual assumption that the game's information sets collectively partition D.

When is a strategy profile and a set of beliefs a sequential equilibrium? We now describe a sequential equilibrium's necessary and sufficient conditions. In short, a sequential equilibrium consists of a strategy profile that is "sequentially rational" *and* a system of beliefs that is "consistent."

Sequential Rationality

Kreps (1990: 427) described sequential rationality as follows: "Roughly speaking, a *sequential equilibrium* is a profile of strategies π and beliefs μ such that starting from every information set h . . . [each player] plays optimally from then on, given that what has transpired previously is given by $\mu(h)$ and what will transpire at subsequent nodes belonging to other players is given by π. This condition is called *sequential rationality*."

A sequentially rational strategy profile is a necessary condition for a sequential equilibrium. It is the requirement that everyone make what he or she believes to be utility-maximizing choices at every stage of the game. In this sense, it is closely related to the better-known Nash equilibrium concept.

Neither sequential rationality nor the Nash equilibrium concept is sufficient for our purposes. The source of the insufficiency is that neither sequential rationality nor the Nash equilibrium concept restricts player beliefs. Restrictions on beliefs are important because communication games can have many sequentially rational (or Nash equilibrium) strategy profiles that require players to have nonsensical belief systems (Kreps 1990: Chapter 12 contains several examples of such equilibria). The sequential equilibrium concept improves on sequential rationality and Nash equilibrium by posing the minimal requirement that strategies and beliefs be somehow "consistent" with each other.

Consistency

Consistency requires that a set of beliefs μ be based on strategy profile π, that is itself based on beliefs μ, and so on. Kreps (1990: 429–30) describes consistency as follows, noting an important set of circumstances where consistency is difficult to define: "Sequential rationality is one part of the definition of a sequential equilibrium. In addition, we want strategies and beliefs to make sense together. . . . At a minimum, we would want to insist that the strategy profile π and the beliefs μ are consistent at the level of Bayes' rule in the following sense: Given the strategy profile π, for any information set h that will be reached with positive probability (if players use the strategies given by π) beliefs at h are computed from the strategies via Bayes' rule. . . . But Bayes' rule will not apply to information sets that are not reached with positive probability in the course of play. And it is precisely at such information sets that beliefs are important. So we might want to insist on rather more consistency than just consistency with Bayes' rule when it applies."

Consistency, while generally easy to define, is problematic when a player finds him- or herself at an information set that he or she believes should occur with zero probability in equilibrium. Such a finding implies that beliefs and strategies are out of sync.

Within the game theory literature, there is substantial disagreement about what to assume about player beliefs at zero-probability information sets. However, if we want to avoid the nonsensical equilibrium possibilities associated with sequential rationality and Nash equilibrium, then we must impose some restriction. The game theorists' disagreement is about which restriction to impose. One popular restriction is to assume that zero-probability information sets cannot occur. For example, the following definition requires "strictly mixed" strategy profiles that preclude zero-probability information sets (as well as some pure strategies) and allow Bayes' rule to be invoked everywhere. A set of beliefs, "(μ, π) is consistent (Kreps and Wilson 1982) if there is a sequence of totally mixed strategy profiles $\pi^n \to \pi$ such that the beliefs μ^n computed from π^n using Bayes' rule converge to μ. A strategy profile is totally mixed if at every information set the associated behavioral strategy puts strictly positive probability on every action. Thus the beliefs associated with a totally mixed strategy profile are completely determined by Bayes' rule" (Fudenberg and Tirole 1991: 241). This restriction, while effective in other contexts, is far too strong for our purposes. Other restrictions are contained within equilibrium refinements, such as Cho and Kreps's (1987) intuitive criterion, Banks and Sobel's (1987) concept of divinity, and Fudenberg and Levine's (1993) steady-state equilibrium. Each refinement requires players to base beliefs at zero-probability information sets on other information available within the game.

We adopt a refinement (developed in the context of a study of both sequential and perfect Bayesian equilibria) offered by Fudenburg and Tirole (1991). We choose this refinement because it was developed using models that are structurally similar to our own. Fudenburg and Tirole's refinement requires that deviations from equilibrium that lead to zero-probability information sets *not* be treated as containing information about things that the deviating player does not know.

In our model, the logic of the Fudenberg and Tirole refinement reduces to the following, innocuous assumption: "if the principal is at a zero-probability information set, then she ignores the speaker's signal." To see why this refinement is innocuous in our model, recall that the speaker can take one of two actions – he can signal B or can signal W. Also recall that the principal does not observe any of nature's three choices. These two facts imply that there are only two information sets at which the principal can find herself – the information set following the principal's observation that $s = B$ and the information set following $s = W$. If there exists an information set that is arrived at in equilibrium with probability 0, then the other information set must be arrived at with probability 1. In essence, it is as if the speaker has a dominant strategy – he does not base his signal on n_b, n_c, or n_k. As a result, the principal cannot infer anything about n_b, n_c, or n_k – and, hence, the consequences of her own actions – from the speaker's deviation. This inference is equivalent to assuming that the principal ignores signals that are off the equilibrium path. Thus, our assumption is innocuous.

The Definition

We now provide a formal definition of a sequential equilibrium in our model. A sequential equilibrium is a strategy profile π and system of beliefs μ that are consistent with each other in the foregoing sense and satisfy sequential rationality at every information set.

We use the vector π_s to denote the speaker's component of strategy profile π. π_s has six scalar elements, one for each speaker information set $h_s \in \{h_1, \ldots, h_6\}$. Note that the speaker's information sets are completely determined by nature's choice vector n and that the information set labels we use, $h_1, \ldots, h_6$, match the labels used in Figure 3.1. Each element, $\pi_s(s;h_j)$, $j = 1, \ldots 6$, is the probability that the speaker signals $s \in \{B, W\}$ if he is at information set h_j. We require that these probabilities sum to 1 for each information set.

We use the vector π_r to denote the principal's component of strategy profile π. This vector has two scalar elements, one for each principal information set $h_r = \{h_B, h_W\}$. Note that the principal's information sets are completely determined by the speaker's signal. Each element, $\pi_r(x; s)$, is the probability that the principal chooses x having heard the signal $s \in \{B, W\}$. $1 - \pi_r(x; s)$ is the probability that the principal chooses y given the same signal. A signal s is "along the path of play" if there exists an information set at which $\pi_s(s; h_s) > 0$.

Definition: A pair of strategy profiles (π_r, π_s) is a *sequential equilibrium* if:

(a) For each $h_s,$ $\pi_s(s; h_s)$ maximizes expected speaker utility given π_r $(x; s)$ for all $s \in \{B, W\}$.

(b) For each s that is along the path of play, $\pi_r(x; s)$ maximizes the principal's expected utility given $\mu(better|s)$ and $\mu(worse|s)$, where μ is computed from π_s by Bayes' rule.

(c) For any s that is not along the path of play, $\pi_r(x; s)$ maximizes expected principal utility given $\mu(better|s) = b$ and $\mu(worse|s) = 1\text{-}b$.

A Note on Equilibrium Selection

In what follows, we identify the set of nonbabbling sequential equilibria. A babbling equilibrium requires either a principal who ignores all signals or a speaker who sends only uninformative signals. In our model, a babbling equilibrium is an equilibrium in which either the speaker does not base his or her signal on n_b or the principal does not base her response on s.

Babbling equilibria generally exist alongside nonbabbling equilibria in economic signaling models (Crawford and Sobel 1982, Farrell and Gibbons 1989). These equilibria exist in our model and provide an important insight – you have no incentive to persuade if you are certain to be ignored, and you have no incentive to be persuaded if you are certain that communication cannot provide useful knowledge. However, there are many circumstances in which babbling equilibria exist even though it is not clear how players would reach such an equilibrium. For example, in any case where a speaker and principal can benefit from the speaker's sending a particular signal to the principal, there exists a babbling equilibrium that leads to a worse outcome for both players than a nonbabbling equilibrium. Now, if an accident of nature leads the speaker in this example to babble and the principal to ignore the speaker's signal, then the "babble-ignore" strategy profile is sustainable in this case. However, we concur with Farrell (1993: 518), who claims that in cases like this, the "babbling equilibrium is implausible. It requires [the speaker] to randomize extensively, saying some very unnatural things, not for his own sake but for the sake of the equilibrium."

More generally, we focus on nonbabbling equilibria because we are interested in determining the conditions under which people *can* persuade one another when they attempt to communicate with one another. This focus is justified by our model of attention. Recall that people who face cognitive opportunity or transaction costs should not attend to stimuli that promise zero benefit. Now consider the plight of a person who has an opportunity to communicate and who anticipates a babbling equilibrium. When compared with not communicating, communication in a babbling equilibrium promises zero benefit to both principal and speaker. If communication entails any opportunity or transaction costs – as we assert that it generally does – then players who anticipate babbling equilibria should make no attempt to communicate. So while we acknowledge their theoretical existence, we do not further pursue "babbling equilibria."

Our equilibrium concept also presupposes agreement on the meaning of the statements "better" and "worse." That is, we focus on non-neologistic equilibria. In our model, a neologistic equilibria *requires* the speaker and principal to agree that the signal *B* means "worse" and not "better" and that the signal *W* means "better" and not "worse." Focusing on non-neologistic equilibria is equivalent to assuming that words have focal meanings (Farrell 1993: 319). Because we allow people to lie and context to affect a signal's persuasiveness, focusing on non-neologistic equilibria is quite unrestrictive.

Conclusions

For notational simplicity, let $\pi = (\pi_s, \pi_r)$, $\pi_{14} = (\pi_s(B;h_1), \pi_s(B;h_2), \pi_s(B;h_3), \pi_s(B;h_4))$, $\pi_5 = \pi_s(B;h_5)$, $\pi_6 = \pi_s(B;h_6)$, and $\pi_r = (\pi_r(x;B), \pi_r(x;W))$.

Proposition 3.1: The only nonbabbling, non-neologistic sequential equilibrium in the basic model is:

$$\pi_{14} = (1, 0, 0, 1)$$
$$\pi_5 = 1; \text{ if } bZ + (1\text{-}b) \underline{Z} \geq 0 \text{ and } \pi_5 = 0 \text{ otherwise.}$$
$$\pi_6 = 1; \text{ if } bZ + (1\text{-}b) \underline{Z} \geq 0 \text{ and } \pi_6 = 0 \text{ otherwise.}$$
$$\pi_r = (1,0)$$

This equilibrium requires Condition A:

$$\frac{[(1\text{-} c)k + [(1\text{-}k) \times [\pi_s(B; h_5)c + \pi_s(B; h_6)(1\text{-}c)]]]}{[ck + [(1\text{-}k) \times [\pi_s(B; h_5)c + \pi_s(B; h_6)(1\text{-}c)]]]} \leq bU/(b\text{-}1)\underline{U}$$

and Condition B:

$$\frac{[ck + [(1\text{-}k) \times [(1\text{-}\pi_s(B; h_5))c + (1\text{-}\pi_s(B; h_6))(1\text{-}c)]]]}{[(1\text{-}c)k + [(\text{-}k) \times [(1\text{-} \pi_s(B; h_5))c + (1\text{-}\pi_s(B; h_6))(1\text{-}c)]]]} \geq bU/(b\text{-}1)\underline{U},$$

where at least one of the inequalities is strict.

Proof

We proceed as follows: First, we define the expected value of every pure strategy at every speaker information set. Second, we identify the

Appendix to Chapter 3

boundaries of the set of potential nonbabbling, non-neologistic sequential equilibria. Third, we identify the sequentially rational strategy profiles within this set. We find that the named equilibrium is this set's only member. Finally, we evaluate the consistency of the sequentially rational strategy profiles.

To see the expected value of every pure strategy at every speaker information set, consider the following relationships. At h_1, the expected utility from $\pi_s(B;h_1) = 1$ is $\pi_r(x;B)Z$. The expected utility from $\pi_s(B;h_1) = 0$ is $\pi_r\,(x;W)Z$. If $\pi_r(x;B) \geq \pi_r(x;W)$, then $\pi_s(B;h_1) = 1$ is the best response. At h_2, the expected utility from $\pi_s(W;\,h_2) = 1$ is $\pi_r(x;\,B)\underline{Z}$. The expected utility from $\pi_s(W;\,h_2) = 0$ is $\pi_r(x;\,W)\underline{Z}$. If $\pi_r(x;B) \geq \pi_r(x;W)$, then $\pi_s(B;h_2) = 0$ is the best response. At h_3, the expected utility from $\pi_s(B;h_3) = 1$ is $\pi_r(x;B)\underline{Z}$. The expected utility from $\pi_s(B;h_3) = 0$ is $\pi_r(x;W)\underline{Z}$. If $\pi_r(x;B) \geq \pi_r(x;W)$, then $\pi_s(B;h_3) = 0$ is the best response. At h_4, the expected utility from $\pi_s(W;\,h_4) = 1$ is $\pi_r(x;\,B)Z$. The expected utility from $\pi_s(W;\,h_2) = 0$ is $\pi_r(x;\,W)Z$. If $\pi_r(x;B) \geq \pi_r(x;W) = 0$, then $\pi_s(B;h_4) = 1$ is the best response. At h_5, the expected utility from $\pi_s(B;h_5) = 1$ is $b\pi_r\,(x;B)Z + (1-b)\,\pi_r(x;\,B)\underline{Z}$. The expected utility from $\pi_s(W;\,h_5) = 0$ is $b\pi_r(x;\,W)Z + (1-b)\,\pi_r(x;\,W)\underline{Z}$. If $\pi_r(x;B) \geq \pi_r\,(x;W)$ and $bZ + (1-b)\underline{Z} \leq 0$, then $\pi_s(B;h_5) = 0$ is the best response. At h_6, the expected utility from $\pi_s(B;h_6) = 1$ is $b\pi_r(x;B)\underline{Z} + (1-b)\,\pi_r(x;\,B)\underline{Z}$. The expected utility from $\pi_s(W;\,h_6) = 0$ is $b\pi_r(x;\,W)\underline{Z} + (1-b)\,\pi_r(x;\,W)Z$. If $\pi_r(x;B) \geq \pi_r(x;W)$ and $b\underline{Z} + (1-b)Z \leq 0$, then $\pi_s(B;h_6) = 0$ is the best response.

> *Lemma 1:* All mixed-strategy sequential equilibria in the model are babbling equilibria.
>
> *Proof of Lemma 1:* A mixed-strategy equilibrium requires that each player choose a strategy which makes the other player indifferent between their two pure strategies. A necessary and sufficient condition for rendering the speaker indifferent between his pure strategies at information sets h_1 through h_4 is to set $\pi_r(x;B) = \pi_r(x;W)$. Setting $\pi_r(x;B) = \pi_r(x;W)$ is also necessary and sufficient to make the speaker indifferent between his two strategies at h_5 if $bZ + (1-b)\underline{Z} \neq 0$ and at h_6 if $b\underline{Z} + (1-b)Z \neq 0$. Setting $\pi_r(x;B) = \pi_r(x;W)$ implies that the principal is not conditioning her strategy on the signal. Anticipating such behavior, the speaker can choose any strategy he likes. These speaker strategies will either make the principal indifferent between her pure strategies, in which case we have a babbling equilibrium, or they will not, in which case we do not have an equilibrium.

If $bZ + (1-b)\underline{Z} = 0$ or $b\underline{Z} + (1-b)Z = 0$, then any principal strategy, including $\pi_r(x;B) = \pi_r\,(x;W)$, makes the speakers at h_5 and h_6 indifferent. Note, however, that the principal has an incentive to choose a mixed strategy other than $0 < \pi_r (x;B) = \pi_r(x;W) < 1$ only if he or she can induce the speaker at h_5 and h_6 to take distinct, knowledge-transferring actions. Because the speaker at h_5 *and* h_6 has no useful private information at either of these information sets, by definition, the requirement cannot be met. Therefore, the only equilibrium that could result from such an adaptation is a babbling equilibrium. **QED.**

From similar logic, it follows that all equilibria for which $\pi_r(x;B) = \pi_r(x;W)$ are babbling equilibria. Moreover, any nonbabbling equilibrium for which $\pi_r(x;B) = 0$ and $\pi_r(x;W) = 1$ requires neologisms (i.e., both players know that B means "worse" and W means "better)." Therefore, nonbabbling, non-neologistic sequential equilibria must include $\pi_r = (1,0)$.

Because nonbabbling, non-neologistic sequential equilibria must include $\pi_r = (1,0)$, they must also include $\pi_{14} = (1, 0, 0, 1)$. The reason for this is that the expected speaker utility at h_1 through h_4 reveals $\pi_{14} = (1, 0, 0, 1)$ to be the unique profile of best responses when $\pi_r (x;B) > \pi_r (x;W)$. Therefore, the set of nonbabbling, non-neologistic sequential equilibria must be contained *within* $\pi = (1, 0, 0, 1, \{0,1\}, \{0,1\}, 1, 0)$, where $\{0,1\}$ within strategy profile π is read as "either 0 or 1." It remains first to identify the sequentially rational strategy profiles within this set and then to evaluate these profiles' consistency.

At h_B, the expected utility from $\pi_r(x;B) = 1$ is:

$$[ckb\pi_s(B;h_1)U + ck(1-b)\pi_s(B;h_2)\underline{U} + (1-c)kb\pi_s(B;h_3)U$$
$$+ (1-c)k(1-b)\pi_s(B;h_4)\underline{U} + c(1-k)b\pi_s(B;h_5)U$$
$$+ c(1-k)(1-b)\pi_s(B;h_5)\underline{U} + (1-c)(1-k)b\pi_s(B;h_6)U$$
$$+ (1-c)(1-k)(1-b)\pi_s(B;h_6)\underline{U}] / [ckb\pi_s(B;h_1) + ck(1-b)\pi_s(B;h_2)$$
$$+ (1-c)kb\pi_s(B;h_3) + (1-c)k(1-b)\pi_s(B;h_4) + c(1-k)b\pi_s(B;h_5)$$
$$+ c(1-k)(1-b)\pi_s(B;h_5) + (1-c)(1-k)b\pi_s(B;h_6)$$
$$+ (1-c)(1-k)(1-b)\pi_s(B;h_6)]$$

At h_W, the expected utility from $\pi_r(x;W) = 1$ is

$$[ckb(1-\pi_s(B;h_1))U + ck(1-b)(1-\pi_s(B;h_2))\underline{U} + (1-c)kb(1-\pi_s(B;h_3))U$$
$$+ (1-c)k(1-b)(1-\pi_s(B;h_4))\underline{U} + c(1-k)b(1-\pi_s(B;h_5))U$$
$$+ c(1-k)(1-b)(1-\pi_s(B;h_5))\underline{U} + (1-c)(1-k)b(1-\pi_s(B;h_6))U$$
$$+ (1-c)(1-k)(1-b)(1-\pi_s(B;h_6))\underline{U}] / [ckb(1-\pi_s(B;h_1))$$
$$+ ck(1-b)(1-\pi_s(B;h_2)) + (1-c)kb(1-\pi_s(B;h_3))$$
$$+ (1-c)k(1-b)(1-\pi_s(B;h_4)) + c(1-k)b(1-\pi_s(B;h_5))$$
$$+ c(1-k)(1-b)(1-\pi_s(B;h_5)) + (1-c)(1-k)b(1-\pi_s(B;h_6))$$
$$+ (1-c)(1-k)(1-b)(1-\pi_s(B;h_6))]$$

Recall that the principal earns utility zero for choosing y. Therefore, $\pi_r(x;B) = 1$ is the best response only if the expected utility from $\pi_r(x;B)=1$ is ≥ 0 and $\pi_r(x;W) = 0$ is a best response only if the expected utility from $\pi_r(x;W) = 1$ is ≤ 0. Since a non-babbling equilibrium requires that the expected utility from $\pi_r(x;B) = 1$ is ≥ 0, that the expected utility from $\pi_r(x;W) = 1$ is ≤ 0, and that one of these inequalities is strict, it requires that one of the inequalities in Conditions A or B be strict.

We now prove that $\pi = (1, 0, 0, 1, 0, 0, 1, 0)$ is a sequential equilibrium under the conditions that we specify in Proposition 3.1. The other cases – $\pi = (1, 0, 0, 1, 0, 1, 1, 0)$, $\pi = (1, 0, 0, 1, 1, 0, 1, 0)$, and $\pi = (1, 0, 0, 1, 1, 1, 1, 0)$ – follow equivalent logic. From the expected utility at information sets h_5 and h_6, we know that this equilibrium holds only if $bZ + (1-b)\underline{Z} \leq$ and $b\underline{Z} + (1-b)Z \leq 0$. This requirement matches the related requirement of Proposition 3.1. From the expected utility at information sets h_1 through h_4 we know that this equilibrium requires the expected utility of $\pi_r (x;B) = 1 \geq 0 \geq$ the expected utility of $\pi_r (x;W) = 1$. We evaluate below the conditions under which this inequality holds.

If $\pi_s = (1, 0, 0, 1, 0, 0)$, then the numerator of the expected utility from $\pi_r (x;W) = 1$ reduces to: $ck(1-b)\underline{U} + (1-c)kbU + c(1-k)bU + c(1-k)(1-b)\underline{U} + (1-c)(1-k)bU + (1-c)(1-k)(1-b)\underline{U}$. Since the denominator of this expected utility is >0, by definition, it is trivial to show that this quantity is ≤ 0 iff $[1-k + ck]/[1-ck] \geq bU/(b-1)\underline{U}$, which is true iff Condition B is true. Similarly, if $\pi_s = (1, 0, 0, 1, 0, 0)$, then the expected utility from $\pi_r (x;B) = 1$ reduces to: $ckbU + (1-c)k(1-b)\underline{U}$. It is trivial to show that this quantity is ≥ 0 iff $bU/(b-1)\underline{U} \geq [1-c]/c$, which is true iff Condition A is true. Therefore, $\pi = (1, 0, 0, 1, 0, 0, 1, 0)$ is sequentially rational under the conditions that we specify in Proposition 3.1.

If the beliefs required to support this profile are consistent, then the profile and beliefs together constitute a sequential equilibrium. Beliefs are consistent iff

$$\mu(better|B) = \frac{(b \times \text{the probability that } s = B \text{ if } n_b = better)}{[(b \times \text{the probability that } s = B \text{ if } n_b = better) + ((1-b) \times \text{the probability that } s = W \text{ if } n_b = better)].}$$

In the proposed equilibrium $\mu(better|B) = 1$; the probability that $s = W$ if $n_b = better$ is zero; and the probability that $s = B$ if $n_b = better$ is non-zero. Therefore, beliefs are consistent. Equivalent logic proves consistency for $\mu(better|W)$, $\mu(worse|B)$, and $\mu(worse|W)$. QED.

Theorem 3.1: The equilibrium in Proposition 3.1 exists only if $c > .5$.

Proof: For notational simplicity, let $f = [(1-k) \times [\pi_s(B; h_5)c + \pi_s(B; h_6)(1-c)]]$ and let $g = [(1-k) \times [(1- \pi_s(B; h_5))c + (1-\pi_s(B; h_6))(1-c)]]$. A necessary, but not sufficient, condition for the satisfaction of Proposition 3.1 is that Conditions A and B hold. A necessary condition for Conditions A and B to hold is that $(k-ck + f)/(ck + f) \leq (ck + g)/(k-ck + g)$. Multiplying each side of the inequality by its denominator and dividing everything by k, which requires $k > 0$, produces $k + f + g \leq 2ck + 2fc + 2gc$. Dividing each side of the inequality by $2k + 2f + 2g$ produces the requirement that $c > .5$. **QED.**

Theorem 3.2: The equilibrium in Proposition 3.1 exists only if $k > 0$.

Proof: If $k = 0$, then both the expected utility from $\pi_r(x;B) = 1$ *and the expected utility from* $\pi_r(x;W) = 1$ equal 0. Therefore, neither of the above mentioned inequalities can be strict. **QED.**

Corollary to Theorem 3.1: The equilibrium in Proposition 3.1 does not require $n_c = common$.

Corollary to Theorem 3.2: The equilibrium in Proposition 3.1 does not require $n_k = n_b$.

The proofs of these corollaries are simple – it is c and k, not the status of n_c or n_k, that determine the equilibria in Proposition 3.1.

EXTENSION 1: VERIFICATION

Premises

The verification extension differs from the basic model in just one way. Now, nature makes a fourth choice $(n_v \in \{n_b, s\})$. As the following time line shows, nature makes this choice after the speaker sends his signal and before the principal makes her choice.

Action:	Nature makes first three choices	The speaker sends a signal.	Nature verifies with probability v. (New)	The principal chooses.

```
  *---------------------------*------------------*-----------------*
```

Sequence:	First, Second, Third	Fourth	Fifth	Last

Nature replaces the speaker's signal with n_b (the true "state of the world") with probability $0 < v < 1$. With probability $1-v$, no replacement occurs. Neither player knows n_v at the time they make their choice. So, if $0 < v < 1$, then the speaker does not know whether or not nature will "verify" his signal and the principal does not know whether the signal she has received is the speaker's statement or nature's verification of the true "state of the world." Note that the case where the principal knows n_v is a trivial variant of the basic model, that the case where $v = 0$ is the basic model, and that the case where $v = 1$ is trivial.

The current definition of a sequential equilibrium differs from the basic model's equilibrium only in that we now replace the strategy $\pi_s(s; h_s)$ with the strategy $\pi_s(s; h_s, v)$; the strategy $\pi_r(x; s)$ with the strategy $\pi_r(x;$

s, v); *and the beliefs* $\mu(better|s)$ *and* $\mu(worse|s)$ *with the beliefs* $\mu(better|s,$
$v)$ *and* $\mu(worse|s, v)$, *respectively.*

Conclusions

Proposition 3.2 describes the set of nonbabbling, non-neologistic equilibria for the basic communication model with verification. The main difference between this set of equilibria and the equilibria of the basic model is that $c > .5$ is no longer a requirement for equilibria. To put it another way, verification is a substitute for common interests.

> *Proposition 3.2:* The only nonbabbling, non-neologistic sequential
> equilibria in the basic model with verification are (with differences
> from Proposition 3.1 in bold): $\pi_{14} = (1, 0, 0, 1)$; $\pi_5 = 1$; if
> $bZ + (1-b)\underline{Z} \geq 0$ and = 0 otherwise; $\pi_6 = 1$; if $b\underline{Z} + (1-b)Z \geq$
> 0 *and* $= 0$ otherwise; and $\pi_r = (1, 0)$.

These equilibria require:

Condition A':
$$\frac{[(1-v) \times [(1-c)k + [(1-k) \times [\pi_s(B; b_5)c + \pi_s(B; b_6)(1-c)]]]}{[(v/b) + [(1-v) \times [ck + [(1-k) \times [\pi_s(B; b_5)c + \pi_s(B; b_6)(1-c)]]]]]} \leq bU/(b-1)\underline{U} \qquad \text{and}$$

Condition B':
$$\frac{[(v/(1-b)) + [(1-v) \times [ck + [(1-k) \times [(1-\pi_s(B; b_5))c + (1-\pi_s(B; b_6))(1-c)]]]]]]}{[(1-v) \times [(1-c)k + [(1-k) \times [(1-\pi_s(B; b_5))c + (1-\pi_s(B; b_6))(1-c)]]]]} \geq bU/(b-1)\underline{U}$$

where at least one of the inequalities is strict.

> *Corollary 1 to Proposition 3.2:* The equilibria in Proposition 3.2
> do not require $c > .5$.
>
> *Corollary 2 to Proposition 3.2: If* $\underline{Z} \neq 0$, *then, in equilibrium,*
> *increases in* v *make participation in the game less valuable for*
> speakers at information sets where there is an incentive to deceive.
> It does not have the same effect on other speakers.

At the request of the publisher, we have moved the proof of this theorem and its corollaries to our website. Note that the logic of these proofs is analogous to the proofs of Proposition 3.1 and its corollaries.

EXTENSION 2: PENALTIES FOR LYING

Premises

Our penalties-for-lying extension differs from the basic model in only one way. Now, if the speaker sends a false signal, then he must pay penalty *pen* ≥ 0. This extension directly affects the speaker's utility. If $n_c =$ *common* and the speaker lies, then the speaker receives utility Z-*pen* when the principal receives utility $U \geq 0$ and receives utility $\underline{Z}$-*pen* ≤ 0

when the principal receives utility $\underline{U} \leq 0$. If $n_c =$ *conflicting* and the speaker lies, then the speaker receives utility $\underline{Z}$ *-pen* ≤ 0 when the principal receives utility $U \geq 0$ and receives utility Z-*pen* when the principal receives utility $\underline{U} \leq 0$. Note that if *pen* $> Z$, then Z-*pen* < 0. If the speaker tells the truth, then the speaker's utility is the same as in the basic model.

A sequential equilibrium in this extension is equivalent to the sequential equilibrium in the basic model. It is a strategy profile π and system of beliefs μ that are consistent with each other and that satisfy sequential rationality at every information set. The only differences are that we replace the strategy $\pi_s(s; h_s)$ with the strategy $\pi_s(s; h_s, pen)$; the strategy $\pi_r(x; s)$ with the strategy $\pi_r(x; s, pen)$; and the beliefs $\mu(better|s)$ and $\mu(worse|s)$ with the beliefs $\mu(better|s, pen)$ and $\mu(worse|s, pen)$, respectively.

Conclusions

Like the previous two cases, there exist nonbabbling, non-neologistic sequential equilibria that contain $\pi_{14} = (1, 0, 0, 1)$ and $\pi_r = (1, 0)$. These are equilibria where knowledgeable speakers with common interests tell the truth while the knowledgeable speakers with conflicting interests lie. However, these equilibria are now possible only if the penalty is less than the smaller of U and $|U|$ (i.e., all possible lies are "worthwhile.") In addition, penalties for lying induce a second set of nonbabbling, non-neologistic sequential equilibria. In these equilibria, the penalty *induces* a speaker to send a truthful signal at information set h_3 and/or h_4.

There are two types of equilibria. In Type I equilibria, penalties for lying can affect persuasion. In Type II equilibria, penalties for lying affect speaker strategies, yet extreme circumstances allow for equilibria where the principal ignores the speaker nevertheless. For notational simplicity, let $\pi_{12} = (\pi_s(B;h_1), \pi_s(B;h_2))$, let $\pi_3 = \pi_s(B;h_3)$, and let $\pi_4 = \pi_s(B;h_4)$.

> *Proposition 3.3:* The only **Type I** nonbabbling, non-neologistic sequential equilibria in the basic model with penalties for lying are (with differences from Proposition 3.1 in **bold**):
>
> $\pi_{12} = (1, 0)$; $\pi_3 = 1$; *if* $\underline{Z} \geq$ *-pen and* $= 0$ *otherwise*; $\pi_4 = 1$; *if* $Z \geq$ **pen** **and** $= 0$ *otherwise*; $\pi_5 = 1$; *if* $bZ + (1-b)(\underline{Z}$ *-pen*$)$ + **bpen** ≥ 0 *and* $\pi_5 = 0$ otherwise; $\pi_6 = 1$; *if* $bZ + (1-b)(Z$-**pen**$)$ + **bpen** ≥ 0 *and* $\pi_6 = 0$ otherwise, and $\pi_r = (1, 0)$
>
> *These equilibria require:*
>
> $$\frac{[(1-c)k\pi_s(B;h_4) + [(1-k) \times [\pi_s(B;h_5)c + \pi_s(B;h_6)(1-c)]]]}{[ck + (1-c)k\pi_s(B;h_3) + (1-k) \times_x [\pi_s(B;h_5)c + \pi_s(B;h_6)(1-c)]]} \leq bU/(b-1)\underline{U} \quad \text{and}$$
>
> $$\frac{[ck + (1-c)k(1-\pi_s(B;h_4)) + [(1-k) \times [(1-\pi_s(B;h_5))c + (1-\pi_s(B;h_6))(1-c)]]]}{[(1-c)k(1-\pi_s(B;h_3)) + [(1-k) \times [(1-\pi_s(B;h_5))c + (1-\pi_s(B;h_6))(1-c)]]]} \geq bU/(b-1)\underline{U}$$

where at least one of the inequalities is strict.

Corollary 1 to Proposition 3.3: The equilibria in Proposition 3.3 do not require $c > .5$

Unlike the equilibria in the basic model, but the equilibrium of the verification extension, $c > .5$ is not a requirement for nonbabbling equilibria. As a result, even a penalty for lying that keeps speakers at some information sets from lying is sufficient to induce persuasion in a range of cases where it is not otherwise possible.

Corollary 2 to Proposition 3.3: The only **Type II** nonbabbling, non-neologistic sequential equilibria are:

- $\pi = (1, 0, 1, 0, 1, 1, 0, 0)$ iff *pen* > 0, $bU/(b-1)\underline{U} \leq (1-k)$ and $b \geq 1/2$.
- $\pi = (1, 0, 1, 0, 0, 0, 1, 1)$ iff *pen* > 0, $bU/(b-1)\underline{U} \geq 1/(1-k)$ and $b \leq 1/2$, and,
- *The following equilibria require $b = 1/2$.*
  - $\pi = (1, 0, 1, 0, 0, 1, 0, 0)$ if *pen* > 0, $bU/(b-1)\underline{U} \leq min((k/(c\text{-}ck))+1, ((1\text{-}k)(1\text{-}c))/(k + ((1\text{-}k)(1\text{-}c))))$.
  - $\pi = (1, 0, 1, 0, 0, 1, 1, 1)$ if *pen* > 0, $bU/(b-1)\underline{U} \geq max((k/(c\text{-}ck)) +1,((1\text{-}k)(1\text{-}c))/(k + ((1\text{-}k)(1\text{-}c))))$.
  - $\pi = (1, 0, 1, 0, 0, 0, 0, 0)$ if *pen* > 0, $bU/(b-1)\underline{U} \leq min(1 + (k/(1\text{-}k)(1\text{-}c)), (c\text{-}ck)/(c + k\text{-}ck))$.
  - $\pi = (1, 0, 1, 0, 0, 0, 1, 1)$ if *pen* > 0, $bU/(b-1)\underline{U} \geq max(1 + (k/(1\text{-}k)(1\text{-}c)), (c\text{-}ck)/(c+k\text{-}ck))$.

At the request of the publisher, we have moved the proof of this theorem and its corollary to our website. Note that the logic of these proofs is analogous to the proofs of Proposition 3.1 and its corollaries.

EXTENSION 3: COSTLY EFFORT WITH CONTINUOUS TYPES

We introduce costly effort to represent cases where the speaker signals through actions instead of words. This extension features continuous types – that is, nature determines player interests and knowledge by selecting one element from a continuum of elements. Previously, nature made each of her choices by choosing one element from a set of two (e.g., previously, $n_b \in \{better, worse\}$). We extend the model in this way to illuminate an important consequence of costly effort that is not easily replicated in the noncontinuous format. Note that our previous theorems hold for the continuous as well as the noncontinuous case (see, e.g., Lupia 1993, n.d.; Lupia and McCubbins 1994a, 1994b, and 1994c.)

Appendix to Chapter 3

Premises

As before, there are two players, the principal and the speaker. The principal has ideal point $p \in [0, 1]$. The speaker has ideal point $sp \in [0, 1]$. The principal chooses one of two alternatives, now defined as $x \in [0, 1]$ and $y \in [0, 1]$. The speaker takes an action that may provide the principal with information about her choice.

The sequence of events begins with two probabilistic moves by nature. The order of these moves is irrelevant. One of nature's choices determines the "state of the world." We denote this choice $n_b = x \in X \subseteq [0,1]$. This choice determines not only whether x is "better" or "worse" for the principal but also how much better or worse x is. For parsimony in discovering the consequences of costly effort, we examine the case where the speaker knows n_b and the principal does not (i.e., in the notation of the previous models, $k = 1$ and $n_k = n_b$). By contrast, the principal may not know, but does have beliefs about, which alternative is better for her.

Specifically, it is common knowledge that the true spatial location of x is determined by a single random draw from the distribution X, where X has support on a known subset of $[0, 1]$. Therefore, the principal has beliefs about the range of possible locations of x and the likelihood that each possible location is the true one. The principal does not, however, know which location was actually drawn. Thus, she may not *know* whether x or y is closer to p.

Nature's other choice, n_c, determines the relationship between the players' interests ($n_c = sp \in SP \subseteq [0,1]$). As before, the speaker knows n_c and the principal does not. In other words, the speaker knows his interests while the principal merely has beliefs about the speaker's interests. Specifically, the principal knows that the true spatial location of sp is determined by a single random draw from the distribution SP, where SP has support on a known subset of $[0, 1]$.

Third, the speaker makes a decision, $s \in \{cost, 0\}$. He must choose whether or not to pay $cost \geq 0$. If the speaker pays, then the principal gets to choose x or y. If the speaker does not pay, then y is the outcome.

The speaker's sole objective is to maximize his utility. If the speaker pays and the principal chooses x, then the speaker earns $-|x\text{-}sp|\text{-}cost$; if the speaker pays and the principal chooses y, then the speaker earns $-|y\text{-}sp|\text{-}cost$; and if the speaker does not pay, then he earns $-|y\text{-}sp|$. To break ties, we make the following innocuous assumption: If paying and not paying provide the speaker with the same expected utility given π_r, then the principal does not pay.

If the speaker pays $cost$, then the principal makes the game's final move by choosing x or y. From her choice the principal earns utility $-|x\text{-}p|$ or $-|y\text{-}p|$, respectively. To break ties, we make the following innocu-

254

ous assumption: If x and y provide the principal with the same expected utility, given π_s and $\mu(x|cost)$, then the principal chooses y.

A sequential equilibrium in this extension is equivalent to the basic model's sequential equilibrium. The differences are: There are now many more information sets; each speaker information set contains only one decision node; $s \in \{B, W\}$ is now $s \in \{cost, 0\}$; and we replace the beliefs $\mu(better|s)$ and $\mu(worse|s)$ with the belief $\mu(x|cost)$.

Conclusions

This model has only one nonbabbling sequential equilibrium. Neologisms have no meaning in this model. The key insight of the nonbabbling equilibrium is as follows: The speaker's objective is to induce the principal to choose the alternative that is closest to sp. However, it is profitable for the speaker to do so only if his action will actually change what the principal does and $|y - sp| - |x - sp| > cost$. That is, if $x \in [y - cost, y + cost]$, then it is not worthwhile for the speaker to influence the principal's choice. Therefore, if the speaker pays cost, then the principal can infer that $x \notin [y - cost, y + cost]$. If this inference is different from the principal's priors, then persuasion can occur.

Proposition 3.4: The only nonbabbling sequential equilibrium for this extension is: $s = cost$ and the principal chooses x if and only if:

$$-\int_{\min(0, y-cost)}^{y-cost} |x-p|\, dX - \int_{\min(y-cost,1)}^{1} |x-p|\, dX > -|y-p| \text{ and}$$
$$-|x-sp|-cost > -|y-sp|.$$

Otherwise, the speaker does not pay and the outcome is y.

Corollary to Proposition 3.4: Persuasion in Proposition 3.4 does not require that the probability of common interests between speaker and principal be $> .5$.

At the request of the publisher, we have moved the proof of this theorem and its corollary to our website (http://polisciexplab.uc-sd.edu). The logic of these proofs is analogous to the logic in Lupia (1992).

Theorem 3.3: The following conditions are individually necessary and collectively sufficient for persuasion: The principal must perceive the speaker to be trustworthy; the principal must perceive the speaker to be knowledgeable; and the signal, if true, must imply that the principal's prior beliefs are insufficient for reasoned choice.

Appendix to Chapter 3

In the absence of all external forces, persuasion requires perceived common interests ($c > .5$) and perceived speaker knowledge ($k >)$). In the presence of external forces, these requirements can be reduced. As the likelihood of verification, the magnitude of the penalty for lying, or the magnitude of costly effort increases, the extent to which common interests are required decreases (c can be less than $.5$). In other words, with respect to persuasion, the external forces can be substitutes for common interests.

> *Proof:* The individual necessity and collective sufficiency of the three conditions is proven in each of Propositions 3.1 through 3.4. The statement about persuasion in the absence of external forces is proven as Theorems 1 and 2. The statement about persuasion in the presence of external forces is proven as Corollary 1 to Proposition 3.2, Corollary 1 to Proposition 3.3, and Corollary 1 to Proposition 3.4. **QED.**

Appendix to Chapter 5

The agent makes the game's first move by choosing whether or not to propose an alternative to the policy status quo, $sq \in [0,1]$. To propose, the agent must pre-commit to pay a cost $k_p (\geq 0)$. If the agent chooses not to pay this cost, then the game ends with the status quo determining each player's payoff. If the agent pays, then he next chooses the proposal's content. We model this choice as the selection of a single point $x \in [0,1]$. We assume that once x is chosen, the agent and speaker know its location, while the principal does not. The agent's sole objective is to maximize his utility, which we represent as $-|outcome - c|$, where $outcome \in \{x, sq\}$.

If the agent makes a proposal, then the speaker makes a statement to the principal. The speaker says either "better" or "worse," where both statements refer to the relative proximity of the proposal to the principal's ideal point. The speaker need not tell the truth.

To identify the dynamics of delegation without verifying our conditions for persuasion, we draw on the lessons from Chapter 3 to simplify the current model. We examine two cases. In the first case, we assume that the principal has no basis for trusting the speaker. As a result, the principal treats the speaker's statement as totally uninformative. In the second case, we assume that the speaker's statement is true and that the principal believes it. Examining these two cases accomplishes three things. First, it provides a simple way to incorporate a substantive reality of delegation – some speakers are not credible to some principals. Second, this simplification is sufficient to show the endpoints of the range of effects that the speaker's statement can have on delegation. Third, this variation keeps us from having to rederive the conditions for persuasion derived in the previous section. That is, in this model, we assume that the speaker's credibility has already been established (exogenous to the interaction described here and, presumably, in the manner described in Chapter 3).

257

This simplification also allows us to employ the subgame perfect Nash equilibrium concept to describe the relationship between the agent and the principal.

If the agent makes a proposal, and after the speaker makes a statement, the principal must choose either the proposal, x, or the status quo, sq. The principal's sole objective is to maximize her utility. We represent that utility as $-|outcome - p|$, where $outcome \in \{x, sq\}$. After this choice has been made, the game ends and the principal receives her payoff.

We also make two innocuous tie-breaking assumptions. First, we assume that if making a proposal and not making a proposal provide the agent with the same expected utility, then he makes no proposal. Second, we assume that if x and sq provide the principal with the same expected utility, then she chooses sq.

The principal knows neither x nor the agent's ideal point c. The principal can, however, form beliefs about the location of x, which can affect her utility. That is, the principal knows that x was chosen by the agent. She also knows the agent's utility function and that c is the result of a single draw from the distribution C, which has density C' and support on a subset of $[0,1]$. The principal can use her initial knowledge to form beliefs about the range of possible locations for x as well as the likelihood of each.

CONCLUSIONS

We now present two propositions that describe equilibrium behaviors and outcomes. Proposition 5.1 applies to the case where the speaker is not persuasive. It is equivalent to the case where the game is played without a speaker. Proposition 5.2 applies to the case where the speaker's statement is true and the principal believes it.

> *Proposition 5.1:* Suppose that the speaker is not persuasive. Then, the agent proposes his ideal point $(x = c)$, the principal accepts the proposal, and c is the outcome if and only if
>
> $c \notin [sq\text{-}k_p, sq + k_p]$ and $- \int_0^{\max(o, sq-k_p)} |c - p| dC' -$
>
> $\int_{\min(sq+p, 1)}^1 |c - p| dC' > -|p - sq|$. Otherwise, the agent does not participate and sq is the outcome.

In words, if the principal correctly perceives her and the agent's interests to be sufficiently similar and there is either no speaker or a nonpersuasive speaker, then delegation succeeds. If, instead, this perception is incorrect, the delegation fails. By contrast, if the principal perceives her and the agent's interests to be dissimilar, then the consequence of delegation is the status quo.

A proof of Proposition 5.1 is provided in Lupia (1992). The crux of the proof is that the principal cannot tell whether the agent sets $x = c$ or whether he chooses a point that is closer to the principal's ideal point. While the principal would like to induce the agent to make a proposal that is more favorable to her, the principal is not sufficiently knowledgeable to induce such behavior. Therefore, both the agent and principal know that if the agent makes a proposal, he can commit to no other proposal strategy than $x = c$. What determines whether the agent makes a proposal is whether $-|c - c| - k_p > -|c - sq|$, which occurs when $c \in [sq - k_p, sq + k_p]$, and whether the principal, who can infer that $x = c$, will approve x, which occurs when the principal's expected payoff from the proposal is greater than her payoff from the status quo (*i.e.*, $-\int_0^{max(0,sq-k_p)} |c -$

$p|dC' - \int_{min(sq+p,1)}^1 |c - p|dC' > -|p - sq|$. The agent makes no proposal if his ideal point is within k_p of the status quo. The reason for this choice is that for all points within k_p of sq, the agent cannot gain enough from making a proposal to recover the cost of doing so. The logic underlying this part of the result is the same as the logic of Proposition 3.4.

We state Proposition 5.2 for the case where $p \le sq$. The case $p > sq$ is equivalent. Let $\varepsilon > 0$ be a very small number and let $k_p > \varepsilon$.

> **Proposition 5.2:** Suppose that the speaker's statement is true and that the principal believes it. Then, if $2 \times |sq - p| > k_p$ and $c \in (max(0, sq - (2 \times |sq - p|)), sq - k_p)$, then the agent proposes his ideal point ($x = c$), and c is the outcome. If $(2 \times |sq - p|)$-ε $> k_p$ and $c \in [0, max (0, sq - (2 \times |sq - p|))]$, then the agent proposes $x = sq - (2 \times |sq - p|) + \varepsilon$, and $sq - (2 \times |sq - p|)$ $+ \varepsilon$ is the outcome. Otherwise, the agent does not participate, and sq is the outcome.

> **Proof:** The agent makes a proposal only if he anticipates that the principal will accept it and that the gain in agent utility from such acceptance is greater than k_p. If the agent either expects the principal to reject the proposal, or the gain in utility is less than k_p, then the agent's best response is to make no proposal. Otherwise, the agent's best response is to choose $x = c$ when $c \in (max(0, sq - (2 \times |sq - p|)), sq - k_p)$ and to *choose* $x = sq - (2 \times |sq - p|) + \varepsilon$ when $c \notin [0, max(0, sq - (2 \times |sq - p|))]$.
>
> In the case where the speaker's statement is believed, the necessary and sufficient condition for the principal to accept the proposal is to hear the statement "better," and the necessary and

sufficient condition for the principal to hear this statement *is* x $\in (sq - (2 \times |sq - p|), sq)$. **QED.**

Had we assumed, instead, that the speaker was persuasive and deceptive, then it follows that the persuasive speaker's effect would be to induce the agent to make proposals that are less favorable to the principal.

> *Corollary to Propositions 5.1 and 5.2:* The introduction of the speaker can influence the agent's proposal. Moreover, if either the agent and the principal have common interests or the speaker speaks in a context where the conditions for enlightenment are satisfied, communication can prevent the failure of delegation and lead to its success.

> *Proof:* To see the validity of this statement, consider the set of cases in Proposition 5.2 where the agent chooses $x \neq c$ or decides not to propose even though there exists an x that is better for him than sq. Had the exact same circumstances applied in the nonpersuasive context, Proposition 5.1 implies that the agent would have chosen $x = c$, which could only be worse for the principal. **QED.**

The proofs of the Chapter 5 theorems follow straightforwardly. The proofs of Theorems 5.1 and 5.3 follow directly from Propositions 5.1 and 5.2 and their Corollary. The proof of Theorem 5.2 follows directly from Theorems 3.1 through 3.3.

References

Aberbach, Joel D. 1990. *Keeping a Watchful Eye: The Politics of Congressional Oversight*. Washington, D.C.: Brookings Institution.

Abramson, Jeffrey. 1994. *We, the Jury: The Jury System and the Ideal of Democracy*. New York: Basic Books.

Alchian, Armen, and Harold Demsetz. 1972. "Production, Information Costs, and Economic Organization." *The American Economic Review* 62: 777–95.

Almond, Gabriel A., and Sidney Verba. 1963. *The Civic Culture*. Princeton, N.J.: Princeton University Press.

Ansolabehere, Stephen, and Shanto Iyengar. 1995. *Going Negative: How Attack Ads Shrink and Polarize the Electorate*. New York: Free Press.

Aristotle. 1954. *Rhetoric*. New York: Modern Library.

Arrow, Kenneth. 1974. *The Limits of Organization*. New York: Norton.

Austen-Smith, David. 1990a. "Credible Debate Equilibria." *Social Choice and Welfare* 7: 75–93.

———. 1990b. "Information Transmission Debate." *American Journal of Political Science* 34: 124–52.

———. 1993. "Information and Influence: Lobbying for Agendas and Votes." *American Journal of Political Science* 37: 799–833.

———. 1994. "Information and Influence: Lobbying for Agendas and Votes." *American Journal of Political Science* 38: 283–93.

Banks, Jeffrey S. 1991. *Signaling Games in Political Science*. Chur, Switzerland: Harwood Academic Publishers.

Banks, Jeffrey S., and Joel Sobel. 1987. "Equilibrium Selection in Signaling Games." *Econometrica* 55: 647–62.

Banks, Jeffrey S., and Barry Weingast. 1992. "The Political Control of Bureaucracies under Asymmetric Information." *American Journal of Political Science*. 36: 509–24.

Barnes, Jonathan, ed. 1984. *The Complete Works of Aristotle: The Revised Oxford Translation*. Princeton, N.J.: Princeton University Press.

Baron, David P. 1989. "A Noncooperative Theory of Legislative Coalitions." *American Journal of Political Science* 33: 1048–84.

———. 1992. *Business and Its Environment*. Englewood Cliffs, N.J.: Prentice-Hall.

References

Barzel, Yoram. 1989. *Economic Analysis of Property Rights*. Cambridge: Cambridge University Press.

Bauer, Raymond A., Ithiel de Sola Pool, and Lewis Anthony Dexter. 1963. *American Business and Public Policy: The Politics of Foreign Trade*. New York: Atherton Press.

Bennett, W. Lance. 1992. *The Governing Crisis: Media, Money, and Marketing in American Elections*. New York: St. Martin's Press.

Berelson, Bernard. 1952. "Democratic Theory and Public Opinion." *Public Opinion Quarterly* XVI: 313–30.

Berelson, Bernard, Paul F. Lazarfeld, and William N. McPhee. 1954. *Voting: A Study of Opinion Formation in a Presidential Campaign*. Chicago: University of Chicago Press.

Bonfield, Arthur Earl, and Michael Asimow. 1989. *State and Federal Administrative Law*. St. Paul, Minn.: West.

Brady, Henry E., and Paul M. Sniderman. 1985. "Attitude Attribution: A Group Basis for Political Reasoning." *American Political Science Review* 79: 1061–78.

Calvert, Randall L. 1985. "The Value of Biased Information: A Rational Choice Model of Political Advice." *Journal of Politics* 47: 530–55.

1986. *Models of Imperfect Information in Politics*. Chur, Switzerland: Harwood Academic Publishers.

Calvert, Randall L., Mathew D. McCubbins, and Barry R. Weingast. 1989. "A Theory of Political Control and Agency Discretion." *American Journal of Political Science* 33: 588–611.

Calvert, Randall L., Mark J. Moran, and Barry R. Weingast. 1987. "Congressional Influence over Policy Making: The Case of the FTC." In Mathew D. McCubbins and Terry Sullivan, eds., *Congress: Structure and Policy*. Cambridge: Cambridge University Press.

Cameron, Charles M., and Joon Pyo Jung. 1992. "Strategic Endorsements." Columbia University. Typescript.

Campbell, Angus, Philip E. Converse, Warren E. Miller, and Donald E. Stokes. 1960. *The American Voter*. New York: Wiley.

Campbell, Donald T., and Julian C. Stanley. 1966. *Experimental and Quasi-Experimental Designs for Research*. Chicago: Rand McNally.

Casady, Robert J., and James M. Lepkowski. 1993. "Stratified Telephone Survey Designs." *Survey Methodology* 19: 103–13.

Cho, In-Koo, and David M. Kreps. 1987. "Signaling Games and Stable Equilibria." *Quarterly Journal of Economics* 102: 179–221.

Churchland, Patricia S., and Terrence J. Sejnowski. 1992. *The Computational Brain*. Cambridge, Mass.: MIT Press.

Churchland, Paul M. 1995. *The Engine of Reason, the Seat of the Soul: A Philosophical Journey into the Brain*. Cambridge, Mass.: MIT Press.

Clark, Andy. 1993. *Associative Engines: Connectionism, Concepts, and Representational Change*. Cambridge, Mass.: MIT Press.

Coase, Ronald. 1937. "The Nature of the Firm." *Economica* 4: 386–405.

Converse, Philip E. 1964. "The Nature of Belief Systems in Mass Publics." In David E. Apter, ed., *Ideology and Discontent*. New York: Free Press.

References

Cook, Thomas D., and Donald T. Campbell. 1979. *Quasi-Experimentation.* Chicago: Rand McNally.

Cooper, Russell, Douglas V. DeJong, Robert Forsythe, and Thomas W. Ross. 1993. "Forward Induction in the Battle-of-the-Sexes Games." *American Economic Review* 83: 1303–16.

Cornell, Nina, Roger G. Noll, and Barry R. Weingast. 1976. "Safety Regulation." In Charles Schultz and H. Owen, eds., *Setting National Priorities.* Washington, D.C.: Brookings Institution.

Cox, Gary W. 1997. *Making Votes Count: Strategic Coordination in the World's Electoral Systems.* Cambridge: Cambridge University Press.

Cox, Gary W., and Mathew D. McCubbins. 1993. *Legislative Leviathan: Party Government in the House.* Berkeley: University of California Press.

——— 1994. "Bonding, Structure, and the Stability of Political Parties: Party Government in the House." *Legislative Studies Quarterly* 19: 215–31.

Crawford, Vincent, and Joel Sobel. 1982. "Strategic Information Transmission." *Econometrica* 50: 1431–51.

Cyert, Richard M., and James G. March. 1963. *A Behavioral Theory of the Firm.* Englewood Cliffs, N.J.: Prentice-Hall.

Dahl, Robert A. 1967. *Pluralist Democracy in the United States: Conflict and Consent.* Chicago: Rand McNally.

Dalton, Russell J. 1989. *Politics in West Germany.* Glenview, Ill.: Scott, Foresman.

Delli Carpini, Michael X., and Scott Keeter. 1991. "Stability and Change in the United States Public's Knowledge of Politics." *Public Opinion Quarterly* 55: 583–612.

——— 1996. *What Americans Know About Politics and Why It Matters.* New Haven, Conn.: Yale University Press.

Demski, Joel S., and Dennis Sappington. 1989. "Hierarchical Structure and Responsibility Accounting." *Journal of Accounting Research* 27: 40–58.

Denzau, Arthur, William Riker, and Kenneth Shepsle. 1985. "Farquharson and Fenno: Sophisticated Voting and Home Style." *American Political Science Review* 79: 1117–34.

Dodd, Lawrence C., and Bruce I. Oppenheimer, eds. 1977. *Congress Reconsidered.* New York: Praeger.

Dodd, Lawrence C., and Richard L. Schott. 1979. *Congress and the Administrative State.* New York: Wiley.

Downs, Anthony. 1957. *An Economic Theory of Democracy.* New York: Harper.

Druckman, James N., Arthur Lupia, and Mathew D. McCubbins. 1998. *Experiments in Politics and Communication.* Unpublished manuscript. University of California, San Diego.

Duverger, Maurice. 1954. *Political Parties: Their Organization and Activity in the Modern State.* New York: Wiley.

Dye, Thomas R., and L. Harmon Zeigler. 1984. *The Irony of Democracy.* Monterey, Calif.: Brooks/Cole.

Eagly, Alice H., and Shelly Chaiken. 1993. *The Psychology of Attitudes.* Fort Worth, Tex.: Harcourt Brace Jovanovich. Enelow, James M., and Melvin J. Hinich. 1984. *The Spatial Theory of Voting: An Introduction.* Cambridge: Cambridge University Press.

References

Eskridge, William N., and John Ferejohn. 1992. "The Article I, Section 7 Game." *The Georgetown Law Journal* 80: 523–64.

Evans, C. Lawrence. 1991a. *Leadership in Committee: A Comparative Analysis of Leadership Behavior in the U.S. Senate.* Ann Arbor: University of Michigan Press.

1991b. "Participation and Policy Making in Senate Committees." *Political Science Quarterly* 106: 479–98.

Farrell, Joseph. 1993. "Meaning and Credibility in Cheap-Talk Games." *Games and Economic Behavior* 5: 514–31.

Farrell, Joseph, and Robert Gibbons. 1989. "Cheap Talk with Two Audiences." *American Economic Review* 79: 1214–23.

Fauconnier, Gilles. 1985. *Mental Spaces: Aspects of Meaning Construction in Natural Language.* Cambridge, Mass.: MIT Press.

Feddersen, Tim, and Wolfgang Pesendorfer. 1995. "Voting Behavior and Information Aggregation in Elections with Private Information." Typescript. Northwestern University.

Fenno, Richard F. 1973. *Congressmen in Committees.* Boston: Little, Brown.

1978. *Home Style: House Members in Their Districts.* Boston: Little, Brown.

Ferejohn, John A. 1987. "The Structure of Agency Decision Processes." In Mathew D. McCubbins and Terry Sullivan, eds., *Congress: Structure and Policy.* Cambridge: Cambridge University Press.

Ferejohn, John A., and James H. Kuklinski, eds. 1990. *Information and Democratic Processes.* Urbana: University of Illinois Press.

Ferejohn, John A., and Charles Shipan. 1990. "Congressional Influence on Bureaucracy." *Journal of Law, Economics, and Organization* 6: 1–20.

Fiorina, Morris P. 1977. *Congress: Keystone of the Washington Establishment.* New Haven, Conn.: Yale University Press.

1981. *Retrospective Voting in American National Elections.* New Haven, Conn.: Yale University Press.

Fiorina, Morris P., and Charles R. Plott. 1978. "Committee Decisions Under Majority Rule." *American Political Science Review* 72: 575–98.

Fishkin, James S. 1991. *Democracy and Deliberation: New Directions for Democratic Reform.* New Haven, Conn.: Yale University Press.

Fodor, Jerry A. 1979. *The Language of Thought.* Cambridge, Mass.: Harvard University Press.

Forsythe, Robert, Forrest Nelson, George R. Neumann, and Jack Wright. 1992. "Anatomy of an Experimental Political Stock Market." *American Economic Review* 82: 1142–61.

Freeman, John Lieper. 1955. *The Political Process: Executive Bureau–Legislative Committee Relations.* New York: Random House.

Friedman, Daniel, and Shyam Sunder. 1994. *Experimental Methods: A Primer for Economists.* Cambridge: Cambridge University Press.

Frolich, Norman, and Joe A. Oppenheimer. 1992. *Choosing Justice: An Experimental Approach to Ethical Theory.* Berkeley: University of California Press.

Fudenberg, Drew, and David K. Levine. 1993. "Steady State Learning and Nash Equilibrium." *Econometrica* 61: 547–73.

References

Fudenberg, Drew, and Jean Tirole. 1991. "Perfect Bayesian Equilibrium and Sequential Equilibrium." *Journal of Economic Theory* 53: 236–60.

Gerber, Elisabeth R., and Arthur Lupia. 1996. "Term Limits, Responsiveness, and the Failures of Increased Competition." In Bernard Grofman, ed., *Legislative Term Limits: Public Choice Perspectives*. Dordrecht, The Netherlands: Kluwer Academic Publishers.

Gerth, H. H., and C. Wright Mills, eds. 1946. *From Max Weber: Essays in Sociology*. New York: Oxford University Press.

Gilligan, Thomas W., and Keith Krehbiel. 1987. "Collective Decision Making and Standing Committees: An Informational Rationale for Restrictive Amendment Procedures." *Journal of Law, Economics, and Organization* 3: 287–335.

1989. "Asymmetric Information and Legislative Rules with a Heterogeneous Committee." *American Journal of Political Science* 33: 459–90.

Goffman, Erving. 1967. *Interaction Ritual: Essays on Face-to-Face Behavior*. Garden City, N.Y.: Anchor Books.

1969. *Strategic Interaction*. Philadelphia: University of Pennsylvania Press.

Goulden, Joseph C. 1969. *Truth Is the First Casualty: The Gulf of Tonkin Affair – Illusion and Reality*. Chicago: Rand McNally.

Greenwood, John D., ed. 1991. *The Future of Folk Psychology*. Cambridge: Cambridge University Press.

Greider, William. 1992. *Who Will Tell the People: The Betrayal of American Democracy*. New York: Simon and Schuster.

Grofman, Bernard, and Scott Feld. 1988. "Rousseau's General Will: A Condorcetian Perspective." *American Political Science Review* 82: 567– 76.

Grofman, Bernard, and Barbara Norrander. 1990. "Efficient Use of Reference Group Cues in a Single Dimension." *Public Choice* 64: 213–27.

Habermas, Jurgen. 1984. *The Theory of Communicative Action*. Boston: Beacon Press.

Hall, Richard L., and Frank W. Wayman. 1990. "Buying Time-Moneyed Interests and the Mobilization of Bias in Congressional Committees." *American Political Science Review* 84: 797–820.

Hamilton, Alexander, John Jay, and James Madison. 1961. *The Federalist Papers* (1787–88). New York: The New American Library of World Literature.

Harris, Joseph. 1964. *Congressional Control of Administration*. Washington D.C.: Brookings Institution.

Harsanyi, John. 1967. "Games with Incomplete Information Played by 'Bayesian' Players, I: The Basic Model." *Management Science* 14 (November 1967), 3: 159–82.

1968a. "Games with Incomplete Information Played by 'Bayesian' Players, II: Bayesian Equilibrium Points." *Management Science* 14 (January 1968), 5: 320–34.

1968b. "Games with Incomplete Information Played by 'Bayesian' Players, III: The Basic Probability Distribution of the Game." *Management Science* 14 (March 1968), 7: 486–502.

Herbert, Robert, "Nation of Nitwits." Commentary Section, *San Jose Mercury News*, March 5, 1995.

References

Herzberg, Donald G., and Jesse Unruh. 1970. *Essays on the State Legislative Process*. New York: Holt, Rinehart and Winston.

Herzberg, Roberta, and Rick Wilson. 1990. "Voting as a Public Bad: Theoretical and Experimental Results on Voting Costs." Typescript, presented at the Western Political Science Association Meetings.

Hinich, Melvin J., and Michael C. Munger. 1994. *Ideology and the Theory of Political Choice*. Ann Arbor: University of Michigan Press.

Hinton, Geoffrey E., and James A. Anderson. 1981. *Parallel Models of Associative Memory*. Hillsdale, N.J.: Erlbaum.

Holland, John H., Keith J. Holyoak, Richard E. Nisbett, and Paul R. Thagard. 1986. *Induction: Processes of Inference, Learning and Discovery*. Cambridge, Mass.: MIT Press.

Holmstrom, Bengt, and Roger B. Myerson. 1983. "Efficient and Durable Decision Rules with Incomplete Information." *Econometrica* 51: 1799–1819.

Hovland, Carl I., Irving L. Janis, and Harold H. Kelley. 1953. *Communication and Persuasion: Psychological Studies of Opinion Change*. New Haven, Conn.: Yale University Press.

Huber, John D. 1992. "Restrictive Legislative Procedures in France and the United States." *American Political Science Review* 86: 675–87.

Hunt, Gaillard, ed. 1910. *The Writings of James Madison*. New York: Putnam.

Iyengar, Shanto. 1987. "Television News and Citizens' Explanations of National Affairs." *American Political Science Review* 81: 815–32.

——— 1990. "Shortcuts to Political Knowledge: The Role of Selective Attention and Accessibility." In John A. Ferejohn and James H. Kuklinski, eds., *Information and Democratic Processes*. Urbana: University of Illinois Press.

——— 1991. *Is Anyone Responsible?: How Television Frames Political Issues*. Chicago: University of Chicago Press.

Iyengar, Shanto, and Donald R. Kinder. 1987. *News That Matters: Television and American Opinion*. Chicago: University of Chicago Press.

Iyengar, Shanto, and William J. McGuire, eds. 1993. *Explorations in Political Psychology*. Durham, N.C.: Duke University Press.

Jackendoff, Ray. 1980. *Consciousness and the Computational Mind*. Cambridge, Mass.: MIT Press.

——— 1994. *Patterns in the Mind: Language and Human Nature*. New York: Basic Books.

Jackson, John E. 1974. *Constituencies and Leaders in Congress: Their Effects on Senate Voting Behavior*. Cambridge, Mass.: Harvard University Press.

Jacobson, Gary C. 1990. "The Effects of Campaign Spending in House Elections: New Evidence for Old Arguments." *American Journal of Political Science* 34: 334–62.

——— 1992. *The Politics of Congressional Elections*. 3rd ed. New York: HarperCollins.

Jensen, Michael C., and William H. Meckling. 1976. "Theory of the Firm: Managerial Behavior, Agency Costs, and Ownership Structure." *Journal of Financial Economics* 3: 305–60.

Johnson, Chalmers. 1975. "Japan: Who Governs? An Essay on Official Bureaucracy." *Journal of Japanese Studies* 2 (Autumn): 1–28.

References

Johnston, Richard, Andre Blais, Henry E. Brady, and Jean Crete. 1992. *Letting the People Decide: Dynamics of a Canadian Election.* Stanford, Calif.: Stanford University Press.

Jones, Bryan D. 1995. *Reconceiving Decision-Making in Democratic Politics: Attention, Choice, and Public Policy.* Chicago: University of Chicago Press.

Joskow, Paul, and Roger G. Noll. 1981. "Regulation in Theory and Practice: An Overview." In Gary Fromm, ed., *Studies of Public Regulation.* Cambridge, Mass.: MIT Press.

Kahn, Alfred. 1988. *The Economics of Regulation: Principles and Institutions.* 2nd ed. New York: Wiley.

Kahneman, Daniel, and Amos Tversky. 1979. "Prospect Theory: An Analysis of Decision under Risk." *Econometrica* 47: 263–91.

1984. "Choices, Values, and Frames." *American Psychologist* 39: 341–50.

Kalton, Graham. 1983. *Introduction to Survey Sampling.* Sage University Papers 35: Quantitative Applications in the Social Sciences.

Kandel, Eric R., James H. Schwartz, and Thomas M. Jessel. 1995. *Essentials of Neural Science and Behavior.* Norwalk, Conn.: Appleton & Lange.

Kaplan, Robert M., James F. Sallis Jr., and Thomas L. Patterson. 1993. *Health and Human Behavior.* New York: McGraw-Hill.

Katz, Richard S., and Peter Mair. 1995. "Changing Models of Party Organization and Party Democracy: The Emergence of the Cartel Party." *Party Politics* 1: 5–28.

Key, V. O. 1966. *The Responsible Electorate: Rationality in Presidential Voting, 1936–1960.* Cambridge, Mass.: Belknap Press of Harvard University Press.

Kiewiet, D. Roderick, and Mathew D. McCubbins. 1991. *The Logic of Delegation: Congressional Parties and the Appropriations Process.* Chicago: University of Chicago Press.

Kinder, Donald R. and Thomas R. Palfrey, eds. 1993. *Experimental Foundations of Political Science.* Ann Arbor: University of Michigan Press.

Kinder, Donald R., and David O. Sears. 1985. "Public Opinion and Political Participation." In G. Lindzey and E. Aronson, eds., *Handbook of Social Psychology.* Reading, Mass.: Addison-Wesley.

Kingdon, John W. 1973. *Congressmen's Voting Decisions.* New York: Harper & Row.

1977. "Models of Legislative Voting." *Journal of Politics* 39: 563–95.

Knight, Jack. 1992. *Institutions and Social Conflict.* Cambridge: Cambridge University Press.

Krehbiel, Keith. 1991. *Information and Legislative Organization.* Ann Arbor: University of Michigan Press.

Kreps, David M. 1990. "Corporate Culture and Economic Theory." In James E. Alt and Kenneth A. Shepsle, eds., *Perspectives on Positive Political Economy.* Cambridge: Cambridge University Press.

Kreps, David M., and Robert Wilson. 1982. "Sequential Equilibria." *Econometrica* 50: 863–94.

Kuklinski, James H., Daniel S. Metlay, and W. D. May. 1982. "Citizen Knowledge and Choice on the Complex Issue of Nuclear Energy." *American Journal of Political Science* 26: 615–42.

References

Ladha, Krishna. 1992. "Condorcet's Jury Theorem, Free Speech and Correlated Votes." *American Journal of Political Science* 36: 617–34.

———. 1993. "Condorcet's Jury Theorem in Light of Definetti Theorem: Majority Rule Voting with Correlated Votes." *Social Choice and Welfare* 10: 69–85.

Laffont, Jean-Jacques, and Jean Tirole. 1993. "Cartelization by Regulation." *Journal of Regulatory Economics* 5: 111–30.

Lakoff, George. 1987. *Women, Fire, and Dangerous Things.* Chicago: University of Chicago Press.

Lane, Robert E. 1995. "What Rational Choice Explains." *Critical Review* 9: 107–26.

Lane, Robert E., and David O. Sears. 1964. *Public Opinion.* Englewood Cliffs, N.J.: Prentice-Hall.

Laver, Michael, and Kenneth A. Shepsle. 1994. *Cabinet Ministers and Parliamentary Government.* Cambridge: Cambridge University Press.

Lijphart, Arend. 1994. *Electoral Systems and Party Systems.* Oxford: Oxford University Press.

Lippmann, Walter. 1922. *Public Opinion.* New York: Macmillan.

Lodge, Milton. 1995. "Toward a Procedural Model of Candidate Evaluation." In Milton Lodge and Kathleen M. McGraw, eds., *Political Judgment: Structure and Process.* Ann Arbor: University of Michigan Press.

Lodge, Milton, and Kathleen M. McGraw, eds. 1995. *Political Judgment: Structure and Process.* Ann Arbor: University of Michigan Press.

Lodge, Milton, Marco Steenbergen, and Shawn Brau. 1995. "The Responsive Voter: Campaign Information and the Dynamics of Candidate Evaluation." *American Political Science Review* 89: 309–26.

Lohmann, Susanne. 1993. "A Signaling Model of Informative and Manipulative Political Action." *American Political Science Review* 87: 319–33.

Lowi, Theodore J. 1979. *The End of Liberalism: The Second Republic of the United States.* 2nd ed. New York: Norton.

Lupia, Arthur. 1992. "Busy Voters, Agenda Control and the Power of Information." *American Political Science Review* 86: 390–404.

———. 1993. "Credibility and Responsiveness of Direct Legislation." In William A. Barnett, Melvin J. Hinich, and Norman J. Schofield, eds., *Political Economy: Institutions, Competition, and Representation.* Cambridge: Cambridge University Press.

———. 1994. "Shortcuts Versus Encyclopedias: Information and Voting Behavior in California Insurance Reform Elections." *American Political Science Review* 88: 63–76.

———. n.d. "Who Can Persuade Whom?: How Simple Cues Affect Political Attitudes." In James H. Kuklinski, ed., *Thinking About Political Psychology.* Forthcoming.

Lupia, Arthur, and Mathew D. McCubbins. 1994a. "Designing Bureaucratic Accountability." *Law and Contemporary Problems* 57: 91–12.

———. 1994b. "Learning from Oversight: Fire Alarms and Police Patrols Reconstructed." *Journal of Law, Economics and Organization* 10: 96–125.

———. 1994c. "Who Controls Information and the Structure of Legislative Decision Making." *Legislative Studies Quarterly* 19: 361–84.

References

Luskin, Robert C. 1987. "Measuring Political Sophistication." *American Journal of Political Science* 31: 856–99.

Macey, Jonathan R. 1992. "Separated Powers and Positive Political Theory – the Tug of War Over Administrative Agencies." *Georgetown Law Review* 80: 671–703.

McCauley, Robert N., ed. 1996. *The Churchlands and Their Critics*. Cambridge, Mass.: Blackwell.

McClosky, Herbert. 1964. "Consensus and Ideology in American Politics." *American Political Science Review* 58: 361–82.

McConachie, Lauros G. 1898. *Congressional Committees*. New York: Thomas Y. Crowell.

McCubbins, Mathew D. 1985. "The Legislative Design of Regulatory Structure." *American Journal of Political Science* 29: 721–48.

McCubbins, Mathew D., and Talbot Page. 1986. "The Congressional Foundations of Agency Performance." *Public Choice* 51: 173–90.

McCubbins, Mathew D., and Gregory W. Noble. 1995a. "The Appearance of Power: Legislators, Bureaucrats, and the Budget Process in the United States and Japan." In Peter F. Cowhey and Mathew D. McCubbins, eds., *Structure and Policy in Japan and the United States*. Cambridge: Cambridge University Press.

1995b. "Perceptions and Realities of Japanese Budgeting." In Peter F. Cowhey and Mathew D. McCubbins, eds., *Structure and Policy in Japan and the United States*. Cambridge: Cambridge University Press.

McCubbins, Mathew D., Roger G. Noll, and Barry R. Weingast. 1987. "Administrative Procedures as an Instrument of Political Control." *Journal of Law, Economics, and Organization* 3: 243–77.

1989. "Structure and Process, Politics and Policy: Administrative Arrangements and the Political Control of Agencies." *Virginia Law Review* 75: 431–82.

1994. "Legislative Intent: The Use of Positive Political Theory in Statutory Interpretation." *Law and Contemporary Problems* 57: 3–37.

McCubbins, Mathew D., and Thomas Schwartz. 1984. "Congressional Oversight Overlooked: Police Patrols Versus Fire Alarms." *American Journal of Political Science* 28: 165–79.

McGuire, William J. 1969. "The Nature of Attitudes and Attitude Change." In G. Lindzey and E. Aronson, eds., *Handbook of Social Psychology,* 2nd ed. Reading, Mass.: Addison-Wesley.

McKelvey, Richard D., and Peter C. Ordeshook. 1986. "Information, Electoral Equilibria, and the Democratic Ideal." *Journal of Politics* 8: 909–37.

1990. "A Decade of Experimental Research on Spatial Models of Elections and Committees." In James M. Enelow and Melvin J. Hinich, eds., *Advances in the Spatial Theory of Voting*. Cambridge: Cambridge University Press.

Macey, Jonathan R. 1992. "Separated Powers and Positive Political Theory – The Tug of War Over Administrative Agencies." *Georgetown Law Review* 80: 671–703.

Machiavelli, Niccolo. 1958. *The Prince*. London: Dent; New York: Dutton.

Madison, James. *Federalist*. In Clinton Rossiter, ed., *The Federalist Papers*. New York: Penguin.

References

Magagna, Victor, and David Mares. Forthcoming. Untitled Manuscript, University of California, San Diego.

March, James G., and Herbert Simon, with Harold Guetzkow. 1958. *Organizations.* New York: Wiley.

Marcus, George E., and Russell L. Hanson.1993. *Reconsidering the Democratic Public.* University Park: Pennsylvania State University Press.

Matthews, Donald, and James Stimson. 1970. "Decision-Making by U.S. Representatives." In S. Sidney Ulmer, ed., *Political Decision Making.* New York: Van Nostrand Reinhold.

——— 1975. *Yeas and Nays.* New York: Wiley.

Meny, Yves. 1990. *Government and Politics in Western Europe: Britain, France, Italy, West Germany.* Oxford: Oxford University Press.

Mezey, Michael L. 1979. *Comparative Legislatures.* Durham, N.C.: Duke University Press.

Milgrom, Paul, and John Roberts. 1986. "Relying on the Information of Interested Parties." *Rand Journal of Economics* 17: 18–31.

Miller, Gary J. 1992. *Managerial Dilemmas: The Political Economy of Hierarchy.* Cambridge: Cambridge University Press.

Miller, Gary, and Joe Oppenheimer. 1982. "Universalism in Experimental Committees." *American Political Science Review* 76: 561–74.

Moe, Terry M. 1990. "The Politics of Structural Choice: Toward a Theory of Public Bureaucracy." In Oliver E. Williamson, ed., *Organization Theory: From Chester Barnard to the Present and Beyond.* New York: Oxford University Press.

Montesquieu, Baron de. 1989. *The Spirit of the Laws,* Translated and edited by Cohler, Anne M., Basia Carolyn Miller, and Harold Samuel Stone. Cambridge: Cambridge University Press.

Morton, Rebecca B. 1993. "Incomplete Information and Ideological Explanations of Platform Divergence." *American Political Science Review* 87: 382–92.

Mutz, Diana C., Paul M. Sniderman, and Richard A. Brody. 1995. *Political Persuasion.* Ann Arbor: University of Michigan Press.

Myerson, Roger B. 1979. "Incentive-Compatibility and the Bargaining Problem." *Econometrica* 47: 61–73.

——— 1983. "Mechanism Design by an Informed Principal." *Econometrica* 51: 1767–97.

——— 1989. "Credible Negotiation Statements and Coherent Plans." *Journal of Economic Theory* 48: 264–303.

Neuman, W. Russell. 1986. *The Paradox of Mass Politics: Knowledge and Opinion in the American Electorate.* Cambridge, Mass.: Harvard University Press.

Newell, Allen. 1990. *Unified Theories of Cognition.* Cambridge, Mass.: Harvard University Press.

Nie, Norman H., Sidney Verba, and John R. Petrocik. 1976. *The Changing American Voter.* Cambridge, Mass.: Harvard University Press.

Niskanen, William A. 1971. *Bureaucracy and Representative Government.* Chicago: Aldine-Atherton.

Noll, Roger. 1971a. "The Behavior of Regulatory Agencies." *Review of Social Economy.* 29: 15–19.

References

1971b. "The Economics and Politics of Regulation." *Virginia Law Review* 57: 1016–32.

1987. "The Political Foundations of Regulatory Policies." In Mathew D. Mc-Cubbins and Terry Sullivan, eds., *Congress: Structure and Policy*. Cambridge: Cambridge University Press.

Noll, Roger, and Bruce Owen. 1983. *Political Economy of Deregulation*. Washington, D.C.: American Enterprise Institute.

North, Douglass C. 1981. *Structure and Change in Economic History*. New York: Norton.

1990. *Institutions, Institutional Change, and Economic Performance*. Cambridge: Cambridge University Press.

Ogul, Morris S. 1976. *Congress Oversees the Bureaucracy: Studies in Legislative Supervision*. Pittsburgh: University of Pittsburgh Press.

Ogul, Morris S., and Bert A. Rockman. 1990. "Overseeing Oversight: New Departures and Old Problems." *Legislative Studies Quarterly* 15: 5–24.

O'Keefe, Daniel J. 1990. *Persuasion: Theory and Research*. Newbury Park, Calif.: Sage.

Ostrom, Elinor. 1990. *Governing the Commons: The Evolution of Institutions for Collective Action*. Cambridge: Cambridge University Press.

Page, Benjamin I., and Robert Y. Shapiro. 1992. *The Rational Public: Fifty Years of Trends in Americans' Policy Preferences*. Chicago: University of Chicago Press.

Page, Benjamin I., Robert Y. Shapiro, and Glenn R. Dempsey. 1987. "What Moves Public Opinion?" *American Political Science Review* 8: 23–44.

Palfrey, Thomas R. 1991. *Laboratory Research in Political Economy*. Ann Arbor: University of Michigan Press.

Parsons, Talcott. 1967. *Sociological Theory and Modern Society*. New York: Free Press.

Petracca, Mark P. 1990. "The Poison of Professional Politics in America." Working Paper 91–21: Institute for Governmental Studies, University of California, Berkeley.

Petty, Richard E., and John T. Cacioppo. 1986. *Communication and Persuasion: Central and Peripheral Routes to Attitude Change*. New York: Springer-Verlag.

Plott, Charles R. 1991. "Will Economics Become an Experimental Science?" *Southern Economic Journal* 57: 901–19.

Polsby, Nelson W. 1968. *The Citizen's Choice: Humphrey or Nixon?* Washington, D.C.: Public Affairs Press.

Polsby, Nelson W., Miriam Gallaher, and Barry Spencer Rundquist. 1969. "The Growth of the Seniority System in the US House of Representatives." *American Political Science Review* 63: 787–807.

Popkin, Samuel L. 1991. *The Reasoning Voter: Communication and Persuasion in Presidential Campaigns*. Chicago: University of Chicago Press.

Popkin, Samuel L., John W. Gorman, Charles Phillips, and Jeffrey A. Smith. 1976. "Comment: What Have You Done for Me Lately? Toward an Investment Theory of Voting." *American Political Science Review* 70: 779–805.

References

Posner, Michael I., ed. 1989. *Foundations of Cognitive Science.* Cambridge, Mass.: MIT Press.

Posner, Richard. 1995. "Juries on Trial." *Commentary* 99: 49–52.

Quattrone, George, and Amos Tversky. 1988. "Contrasting Rational and Psychological Analyses of Political Choice." *American Political Science Review* 82: 719–36.

Rae, Douglas W. 1971. *The Political Consequences of Electoral Laws.* New Haven, Conn.: Yale University Press.

Rahn, Wendy M., Brian Kroeger, and Cynthia M. Kite. 1996. "A Framework for the Study of Public Mood." *Political Psychology* 17: 29–58.

Ramseyer, J. Mark, and Frances McCall Rosenbluth. 1993. *Japan's Political Marketplace.* Cambridge, Mass.: Harvard University Press.

Riemer, Neal. 1986. *James Madison: Creating the American Constitution.* Washington, D.C.: Congressional Quarterly.

Ripley, Randall B. 1983. *Congress: Process and Policy.* 3rd ed. New York: Norton.

Rohde, David. 1991. *Parties and Leaders in Postreform House.* Chicago: University of Chicago Press.

Rohde, David, and Kenneth Shepsle. 1973. "Democratic Committee Assignments in the House of Representatives: Strategic Aspects of a Social Choice Process." *American Political Science Review* 67: 889–905.

Romer, Thomas, and Howard Rosenthal. 1978. "Political Resource Allocation, Controlled Agendas, and the Status Quo." *Public Choice* 33: 27–44.

Rose-Ackerman, Susan. 1994. "American Administrative Law Under Siege: Is Germany a Model?" *Harvard Law Review* 107: 1279–1302.

Rosenbluth, Frances McCall. 1989. *Financial Politics in Contemporary Japan.* Ithaca, N.Y.: Cornell University Press.

Ross, Stephen. 1973. "The Economic Theory of Agency: The Principal's Problem." *American Economic Review* 63: 134–9.

Roth, Alvin E., ed. 1987. *Laboratory Experimentation in Economics: Six Points of View.* Cambridge: Cambridge University Press.

Rumelhart, David E., James L. McClelland, and the PDP Research Group. 1986. *Parallel Distributed Processing: Explorations in the Microstructure of Cognition.* Cambridge, Mass.: MIT Press.

Sabato, Larry J. 1991. *Feeding Frenzy.* New York: Free Press.

Savoie, Donald J. 1990. *The Politics of Public Spending in Canada.* Toronto: University of Toronto Press.

Satz, Debra, and John A. Ferejohn. 1994. "Rational Choice and Social Theory." *Journal of Philosophy* 91: 71–87.

Schattschneider, Elmer Eric. 1960. *The Semisovereign People: A Realist's View of Democracy in America.* New York: Holt, Rinehart and Winston.

Schick, Allen. 1976. "Congress and the 'Details' of Administration." *Public Administration Review* 36: 516–28.

Schickler, Eric, and Andrew Rich. 1997. "Controlling the Floor: Politics as Procedural Coalitions in the House." *American Journal of Political Science.* Forthcoming.

References

Schumpeter, Joseph Alois. 1942. *Capitalism, Socialism, and Democracy.* New York: Harper.

Schwartz, Thomas A. 1980. *The Art of Logical Reasoning.* New York: Random House.

Shapiro, Martin. 1986. "APA: Past, Present, and Future." *Virginia Law Review* 72: 447–92.

Shepsle, Kenneth A. 1978. *The Giant Jigsaw Puzzle: Democratic Committee Assignments in the Modern House.* Chicago: University of Chicago Press.

——— 1979. "Institutional Arrangements and Equilibrium in Multidimensional Voting Models." *American Journal of Political Science* 23: 27–60.

Shepsle, Kenneth A., and Barry R. Weingast. 1981. "Structure Induced Equilibrium and Legislative Choice." *Public Choice* 37: 503–19.

——— 1987. "The Institutional Foundations of Committee Power." *American Political Science Review* 81: 85–104.

Sherif, Carolyn W., Muzafer Sherif, and Roger E. Nebergall. 1965. *Attitude and Attitude Change: The Social Judgment–Involvement Approach.* Philadelphia: Saunders.

Simon, Herbert A. 1955. "A Behavioral Model of Rational Choice." *Quarterly Journal of Economics* 69: 99–118.

——— 1959. "Theories of Decision Making in Economics and Behavioral Science." *American Economic Review* 253–83.

——— 1979. *Models of Thought.* New Haven, Conn.: Yale University Press.

——— 1982. *Models of Bounded Rationality.* Cambridge, Mass.: MIT Press.

——— 1985. "Human Nature in Politics: The Dialogue of Psychology with Political Science." *American Political Science Review* 79: 293–304.

——— 1995. "Rationality in Political Behavior." *Political Psychology* 16: 45–61.

Smith, Adam. 1965. "The Wealth of Nations." In Edwin Cannan, ed., *An Inquiry into the Nature and Causes of the Wealth of Nations.* New York: Modern Library.

Smith, Eric R.A.N. 1989. *The Unchanging American Voter.* Berkeley: University of California Press.

Smith, Steven S. 1988. "An Essay on Sequence, Position, Goals, and Committee Power." *Legislative Studies Quarterly* 8: 151–77.

Smith, Steven S., and Christopher J. Deering. 1990. *Committees in Congress.* Washington, D.C.: Congressional Quarterly Press.

Smith, Vernon L. 1976. "Experimental Economics: Induced Value Theory." *American Economic Review* 66: 274–9.

——— 1982. "Microeconomic Systems as an Experimental Science." *American Economic Review* 82: 923–55.

Sniderman, Paul M. 1993. "The New Look in Public Opinion Research." In Ada W. Finifter, ed., *Political Science: The State of the Discipline II.* Washington, D.C.: American Political Science Association.

Sniderman, Paul M., Richard A. Brody, and Philip E. Tetlock. 1991. *Reasoning and Choice: Explorations in Political Psychology.* Cambridge: Cambridge University Press.

Sobel, Joel. 1985. "A Theory of Credibility." *The Review of Economic Studies* 52: 557–73.

273

References

Spence, Michael. 1973. "Job Market Signaling." *Quarterly Journal of Economics* 87: 355–74.

 1974. *Market Signaling: Informational Transfer in Hiring and Related Screening Processes.* Cambridge, Mass.: Harvard University Press.

Spiller, Pablo T. 1990. "Agency and the Role of Political Institutions." In John Ferejohn and James Kuklinski, eds., *Information and Democratic Process.* Urbana: University of Illinois Press.

 1996. "A Positive Political Theory of Regulatory Instruments: Contracts, Administrative Law or Regulatory Specificity." *Southern California Law Review* 69: 477–514.

Spiller, Pablo T., and John Ferejohn. 1992. "The Economics and Politics of Administrative Law and Procedures – An Introduction." *Journal of Law, Economics, and Organization* 8: 1–7.

Spiller, Pablo T., and Santiago Urbiztondo. 1994. "Political Appointees vs. Civil Servants: A Multiple-Principles Theory of Political Institutions." *European Journal of Political Economy* 10: 465–97.

Steinberger, Peter J. 1993. *The Concept of Political Judgment.* Chicago: University of Chicago Press.

Stewart, Charles H. 1989. *Budget Reform Politics: The Design of the Appropriations Process in the House of Representatives, 1865–1921.* Cambridge: Cambridge University Press.

Stone, Alan, and Richard P. Barke. 1989. *Governing the American Republic: Economics, Law, and Politics.* New York: St. Martin's Press.

Sundquist, James L. 1981. *The Decline and Resurgence of Congress.* Washington, D.C.: Brookings Institution.

Tirole, Jean. 1988. *The Theory of Industrial Organization.* Cambridge, Mass.: MIT Press.

Tsebelis, George. 1990. *Nested Games: Rational Choice Perspective in Comparative Politics.* Berkeley: University of California Press.

 1995. "Veto Players and Law Production in Parliamentary Democracies." In Herbert Doring, ed., *Parliaments and Majority Rule in Western Europe.* New York: St. Martin's Press.

Turner, Mark. 1991. *Reading Minds: The Study of English in the Age of Cognitive Science.* Princeton, N.J.: Princeton University Press.

Tversky, Amos, and Daniel Kahneman. 1974. "Judgment under Uncertainty: Heuristics and Biases." *Science* 185: 1124–131.

Weaver, R. Kent, and Bert A. Rockman, eds. 1993. *Do Institutions Matter?: Government Capabilities in the United States and Abroad.* Washington, D.C.: Brookings Institution.

Weber, Max. 1946. "Economy and Society." In H. H. Gerth and C. Wright Mills, eds., *From Max Weber: Essays in Sociology.* New York: Oxford University Press.

Weingast, Barry R. 1979. "A Rational Choice Perspective on Congressional Norms." *American Journal of Political Science* 23: 245–62.

 1984. "The Congressional Bureaucratic System: A Principal–Agent Perspective." *Public Choice* 44: 147–92.

References

Weingast, Barry R., and William J. Marshall. 1988. "The Industrial Organization of Congress: or, Why Legislatures, Like Firms, Are Not Organized as Markets." *Journal of Political Economy* 96: 132–63.

Weingast, Barry R., and Mark J. Moran. 1983. "Bureaucracy Discretion or Congressional Control? Regulatory Policymaking by the Federal Trade Commission." *Journal of Political Economy* 91: 765–800.

Weisberg, Herbert F., ed. 1995. *Democracy's Feast: Elections in America.* Chatham, N.J.: Chatham House.

Wildavsky, Aaron B. 1974. *The Politics of the Budgetary Process,* 2nd ed. Boston: Little, Brown.

Will, George F. 1992. *Restoration: Congress, Term Limits and the Recovery of Deliberative Democracy.* New York: Free Press.

Williams, Kenneth C. 1991. "Advertising and Political Expenditure in a Spatial Election Game – An Experimental Investigation." *Simulation and Gaming* 22: 421–42.

Williamson, Oliver E. 1975. *Markets and Hierarchies, Analysis and Antitrust Implications: A Study in the Economics of Internal Organization.* New York: Free Press.

Wilmerding, Lucius. 1943. *The Spending Power: A History of the Efforts of Congress to Control Expenditures.* New Haven, Conn.: Yale University Press.

Wilson, Woodrow. 1885. *Congressional Government: A Study in American Politics.* Boston: Houghton Mifflin.

Wittman, Donald A. 1995. *The Myth of Democratic Failure: Why Political Institutions Are Efficient.* Chicago: University of Chicago Press.

Wood, B. Dan. 1988. "Principals, Bureaucrats, and Responsiveness in Clean Air Enforcements." *American Political Science Review,* Volume 82, Number 1, March 1988: 213–34.

Wright, John R. 1990. "Contributions, Lobbying, and Committee Voting in the US House of Representatives." *American Political Science Review* 84: 417–38.

Zaller, John. 1992. *The Nature and Origins of Mass Opinion.* Cambridge: Cambridge University Press.

Zaller, John, and Stanley Feldman. 1992. "A Simple Theory of the Survey Response: Answering Questions Versus Revealing Preferences." *American Journal of Political Science* 36: 579–616.

Author Index

Aberbach, Joel D., 220fn
Abramson, Jeffrey, 4
Alchian, Armen, 91, 205fn
Almond, Gabriel A., 34fn
Anderson, James A., 32
Ansolabehere, Stephen, 69
Aristotle, 8, 41 3, 41fn, 53, 55, 60, 63, 70, 74, 101
Arrow, Kenneth, 17
Asimow, Michael, 222, 223
Austen-Smith, David, 48fn, 50fn

Banks, Jeffrey S., 5, 44, 220, 243
Barke, Richard P., 72
Barnes, Jonathan, 41
Baron, David P., 42fn, 205fn
Barzel, Yoram, 26fn
Bauer, Raymond A., 221
Bennett, W. Lance, 3
Berelson, Bernard, 3, 4, 7, 8
Bonfield, Arthur Earl, 222, 223
Brady, Henry E., 40
Brau, Shawn, 8, 69
Brody, Richard, 5, 8, 29fn, 37, 40fn, 43fn, 100fn, 184fn, 206

Cacioppo, John T., 5, 43fn, 44, 44fn, 99, 196
Calvert, Randall L., 5, 8, 40, 44, 61fn, 215
Cameron, Charles M., 212fn
Campbell, Angus, 3, 17fn, 100fn, 206
Campbell, Donald T., 99
Casady, Robert J., 187fn
Chaiken, Shelly, 5, 43fn, 44, 44fn
Cho, In-Koo, 243
Churchland, Patricia S., 5, 6, 19fn, 33fn, 44
Churchland, Paul M., 19, 20
Cicero, 3
Clark, Andy, 19fn

Coase, Ronald, 26fn
Converse, Philip E., 3, 17
Cook, Thomas D., 99
Cooper, Russell, 110fn
Cornell, Nina, 216
Cox, Gary W., 207, 210, 210fn, 211, 212, 225
Crawford, Vincent, 5, 43fn, 44, 44fn, 45, 46, 48fn, 50fn, 192, 245
Cyert, Richard M., 31fn

Dahl, Robert A., 3
Dalton, Russell J., 208, 208fn
Deering, Christopher J., 210
Delli Carpini, 3, 17
Dempsey, Glenn R., 8
Demsetz, Harold, 91, 205fn
Demski, Joel S., 205fn
Denzau, Arthur, 208fn
Dexter, Lewis Anthony, 221
Dodd, Lawrence C., 80fn
Downs, Anthony, 4, 8, 20fn, 40, 206, 226
Duverger, Maurice, 207
Dye, Thomas R., 36fn

Eagly, Alice H., 5, 43fn, 44, 44fn
Enelow, James M., 206
Eskridge, William N., 218
Evans, C. Lawrence, 211

Farrell, Joseph, 5, 44, 61fn, 245
Fauconnier, Gilles, 49fn
Feddersen, Tim, 62
Feld, Scott, 62
Feldman, Stanley, 3
Fenno, Richard F., 210, 211
Ferejohn, John A., 5, 23fn, 216, 218
Fiorina, Morris P., 5, 8, 20, 40, 99, 206, 219, 226
Fishkin, James S., 226
Fodor, Jerry A., 32

Author Index

Author Index

Milgrom, Paul, 8, 40, 212fn
Miller, Gary J., 11, 149, 205fn
Miller, Warren E., 99
Mills, H.C. Wright, 3
Moe, Terry M, 218
Montesquieu, Baron de, 205fn, 212
Morton, Rebecca B., 99
Munger, Michael C., 37fn
Mutz, Diana C., 43fn
Myerson, Roger B., 42fn, 205fn, 234

Nebergall, Roger E., 43fn
Neuman, W. Russell, 3, 17
Newell, Allen, 18fn, 24fn
Nie, Norman H., 17fn, 100fn, 206
Nisbett, Richard E., 18fn
Niskanen, William A., 3, 79, 80fn, 215
Noble, Gregory W., 215
Noll, Roger W., 45fn, 216
Norrander, Barbara, 5, 43fn
North, Douglass C., 26fn, 205fn

Ogul, Morris S., 80fn, 220fn
O'Keefe, Daniel J., 99, 196
Ordeshook, Peter C., 5, 8, 40, 42fn, 44, 99
Oppenheimer, Bruce I., 80fn
Oppenheimer, Joe A., 99
Ostrom, Elinor, 205fn
Owen, Bruce, 216

Page, Benjamin I., 8, 40, 207
Page, Talbot, 220
Palfrey, Thomas R., 99
Parsons, Talcott, 17fn
Patterson, Thomas L., 27fn
PDP Research Group, 32
Pesendorfer, Wolfgang, 62
Petracca, Mark P., 226fn
Petrocik, John R., 17fn, 100fn, 206
Petty, Richard E., 5, 43fn, 44, 44fn, 99, 196
Plott, Charles R., 99
Polsby, Nelson W, 210
Popkin, Samuel L., 5, 8, 29fn, 37, 40, 43fn, 67, 69, 206
Pool, Ithiel de Sola, 221
Posner, Michael I.,, 4, 32

Quattrone, George, 23fn

Rae, Douglas W., 207
Rahn, Wendy M., 40
Ramseyer, J. Mark, 214, 218
Rich, Andrew, 211
Riemer, Neal, 1fn
Riker, William, 208fn

Ripley, Randall B., 18, 80fn
Roberts, John, 8, 40, 212fn
Rockman, Bert, 218, 220fn
Rohde, David, 210, 210fn
Romer, Thomas, 80fn
Rose-Ackerman, Susan, 218
Rosenbluth, Frances McCall, 211, 214, 218
Rosenthal, Howard, 80fn
Ross, Stephen., 80fn
Roth, Alvin E., 99
Rumelhart, David E., 32
Rundquist, Barry Spencer, 210

Sabato, Larry J., 3
Sallis, James F., Jr., 27fn
Sappington, Dennis, 205fn
Savoie, Donald J., 18fn
Satz, Debra, 23fn
Schattschneider, Elmer Eric., 3
Schick, Allen, 80fn
Schickler, Eric, 211
Schott, Richard L., 80fn
Schumpeter, Joseph Alois, 3, 4, 17fn, 81
Schwartz, James H., 18fn
Schwartz, Thomas, 7, 43fn, 82fn, 97, 215, 218fn, 219
Sears, David O., 3, 17
Sejonowski, Terrence J., 5, 6, 19fn, 33fn, 44
Shapiro, Martin, 218fn
Shapiro, Robert Y., 8, 40, 207
Shepsle, Kenneth A., 80fn, 205, 208fn, 210, 210fn
Sherif, Muzafer, 43fn
Sherif, Carolyn W., 43fn
Shipan, Charles, 216
Simon, Herbert A., 5, 6, 7, 23fn, 24, 29fn, 30 1, 31fn, 44, 45fn, 49fn, 186
Smith, Adam., 205
Smith, Eric R.A.N., 17fn
Smith, Steven S., 18, 210
Smith, Vernon L. 108fn
Sniderman, Paul M., 5, 8, 29fn, 37, 40, 43fn, 100fn, 184fn, 206
Sobel, Joel, 5, 40, 43fn, 44, 44fn, 45, 46, 50fn, 192, 243, 245
Spence, Michael, 5, 44, 44fn, 58fn, 91, 91fn, 216
Spiller, Pablo T., 216, 216fn, 220
Stanley, Julian C., 99
Steenbergen, Marco, 8, 69
Steinberger, Peter J., 36
Stewart, Charles H., 210fn
Stimson, James, 75fn, 211
Stone, Alan, 72

279

Author Index

Sunder, Shyam, 99
Sundquist, James L, 215

Tetlock, Philip, 5, 8, 29fn, 37, 40, 43fn, 100fn, 184fn, 206
Thagard, Paul R., 18fn
Tirole, Jean, 91, 205fn, 243, 244
Tsebelis, George, 210fn
Turner, Mark, 41fn, 49fn
Tversky, Amos, 8fn, 23fn

Unruh, Jess, 211
Urbiztondo, Santiago, 216fn

Verba, Sidney, 17fn, 34fn, 100fn, 206

Wayman, Frank W., 211
Weaver, R. Kent, 218

Weber, Max., 3, 18, 81
Weingast, Barry, 80fn, 205fn, 210fn, 219, 220
Weisberg, Herbert F., 100fn
Wildavsky, Aaron B., 215
Will, George F., 226fn
Williams, Kenneth C., 99
Williamson, Oliver E., 26fn, 31fn, 42fn
Wilmerding, Lucius, 215
Wilson, Rick, 99
Wilson, Robert, 243
Wilson, Woodrow, 18
Wittman, Donald A., 23fn
Wood, B. Dan, 218
Wright, John R., 211

Zaller, John, 3, 40, 43fn
Zeigler, L. Harmon, 36fn

Subject Index

accurate prediction, 18, 20, 24–5, 26,
    68–9, 68fn, 227, 229
attention
    benefits of, 25, 26, 28
    calculus of, 25–30
    model of, 234–9, 246
    opportunity costs of, 25
    returns from, 25
    transactions costs of, 25, 26

brand names, 21, 35–6, 207

cheap talk, 45, 46–9, 57, 192, 194
cognitive stock market, 30–35
connectionism, 18–19, 31–2
costly effort, 9–10, 54–5, 58–60, 62, 75,
    85, 86, 88, 89, 98, 107, 110,
    114, 206
    case studies, 209–10, 214–15, 222–3
    definition, 58
    experiments, 139–44
    figure, 59
    theory, 58–9, 253–6
credibility, 30fn, 44fn, 42, 63, 66, 75,
    221

deception, 2, 4, 7–11, 49, 53, 57, 68–9,
    88, 98, 102, 103, 104, 147, 148
    conditions for, 70, 72–4
    predictions, 98
    willful, 70
delegation
    case studies
        bureaucracy, 215–23
        elections, 206–10
        juries, 223–5
        legislation, 210–15
    experiments, 149–83
        design of, 150–7
        frequency of persuasion and reasoned
            choice in these experiments,
            182–3

types
    penalty for lying, 174–8
    speaker interest, 166, 168–74
    speaker knowledge, 158–66, 167
    verification, 178–82
  our theory, 82–92, 257–60
  predictions, 98
  success and failure
    conditions for, 85–92
    original definition, 79
    tougher definition, 91–2
democracy, 1, 2, 2fn, 3–4, 37, 70, 74, 77
    8, 205, 206, 226, 229
  critiques of, 6, 10, 54fn, 77, 81
  delegation and, 11, 79–80, 92–3,
    149–50
democratic dilemma, 1, 2, 12–13, 205,
    227, 229

enlightenment, 8, 11, 68, 74, 75, 77, 88,
    92, 102–4, 122, 132, 137,
    145–8, 157–9, 161, 168, 169,
    182, 185, 205, 208, 214, 216,
    221, 223, 226
  compared with deliberation, 227
  conditions for, 69–71
  prediction, 98
equilibrium
  perfect Bayesian, 243–4
  sequential, 241–6, 251, 254–6
external forces, 9, 42, 42fn, 43, 45, 50,
    53–62, 64, 69, 70, 72, 75, 85,
    98, 102, 110, 114, 155, 185,
    198, 211, 255–6

ideology, 9–11, 43, 55, 63, 64, 67, 99fn,
    188, 191, 196, 199 201, 208
incentive condition, 12, 85–6, 89, 92,
    149, 216, 226
incentives, 2, 9, 11, 29, 30, 43, 53, 55,
    62, 70, 100, 101, 205, 217, 219,
    237–9

281

Printed in the United States
84254LV00006B/64-66/A